DUTCH
VOCABULARY

ENGLISH-DUTCH

The most useful words
To expand your lexicon and sharpen
your language skills

9000 words

Dutch vocabulary for English speakers - 9000 words

By Andrey Taranov

T&P Books vocabularies are intended for helping you learn, memorize and review foreign words. The dictionary is divided into themes, covering all major spheres of everyday activities, business, science, culture, etc.

The process of learning words using T&P Books' theme-based dictionaries gives you the following advantages:

- Correctly grouped source information predetermines success at subsequent stages of word memorization
- Availability of words derived from the same root allowing memorization of word units (rather than separate words)
- Small units of words facilitate the process of establishing associative links needed for consolidation of vocabulary
- Level of language knowledge can be estimated by the number of learned words

T&P Books Publishing
www.tpbooks.com

ISBN: 978-1-78071-812-5

This book is also available in E-book formats.
Please visit www.tpbooks.com or the major online bookstores.

DUTCH VOCABULARY
for English speakers

T&P Books vocabularies are intended to help you learn, memorize, and review foreign words. The vocabulary contains over 9000 commonly used words arranged thematically.

- Vocabulary contains the most commonly used words
- Recommended as an addition to any language course
- Meets the needs of beginners and advanced learners of foreign languages
- Convenient for daily use, revision sessions, and self-testing activities
- Allows you to assess your vocabulary

Special features of the vocabulary

- Words are organized according to their meaning, not alphabetically
- Words are presented in three columns to facilitate the reviewing and self-testing processes
- Words in groups are divided into small blocks to facilitate the learning process
- The vocabulary offers a convenient and simple transcription of each foreign word

The vocabulary has 256 topics including:

Basic Concepts, Numbers, Colors, Months, Seasons, Units of Measurement, Clothing & Accessories, Food & Nutrition, Restaurant, Family Members, Relatives, Character, Feelings, Emotions, Diseases, City, Town, Sightseeing, Shopping, Money, House, Home, Office, Working in the Office, Import & Export, Marketing, Job Search, Sports, Education, Computer, Internet, Tools, Nature, Countries, Nationalities and more ...

T&P BOOKS' THEME-BASED DICTIONARIES

The Correct System for Memorizing Foreign Words

Acquiring vocabulary is one of the most important elements of learning a foreign language, because words allow us to express our thoughts, ask questions, and provide answers. An inadequate vocabulary can impede communication with a foreigner and make it difficult to understand a book or movie well.

The pace of activity in all spheres of modern life, including the learning of modern languages, has increased. Today, we need to memorize large amounts of information (grammar rules, foreign words, etc.) within a short period. However, this does not need to be difficult. All you need to do is to choose the right training materials, learn a few special techniques, and develop your individual training system.

Having a system is critical to the process of language learning. Many people fail to succeed in this regard; they cannot master a foreign language because they fail to follow a system comprised of selecting materials, organizing lessons, arranging new words to be learned, and so on. The lack of a system causes confusion and eventually, lowers self-confidence.

T&P Books' theme-based dictionaries can be included in the list of elements needed for creating an effective system for learning foreign words. These dictionaries were specially developed for learning purposes and are meant to help students effectively memorize words and expand their vocabulary.

Generally speaking, the process of learning words consists of three main elements:

- Reception (creation or acquisition) of a training material, such as a word list
- Work aimed at memorizing new words
- Work aimed at reviewing the learned words, such as self-testing

All three elements are equally important since they determine the quality of work and the final result. All three processes require certain skills and a well-thought-out approach.

New words are often encountered quite randomly when learning a foreign language and it may be difficult to include them all in a unified list. As a result, these words remain written on scraps of paper, in book margins, textbooks, and so on. In order to systematize such words, we have to create and continually update a "book of new words." A paper notebook, a netbook, or a tablet PC can be used for these purposes.

This "book of new words" will be your personal, unique list of words. However, it will only contain the words that you came across during the learning process. For example, you might have written down the words "Sunday," "Tuesday," and "Friday." However, there are additional words for days of the week, for example, "Saturday," that are missing, and your list of words would be incomplete. Using a theme dictionary, in addition to the "book of new words," is a reasonable solution to this problem.

The theme-based dictionary may serve as the basis for expanding your vocabulary.

It will be your big "book of new words" containing the most frequently used words of a foreign language already included. There are quite a few theme-based dictionaries available, and you should ensure that you make the right choice in order to get the maximum benefit from your purchase.

Therefore, we suggest using theme-based dictionaries from T&P Books Publishing as an aid to learning foreign words. Our books are specially developed for effective use in the sphere of vocabulary systematization, expansion and review.

Theme-based dictionaries are not a magical solution to learning new words. However, they can serve as your main database to aid foreign-language acquisition. Apart from theme dictionaries, you can have copybooks for writing down new words, flash cards, glossaries for various texts, as well as other resources; however, a good theme dictionary will always remain your primary collection of words.

T&P Books' theme-based dictionaries are specialty books that contain the most frequently used words in a language.

The main characteristic of such dictionaries is the division of words into themes. For example, the *City* theme contains the words "street," "crossroads," "square," "fountain," and so on. The *Talking* theme might contain words like "to talk," "to ask," "question," and "answer".

All the words in a theme are divided into smaller units, each comprising 3-5 words. Such an arrangement improves the perception of words and makes the learning process less tiresome. Each unit contains a selection of words with similar meanings or identical roots. This allows you to learn words in small groups and establish other associative links that have a positive effect on memorization.

The words on each page are placed in three columns: a word in your native language, its translation, and its transcription. Such positioning allows for the use of techniques for effective memorization. After closing the translation column, you can flip through and review foreign words, and vice versa. "This is an easy and convenient method of review – one that we recommend you do often."

Our theme-based dictionaries contain transcriptions for all the foreign words. Unfortunately, none of the existing transcriptions are able to convey the exact nuances of foreign pronunciation. That is why we recommend using the transcriptions only as a supplementary learning aid. Correct pronunciation can only be acquired with the help of sound. Therefore our collection includes audio theme-based dictionaries.

The process of learning words using T&P Books' theme-based dictionaries gives you the following advantages:

- You have correctly grouped source information, which predetermines your success at subsequent stages of word memorization
- Availability of words derived from the same root (lazy, lazily, lazybones), allowing you to memorize word units instead of separate words
- Small units of words facilitate the process of establishing associative links needed for consolidation of vocabulary
- You can estimate the number of learned words and hence your level of language knowledge
- The dictionary allows for the creation of an effective and high-quality revision process
- You can revise certain themes several times, modifying the revision methods and techniques
- Audio versions of the dictionaries help you to work out the pronunciation of words and develop your skills of auditory word perception

The T&P Books' theme-based dictionaries are offered in several variants differing in the number of words: 1.500, 3.000, 5.000, 7.000, and 9.000 words. There are also dictionaries containing 15,000 words for some language combinations. Your choice of dictionary will depend on your knowledge level and goals.

We sincerely believe that our dictionaries will become your trusty assistant in learning foreign languages and will allow you to easily acquire the necessary vocabulary.

TABLE OF CONTENTS

Medicine

HUMAN HABITAT
City

Dwelling. House. Home

HUMAN ACTIVITIES 107
Job. Business. Part 1 107

Education

Arts

Rest. Entertainment. Travel

TECHNICAL EQUIPMENT. TRANSPORTATION
Technical equipment

MISCELLANEOUS

MAIN 500 VERBS

PRONUNCIATION GUIDE

T&P phonetic alphabet	Dutch example	English example
[a]	plasje	shorter than in ask
[ā]	kraag	calf, palm
[o], [ɔ]	zondag	drop, baught
[o]	geografie	pod, John
[ō]	oorlog	fall, bomb
[e]	nemen	elm, medal
[ē]	wreed	longer than in bell
[ɛ]	ketterij	man, bad
[ɛ:]	crème	longer than bed, fell
[ə]	tachtig	driver, teacher
[i]	alpinist	shorter than in feet
[ī]	referee	feet, meter
[y]	stadhuis	fuel, tuna
[œ]	druif	German Hölle
[ø]	treurig	eternal, church
[u]	schroef	book
[ʉ]	zuchten	youth, usually
[ū]	minuut	fuel, tuna
[b]	oktober	baby, book
[d]	diepte	day, doctor
[f]	fierheid	face, food
[g]	golfclub	game, gold
[h]	horizon	home, have
[j]	jaar	yes, New York
[k]	klooster	clock, kiss
[l]	politiek	lace, people
[m]	melodie	magic, milk
[n]	netwerk	sang, thing
[p]	peper	pencil, private
[r]	rechter	rice, radio
[s]	smaak	city, boss
[t]	telefoon	tourist, trip
[v]	vijftien	very, river
[w]	waaier	vase, winter

T&P phonetic alphabet	Dutch example	English example
[z]	zacht	zebra, please
[dʒ]	manager	joke, general
[ʃ]	architect	machine, shark
[ŋ]	behang	English, ring
[ʧ]	beertje	church, French
[ʒ]	bougie	forge, pleasure
[x]	acht, gaan	as in Scots 'loch'

ABBREVIATIONS
used in the vocabulary

English abbreviations

ab.	-	about
adj	-	adjective
adv	-	adverb
anim.	-	animate
as adj	-	attributive noun used as adjective
e.g.	-	for example
etc.	-	et cetera
fam.	-	familiar
fem.	-	feminine
form.	-	formal
inanim.	-	inanimate
masc.	-	masculine
math	-	mathematics
mil.	-	military
n	-	noun
pl	-	plural
pron.	-	pronoun
sb	-	somebody
sing.	-	singular
sth	-	something
v aux	-	auxiliary verb
vi	-	intransitive verb
vi, vt	-	intransitive, transitive verb
vt	-	transitive verb

Dutch abbreviations

mv.	-	plural

Dutch articles

de	-	common gender
de/het	-	neuter, common gender
het	-	neuter

BASIC CONCEPTS

Basic concepts. Part 1

1. Pronouns

I, me	ik	[ik]
you	jij, je	[jɛj], [jə]
he	hij	[hɛj]
she	zij, ze	[zɛj], [zə]
it	het	[ət]
we	wij, we	[wɛj], [wə]
you (to a group)	jullie	['juli]
they	zij, ze	[zɛj], [zə]

2. Greetings. Salutations. Farewells

Hello! (fam.)	Hallo! Dag!	[ha'lo dax]
Hello! (form.)	Hallo!	[ha'lo]
Good morning!	Goedemorgen!	['xudə·'mɔrxən]
Good afternoon!	Goedemiddag!	['xudə·'midax]
Good evening!	Goedenavond!	['xudən·'avɔnt]
to say hello	gedag zeggen	[xe'dax 'zexən]
Hi! (hello)	Hoi!	[hɔj]
greeting (n)	groeten (het)	['xrutən]
to greet (vt)	verwelkomen	[vər'wɛlkɔmən]
How are you?	Hoe gaat het?	[hu xāt ət]
What's new?	Is er nog nieuws?	[is ɛr nɔx 'nius]
Goodbye!	Tot ziens!	[tɔt 'tsins]
Bye!	Doei!	['dui]
See you soon!	Tot snel!	[tɔt snɛl]
Farewell!	Vaarwel!	[vār'wɛl]
to say goodbye	afscheid nemen	['afsxɛjt 'nemən]
So long!	Tot kijk!	[tɔt kɛjk]
Thank you!	Dank u!	[dank ju]
Thank you very much!	Dank u wel!	[dank ju wɛl]
You're welcome	Graag gedaan	[xrāx xə'dān]
Don't mention it!	Geen dank!	[xēn dank]

It was nothing	Geen moeite.	[xēn 'mujtə]
Excuse me!	Excuseer me, …	[ɛkskʉ'zēr mə]
to excuse (forgive)	excuseren	[ɛkskʉ'zerən]

to apologize (vi)	zich verontschuldigen	[zih vərɔnt'sxʉldəxən]
My apologies	Mijn excuses	[mɛjn ɛks'kʉzəs]
I'm sorry!	Het spijt me!	[ət spɛjt mə]
to forgive (vt)	vergeven	[vər'xevən]
It's okay! (that's all right)	Maakt niet uit!	[māk nit œʏt]
please (adv)	alsjeblieft	[alstʉ'blift]

Don't forget!	Vergeet het niet!	[vər'xēt ət nit]
Certainly!	Natuurlijk!	[na'tūrlək]
Of course not!	Natuurlijk niet!	[na'tūrlək nit]
Okay! (I agree)	Akkoord!	[a'kōrt]
That's enough!	Zo is het genoeg!	[zɔ is ət xə'nux]

3. How to address

Excuse me, …	Excuseer me, …	[ɛkskʉ'zēr mə]
mister, sir	meneer	[mə'nēr]
ma'am	mevrouw	[məv'rau]
miss	juffrouw	[ju'frau]
young man	jongeman	[jɔŋə'man]
young man (little boy, kid)	jongen	['jɔŋən]
miss (little girl)	meisje	['mɛjɕə]

4. Cardinal numbers. Part 1

0 zero	nul	[nʉl]
1 one	een	[en]
2 two	twee	[twē]
3 three	drie	[dri]
4 four	vier	[vir]

5 five	vijf	[vɛjf]
6 six	zes	[zɛs]
7 seven	zeven	['zevən]
8 eight	acht	[axt]
9 nine	negen	['nexən]

10 ten	tien	[tin]
11 eleven	elf	[ɛlf]
12 twelve	twaalf	[twālf]
13 thirteen	dertien	['dɛrtin]
14 fourteen	veertien	['vērtin]
15 fifteen	vijftien	['vɛjftin]
16 sixteen	zestien	['zɛstin]

17 seventeen	**zeventien**	['zevəntin]
18 eighteen	**achttien**	['axtin]
19 nineteen	**negentien**	['nexəntin]
20 twenty	**twintig**	['twintəx]
21 twenty-one	**eenentwintig**	['ēnən·'twintəx]
22 twenty-two	**tweeëntwintig**	['twēɛn·'twintəx]
23 twenty-three	**drieëntwintig**	['driɛn·'twintəx]
30 thirty	**dertig**	['dɛrtəx]
31 thirty-one	**eenendertig**	['ēnən·'dɛrtəx]
32 thirty-two	**tweeëndertig**	['twēɛn·'dɛrtəx]
33 thirty-three	**drieëndertig**	['driɛn·'dɛrtəx]
40 forty	**veertig**	['vērtəx]
41 forty-one	**eenenveertig**	['ēnən·'vertəx]
42 forty-two	**tweeënveertig**	['twēɛn·'vertəx]
43 forty-three	**drieënveertig**	['driɛn·'vērtəx]
50 fifty	**vijftig**	['vɛjftəx]
51 fifty-one	**eenenvijftig**	['ēnən·'vɛjftəx]
52 fifty-two	**tweeënvijftig**	['twēɛn·'vɛjftəx]
53 fifty-three	**drieënvijftig**	['driɛn·'vɛjftəx]
60 sixty	**zestig**	['zɛstəx]
61 sixty-one	**eenenzestig**	['ēnən·'zɛstəx]
62 sixty-two	**tweeënzestig**	['twēɛn·'zɛstəx]
63 sixty-three	**drieënzestig**	['driɛn·'zɛstəx]
70 seventy	**zeventig**	['zevəntəx]
71 seventy-one	**eenenzeventig**	['ēnən·'zevəntəx]
72 seventy-two	**tweeënzeventig**	['twēɛn·'zevəntəx]
73 seventy-three	**drieënzeventig**	['driɛn·'zevəntəx]
80 eighty	**tachtig**	['tahtəx]
81 eighty-one	**eenentachtig**	['ēnən·'tahtəx]
82 eighty-two	**tweeëntachtig**	['twēɛn·'tahtəx]
83 eighty-three	**drieëntachtig**	['driɛn·'taxtəx]
90 ninety	**negentig**	['nexəntəx]
91 ninety-one	**eenennegentig**	['ēnən·'nexəntəx]
92 ninety-two	**tweeënnegentig**	['twēɛn·'nexəntəx]
93 ninety-three	**drieënnegentig**	['driɛn·'nexəntəx]

5. Cardinal numbers. Part 2

100 one hundred	**honderd**	['hɔndərt]
200 two hundred	**tweehonderd**	[twē·'hɔndərt]
300 three hundred	**driehonderd**	[dri·'hɔndərt]
400 four hundred	**vierhonderd**	[vir·'hɔndərt]

500 five hundred	**vijfhonderd**	[vɛjf·'hɔndərt]
600 six hundred	**zeshonderd**	[zɛs·'hɔndərt]
700 seven hundred	**zevenhonderd**	['zevən·'hɔndərt]
800 eight hundred	**achthonderd**	[axt·'hɔndərt]
900 nine hundred	**negenhonderd**	['nexən·'hɔndərt]
1000 one thousand	**duizend**	['dœyzənt]
2000 two thousand	**tweeduizend**	[twē·'dœyzənt]
3000 three thousand	**drieduizend**	[dri·'dœyzənt]
10000 ten thousand	**tienduizend**	[tin·'dœyzənt]
one hundred thousand	**honderdduizend**	['hɔndərt·'dœyzənt]
million	**miljoen (het)**	[mi'ljun]
billion	**miljard (het)**	[mi'ljart]

6. Ordinal numbers

first (adj)	**eerste**	['ērstə]
second (adj)	**tweede**	['twēdə]
third (adj)	**derde**	['dɛrdə]
fourth (adj)	**vierde**	['virdə]
fifth (adj)	**vijfde**	['vɛjfdə]
sixth (adj)	**zesde**	['zɛsdə]
seventh (adj)	**zevende**	['zevəndə]
eighth (adj)	**achtste**	['axtstə]
ninth (adj)	**negende**	['nexəndə]
tenth (adj)	**tiende**	['tində]

7. Numbers. Fractions

fraction	**breukgetal (het)**	['brøkxə'tal]
one half	**half**	[half]
one third	**een derde**	[en 'dɛrdə]
one quarter	**kwart**	['kwart]
one eighth	**een achtste**	[en 'axtstə]
one tenth	**een tiende**	[en 'tində]
two thirds	**twee derde**	[twē 'dɛrdə]
three quarters	**driekwart**	['drikwart]

8. Numbers. Basic operations

subtraction	**aftrekking (de)**	['aftrɛkiŋ]
to subtract (vi, vt)	**aftrekken**	['aftrɛkən]
division	**deling (de)**	['deliŋ]
to divide (vt)	**delen**	['delən]

addition	optelling (de)	['ɔptɛliŋ]
to add up (vt)	erbij optellen	[ɛr'bɛj 'ɔptɛlən]
to add (vi, vt)	optellen	['ɔptɛlən]
multiplication	vermenigvuldiging (de)	[vər'menix·'vʉldixiŋ]
to multiply (vt)	vermenigvuldigen	[vər'menix·'vʉldixən]

9. Numbers. Miscellaneous

digit, figure	cijfer (het)	['sɛjfər]
number	nummer (het)	['nʉmər]
numeral	telwoord (het)	[tɛl'wõrt]
minus sign	minteken (het)	['min·tekən]
plus sign	plusteken (het)	['plʉs·tekən]
formula	formule (de)	[fɔr'mʉlə]

calculation	berekening (de)	[bə'rekəniŋ]
to count (vi, vt)	tellen	['tɛlən]
to count up	bijrekenen	[bɛj'rekənən]
to compare (vt)	vergelijken	[vɛrxə'lɛjkən]

How much?	Hoeveel?	[hu'vēl]
sum, total	som (de), totaal (het)	[sɔm], [to'tāl]
result	uitkomst (de)	['œytkɔmst]
remainder	rest (de)	[rɛst]

a few (e.g., ~ years ago)	enkele	['ɛnkələ]
little (I had ~ time)	weinig	['wɛjnəx]
a little (~ tired)	een beetje	[en 'bētʃə]
the rest	restant (het)	[rɛs'tant]
one and a half	anderhalf	[andər'half]
dozen	dozijn (het)	[do'zɛjn]

in half (adv)	middendoor	[midən'dõr]
equally (evenly)	even	['ɛvən]
half	helft (de)	[hɛlft]
time (three ~s)	keer (de)	[kēr]

10. The most important verbs. Part 1

to advise (vt)	adviseren	[atvi'zirən]
to agree (say yes)	instemmen	['instɛmən]
to answer (vi, vt)	antwoorden	['antwõrdən]
to apologize (vi)	zich verontschuldigen	[zih verɔnt'sxʉldəxən]
to arrive (vi)	aankomen	['ānkɔmən]

to ask (~ oneself)	vragen	['vraxən]
to ask (~ sb to do sth)	verzoeken	[vər'zukən]
to be (vi)	zijn	[zɛjn]

to be afraid	bang zijn	['baŋ zɛjn]
to be hungry	honger hebben	['hɔŋər 'hɛbən]
to be interested in ...	zich interesseren voor ...	[zix interə'serən vōr]
to be needed	nodig zijn	['nɔdəx zɛjn]
to be surprised	verbaasd zijn	[vər'bāst zɛjn]

to be thirsty	dorst hebben	[dɔrst 'hɛbən]
to begin (vt)	beginnen	[bə'xinən]
to belong to ...	toebehoren aan ...	['tubəhɔrən ān]
to boast (vi)	opscheppen	['ɔpsxepən]
to break (split into pieces)	breken	['brekən]

to call (~ for help)	roepen	['rupən]
can (v aux)	kunnen	['kʉnən]
to catch (vt)	vangen	['vaŋən]
to change (vt)	veranderen	[və'randərən]
to choose (select)	kiezen	['kizən]

to come down (the stairs)	afdalen	['afdalən]
to compare (vt)	vergelijken	[vɛrxə'lɛjkən]
to complain (vi, vt)	klagen	['klaxən]
to confuse (mix up)	verwarren	[vər'warən]
to continue (vt)	vervolgen	[vər'vɔlxən]
to control (vt)	controleren	[kɔntrɔ'lerən]

to cook (dinner)	bereiden	[bə'rɛjdən]
to cost (vt)	kosten	['kostən]
to count (add up)	tellen	['tɛlən]
to count on ...	rekenen op ...	['rekənən ɔp]
to create (vt)	creëren	[kre'jerən]
to cry (weep)	huilen	['hœylən]

11. The most important verbs. Part 2

to deceive (vi, vt)	bedriegen	[bə'drixən]
to decorate (tree, street)	versieren	[vər'sirən]
to defend (a country, etc.)	verdedigen	[vər'dedixən]
to demand (request firmly)	eisen	['ɛjsən]
to dig (vt)	graven	['xravən]

to discuss (vt)	bespreken	[bə'sprekən]
to do (vt)	doen	[dun]
to doubt (have doubts)	twijfelen	['twɛjfelən]
to drop (let fall)	laten vallen	['latən 'valən]
to enter (room, house, etc.)	binnengaan	['binənxān]

to excuse (forgive)	excuseren	[ɛkskʉ'zerən]
to exist (vi)	existeren	[ɛksis'tɛrən]
to expect (foresee)	voorzien	[vōr'zin]

to explain (vt)	verklaren	[vər'klarən]
to fall (vi)	vallen	['valən]
to find (vt)	vinden	['vindən]
to finish (vt)	beëindigen	[be'ɛjndəxən]
to fly (vi)	vliegen	['vlixən]
to follow ... (come after)	volgen	['vɔlxən]
to forget (vi, vt)	vergeten	[vər'xetən]
to forgive (vt)	vergeven	[vər'xevən]
to give (vt)	geven	['xevən]
to give a hint	een hint geven	[en hint 'xevən]
to go (on foot)	gaan	[xān]
to go for a swim	gaan zwemmen	[xān 'zwɛmən]
to go out (for dinner, etc.)	uitgaan	['œʏtxān]
to guess (the answer)	goed raden	[xut 'radən]
to have (vt)	hebben	['hɛbən]
to have breakfast	ontbijten	[ɔn'bɛjtən]
to have dinner	souperen	[su'perən]
to have lunch	lunchen	['lʏnʃən]
to hear (vt)	horen	['horən]
to help (vt)	helpen	['hɛlpən]
to hide (vt)	verbergen	[vər'bɛrxən]
to hope (vi, vt)	hopen	['hopən]
to hunt (vi, vt)	jagen	['jaxən]
to hurry (vi)	zich haasten	[zix 'hāstən]

12. The most important verbs. Part 3

to inform (vt)	informeren	[infɔr'merən]
to insist (vi, vt)	aandringen	['āndriŋən]
to insult (vt)	beledigen	[bə'ledəxən]
to invite (vt)	uitnodigen	['œʏtnɔdixən]
to joke (vi)	grappen maken	['xrapən 'makən]
to keep (vt)	bewaren	[bə'warən]
to keep silent	zwijgen	['zwɛjxən]
to kill (vt)	doden	['dodən]
to know (sb)	kennen	['kɛnən]
to know (sth)	weten	['wetən]
to laugh (vi)	lachen	['laxən]
to liberate (city, etc.)	bevrijden	[bə'vrɛjdən]
to like (I like ...)	bevallen	[bə'valən]
to look for ... (search)	zoeken	['zukən]
to love (sb)	liefhebben	['lifhɛbən]
to make a mistake	zich vergissen	[zih vər'xisən]

to manage, to run	beheren	[bə'herən]
to mean (signify)	betekenen	[bə'tekənən]
to mention (talk about)	vermelden	[vər'mɛldən]
to miss (school, etc.)	verzuimen	[vər'zœymən]
to notice (see)	opmerken	['ɔpmɛrkən]
to object (vi, vt)	weerspreken	[wěr'sprekən]
to observe (see)	waarnemen	['wārnemən]
to open (vt)	openen	['ɔpənən]
to order (meal, etc.)	bestellen	[bə'stɛlən]
to order (mil.)	bevelen	[bə'velən]
to own (possess)	bezitten	[bə'zitən]
to participate (vi)	deelnemen	['dělnemən]
to pay (vi, vt)	betalen	[bə'talən]
to permit (vt)	toestaan	['tustān]
to plan (vt)	plannen	['planən]
to play (children)	spelen	['spelən]
to pray (vi, vt)	bidden	['bidən]
to prefer (vt)	prefereren	[prəfe'rerən]
to promise (vt)	beloven	[bə'lovən]
to pronounce (vt)	uitspreken	['œytsprekən]
to propose (vt)	voorstellen	['vōrstɛlən]
to punish (vt)	bestraffen	[bə'strafən]

13. The most important verbs. Part 4

to read (vi, vt)	lezen	['lezən]
to recommend (vt)	aanbevelen	['āmbəvelən]
to refuse (vi, vt)	weigeren	['wɛjxərən]
to regret (be sorry)	betreuren	[bə'trørən]
to rent (sth from sb)	huren	['hʉrən]
to repeat (say again)	herhalen	[hɛr'halən]
to reserve, to book	reserveren	[rezɛr'verən]
to run (vi)	rennen	['renən]
to save (rescue)	redden	['rɛdən]
to say (~ thank you)	zeggen	['zexən]
to scold (vt)	uitvaren tegen	['œytvarən 'texən]
to see (vt)	zien	[zin]
to sell (vt)	verkopen	[vɛr'kopən]
to send (vt)	sturen	['stʉrən]
to shoot (vi)	schieten	['sxitən]
to shout (vi)	schreeuwen	['sxrěwən]
to show (vt)	tonen	['tonən]
to sign (document)	ondertekenen	['ɔndər'tekənən]
to sit down (vi)	gaan zitten	[xān 'zitən]

to smile (vi)	glimlachen	['xlimlahən]
to speak (vi, vt)	spreken	['sprekən]
to steal (money, etc.)	stelen	['stelən]
to stop (for pause, etc.)	stoppen	['stɔpən]
to stop (please ~ calling me)	ophouden	['ɔphaudən]

to study (vt)	studeren	[stʉ'derən]
to swim (vi)	zwemmen	['zwɛmən]
to take (vt)	nemen	['nemən]
to think (vi, vt)	denken	['dɛnkən]
to threaten (vt)	bedreigen	[bə'drɛjxən]

to touch (with hands)	aanraken	['ānrakən]
to translate (vt)	vertalen	[vər'talən]
to trust (vt)	vertrouwen	[vər'trauwən]
to try (attempt)	proberen	[prɔ'berən]
to turn (e.g., ~ left)	afslaan	['afslān]

to underestimate (vt)	onderschatten	['ɔndər'sxatən]
to understand (vt)	begrijpen	[bə'xrɛjpən]
to unite (vt)	verenigen	[və'rɛnixən]
to wait (vt)	wachten	['waxtən]

to want (wish, desire)	willen	['wilən]
to warn (vt)	waarschuwen	['wārsxjuvən]
to work (vi)	werken	['wɛrkən]
to write (vt)	schrijven	['sxrɛjvən]
to write down	opschrijven	['ɔpsxrɛjvən]

14. Colors

color	kleur (de)	['klør]
shade (tint)	tint (de)	[tint]
hue	kleurnuance (de)	['klør·nʉ'waŋsə]
rainbow	regenboog (de)	['rexən·bōx]

white (adj)	wit	[wit]
black (adj)	zwart	[zwart]
gray (adj)	grijs	[xrɛjs]

green (adj)	groen	[xrun]
yellow (adj)	geel	[xēl]
red (adj)	rood	[rōt]

blue (adj)	blauw	['blau]
light blue (adj)	lichtblauw	['lixt·blau]
pink (adj)	roze	['rɔzə]
orange (adj)	oranje	[ɔ'ranjə]
violet (adj)	violet	[viɔ'lɛt]

brown (adj)	bruin	['brœyn]
golden (adj)	goud	['xaut]
silvery (adj)	zilverkleurig	['zilvər·'klørəx]

beige (adj)	beige	['bɛ:ʒ]
cream (adj)	roomkleurig	['rōm·'klørix]
turquoise (adj)	turkoois	[tʉrk'was]
cherry red (adj)	kersrood	['kɛrs·rōt]
lilac (adj)	lila	['lila]
crimson (adj)	karmijnrood	['karmɛjn·'rōt]

light (adj)	licht	[lixt]
dark (adj)	donker	['dɔnkər]
bright, vivid (adj)	fel	[fel]

colored (pencils)	kleur-, kleurig	['klør], ['klørəx]
color (e.g., ~ film)	kleuren-	['klørən]
black-and-white (adj)	zwart-wit	[zwart-wit]
plain (one-colored)	eenkleurig	[ēn'klørəx]
multicolored (adj)	veelkleurig	[vēl'klørəx]

15. Questions

Who?	Wie?	[wi]
What?	Wat?	[wat]
Where? (at, in)	Waar?	[wār]
Where (to)?	Waarheen?	[wār'hēn]
From where?	Waarvandaan?	[uăr·van'dān]
When?	Wanneer?	[wa'nēr]
Why? (What for?)	Waarom?	[wār'ɔm]
Why? (~ are you crying?)	Waarom?	[wār'ɔm]

What for?	Waarvoor dan ook?	[wār'vōr dan 'ōk]
How? (in what way)	Hoe?	[hu]
What? (What kind of ...?)	Wat voor ...?	[wat vɔr]
Which?	Welk?	[wɛlk]
To whom?	Aan wie?	[ān wi]
About whom?	Over wie?	['ɔvər wi]
About what?	Waarover?	[wār'ɔvər]
With whom?	Met wie?	[mɛt 'wi]

| How many? How much? | Hoeveel? | [hu'vēl] |
| Whose? | Van wie? | [van 'wi] |

16. Prepositions

| with (accompanied by) | met | [mɛt] |
| without | zonder | ['zɔndər] |

to (indicating direction)	naar	[nār]
about (talking ~ ...)	over	['ɔvər]
before (in time)	voor	[vōr]
in front of ...	voor	[vōr]

under (beneath, below)	onder	['ɔndər]
above (over)	boven	['bovən]
on (atop)	op	[ɔp]
from (off, out of)	van	[van]
of (made from)	van	[van]

| in (e.g., ~ ten minutes) | over | ['ɔvər] |
| over (across the top of) | over | ['ɔvər] |

17. Function words. Adverbs. Part 1

Where? (at, in)	Waar?	[wār]
here (adv)	hier	[hir]
there (adv)	daar	[dār]

| somewhere (to be) | ergens | ['ɛrxəns] |
| nowhere (not anywhere) | nergens | ['nɛrxəns] |

| by (near, beside) | bij ... | [bɛj] |
| by the window | bij het raam | [bɛj het 'rām] |

Where (to)?	Waarheen?	[wār'hēn]
here (e.g., come ~!)	hierheen	[hir'hēn]
there (e.g., to go ~)	daarheen	[dār'hēn]
from here (adv)	hiervandaan	[hirvan'dān]
from there (adv)	daarvandaan	[darvan'dān]

| close (adv) | dichtbij | [dix'bɛj] |
| far (adv) | ver | [vɛr] |

near (e.g., ~ Paris)	in de buurt	[in də būrt]
nearby (adv)	dichtbij	[dix'bɛj]
not far (adv)	niet ver	[nit vɛr]

left (adj)	linker	['linkər]
on the left	links	[links]
to the left	linksaf, naar links	['linksaf], [nār 'links]

right (adj)	rechter	['rɛxtər]
on the right	rechts	[rɛxts]
to the right	rechtsaf, naar rechts	['rɛxtsaf], [nār 'rɛxts]

in front (adv)	vooraan	[võ'rān]
front (as adj)	voorste	['võrstə]
ahead (the kids ran ~)	vooruit	[võr'œyt]

behind (adv)	achter	['axtər]
from behind	van achteren	[van 'axtərən]
back (towards the rear)	achteruit	['axtərœʏt]

| middle | midden (het) | ['midən] |
| in the middle | in het midden | [in ət 'midən] |

at the side	opzij	[ɔp'sɛj]
everywhere (adv)	overal	[ɔvə'ral]
around (in all directions)	omheen	[ɔm'hēn]

from inside	binnenuit	['binənœʏt]
somewhere (to go)	naar ergens	[nār 'ɛrxəns]
straight (directly)	rechtdoor	[rɛx'dōr]
back (e.g., come ~)	terug	[te'rʉx]

| from anywhere | ergens vandaan | ['ɛrxəns van'dān] |
| from somewhere | ergens vandaan | ['ɛrxəns van'dān] |

firstly (adv)	ten eerste	[tən 'ērstə]
secondly (adv)	ten tweede	[tən 'twēdə]
thirdly (adv)	ten derde	[tən 'dɛrdə]

suddenly (adv)	plotseling	['plɔtseliŋ]
at first (in the beginning)	in het begin	[in ət bə'xin]
for the first time	voor de eerste keer	[vōr də 'ērstə kēr]
long before ...	lang voor ...	[laŋ vōr]
anew (over again)	opnieuw	[ɔp'niu]
for good (adv)	voor eeuwig	[vōr 'ēwəx]

never (adv)	nooit	[nōjt]
again (adv)	weer	[wēr]
now (adv)	nu	[nʉ]
often (adv)	vaak	[vāk]
then (adv)	toen	[tun]
urgently (quickly)	urgent	[jurxənt]
usually (adv)	meestal	['mēstal]

by the way, ...	trouwens, ...	['trauwəns]
possible (that is ~)	mogelijk	['mɔxələk]
probably (adv)	waarschijnlijk	[wār'sxɛjnlək]
maybe (adv)	misschien	[mis'xin]
besides ...	trouwens	['trauwəns]
that's why ...	daarom ...	[dā'rɔm]
in spite of ...	in weerwil van ...	[in 'wērwil van]
thanks to ...	dankzij ...	[dank'zɛj]

what (pron.)	wat	[wat]
that (conj.)	dat	[dat]
something	iets	[its]
anything (something)	iets	[its]
nothing	niets	[nits]

who (pron.)	wie	[wi]
someone	iemand	['imant]
somebody	iemand	['imant]

nobody	niemand	['nimant]
nowhere (a voyage to ~)	nergens	['nɛrxəns]
nobody's	niemands	['nimants]
somebody's	iemands	['imants]

so (I'm ~ glad)	zo	[zɔ]
also (as well)	ook	[ōk]
too (as well)	alsook	[al'sōk]

18. Function words. Adverbs. Part 2

Why?	Waarom?	[wār'ɔm]
for some reason	om een bepaalde reden	[ɔm en be'pāldə 'redən]
because ...	omdat ...	[ɔm'dat]
for some purpose	voor een bepaald doel	[vōr en be'pālt dul]

and	en	[en]
or	of	[ɔf]
but	maar	[mār]
for (e.g., ~ me)	voor	[vōr]

too (~ many people)	te	[te]
only (exclusively)	alleen	[a'lēn]
exactly (adv)	precies	[prə'sis]
about (more or less)	ongeveer	[ɔnxə'vēr]

approximately (adv)	ongeveer	[ɔnxə'vēr]
approximate (adj)	bij benadering	[bɛj bə'nadəriŋ]
almost (adv)	bijna	['bɛjna]
the rest	rest (de)	[rɛst]

the other (second)	de andere	[də 'andərə]
other (different)	ander	['andər]
each (adj)	elk	[ɛlk]
any (no matter which)	om het even welk	[ɔm ət ɛvən wɛlk]
many, much (a lot of)	veel	[vēl]
many people	veel mensen	[vēl 'mɛnsən]
all (everyone)	iedereen	[idə'rēn]

in return for ...	in ruil voor ...	[in 'rœyl vōr]
in exchange (adv)	in ruil	[in 'rœyl]
by hand (made)	met de hand	[mɛt də 'hant]
hardly (negative opinion)	onwaarschijnlijk	[ɔnwār'sxɛjnlək]

| probably (adv) | waarschijnlijk | [wār'sxɛjnlək] |
| on purpose (intentionally) | met opzet | [mɛt 'ɔpzət] |

by accident (adv)	**toevallig**	[tuˈvaləx]
very (adv)	**zeer**	[zēr]
for example (adv)	**bijvoorbeeld**	[bɛjˈvõrbēlt]
between	**tussen**	[ˈtʉsən]
among	**tussen**	[ˈtʉsən]
so much (such a lot)	**zoveel**	[zɔˈvēl]
especially (adv)	**vooral**	[võˈral]

Basic concepts. Part 2

19. Weekdays

Monday	maandag (de)	['māndax]
Tuesday	dinsdag (de)	['dinsdax]
Wednesday	woensdag (de)	['wunsdax]
Thursday	donderdag (de)	['dondərdax]
Friday	vrijdag (de)	['vrɛjdax]
Saturday	zaterdag (de)	['zatərdax]
Sunday	zondag (de)	['zɔndax]
today (adv)	vandaag	[van'dāx]
tomorrow (adv)	morgen	['mɔrxən]
the day after tomorrow	overmorgen	[ɔvər'mɔrxən]
yesterday (adv)	gisteren	['xistərən]
the day before yesterday	eergisteren	[ēr'xistərən]
day	dag (de)	[dax]
working day	werkdag (de)	['wɛrk·dax]
public holiday	feestdag (de)	['fēst·dax]
day off	verlofdag (de)	[vər'lɔfdax]
weekend	weekend (het)	['wikənt]
all day long	de hele dag	[də 'helə dah]
the next day (adv)	de volgende dag	[də 'vɔlxəndə dax]
two days ago	twee dagen geleden	[twē 'daxən xə'ledən]
the day before	aan de vooravond	[ān də vō'ravɔnt]
daily (adj)	dag-, dagelijks	[dax], ['daxələks]
every day (adv)	elke dag	['ɛlkə dax]
week	week (de)	[wēk]
last week (adv)	vorige week	['vɔrixə wēk]
next week (adv)	volgende week	['vɔlxəndə wēk]
weekly (adj)	wekelijks	['wekələks]
every week (adv)	elke week	['ɛlkə wēk]
twice a week	twee keer per week	[twē ker pər vēk]
every Tuesday	elke dinsdag	['ɛlkə 'dinsdax]

20. Hours. Day and night

morning	morgen (de)	['mɔrxən]
in the morning	's morgens	[s 'mɔrxəns]
noon, midday	middag (de)	['midax]

in the afternoon	**'s middags**	[s 'midax]
evening	**avond (de)**	['avɔnt]
in the evening	**'s avonds**	[s 'avɔnts]
night	**nacht (de)**	[naxt]
at night	**'s nachts**	[s naxts]
midnight	**middernacht (de)**	['midər·naxt]
second	**seconde (de)**	[se'kɔndə]
minute	**minuut (de)**	[mi'nūt]
hour	**uur (het)**	[ūr]
half an hour	**halfuur (het)**	[half 'ūr]
a quarter-hour	**kwartier (het)**	['kwar'tir]
fifteen minutes	**vijftien minuten**	['vɛjftin mi'nutən]
24 hours	**etmaal (het)**	['ɛtmāl]
sunrise	**zonsopgang (de)**	[zɔns'ɔpxaŋ]
dawn	**dageraad (de)**	['daxərāt]
early morning	**vroege morgen (de)**	['vruxə 'mɔrxen]
sunset	**zonsondergang (de)**	[zɔns'ɔndərxaŋ]
early in the morning	**'s morgens vroeg**	[s 'mɔrxəns vrux]
this morning	**vanmorgen**	[van'mɔrxen]
tomorrow morning	**morgenochtend**	['mɔrxən·'ɔhtənt]
this afternoon	**vanmiddag**	[van'midax]
in the afternoon	**'s middags**	[s 'midax]
tomorrow afternoon	**morgenmiddag**	['mɔrxən·'midax]
tonight (this evening)	**vanavond**	[va'navɔnt]
tomorrow night	**morgenavond**	['mɔrxən·'avɔnt]
at 3 o'clock sharp	**klokslag drie uur**	['klɔkslax dri ūr]
about 4 o'clock	**ongeveer vier uur**	[ɔnxə'vēr vir ūr]
by 12 o'clock	**tegen twaalf uur**	['texən twālf ūr]
in 20 minutes	**over twintig minuten**	['ɔvər 'twintix mi'nutən]
in an hour	**over een uur**	['ɔvər en ūr]
on time (adv)	**op tijd**	[ɔp tɛjt]
a quarter of ...	**kwart voor ...**	['kwart vōr]
within an hour	**binnen een uur**	['binən en ūr]
every 15 minutes	**elk kwartier**	['ɛlk kwar'tir]
round the clock	**de klok rond**	[də klɔk rɔnt]

21. Months. Seasons

January	**januari (de)**	[janu'ari]
February	**februari (de)**	[febru'ari]
March	**maart (de)**	[mārt]
April	**april (de)**	[ap'ril]

| May | mei (de) | [mɛj] |
| June | juni (de) | ['juni] |

July	juli (de)	['juli]
August	augustus (de)	[au'xʉstʉs]
September	september (de)	[sɛp'tɛmbər]
October	oktober (de)	[ɔk'tɔbər]
November	november (de)	[nɔ'vɛmbər]
December	december (de)	[de'sɛmbər]

spring	lente (de)	['lɛntə]
in spring	in de lente	[in də 'lɛntə]
spring (as adj)	lente-	['lɛntə]

summer	zomer (de)	['zɔmər]
in summer	in de zomer	[in də 'zɔmər]
summer (as adj)	zomer-, zomers	['zɔmər], ['zɔmərs]

fall	herfst (de)	[hɛrfst]
in fall	in de herfst	[in də hɛrfst]
fall (as adj)	herfst-	[hɛrfst]

winter	winter (de)	['wintər]
in winter	in de winter	[in də 'wintər]
winter (as adj)	winter-	['wintər]

month	maand (de)	[mānt]
this month	deze maand	['dezə mānt]
next month	volgende maand	['vɔlxəndə mānt]
last month	vorige maand	['vɔrixə mānt]

a month ago	een maand geleden	[en mānt xə'ledən]
in a month (a month later)	over een maand	['ɔvər en mānt]
in 2 months (2 months later)	over twee maanden	['ɔvər twē 'māndən]
the whole month	de hele maand	[də 'helə mānt]
all month long	een volle maand	[en 'vɔlə mānt]

monthly (~ magazine)	maand-, maandelijks	[mānt], ['māndələks]
monthly (adv)	maandelijks	['māndələks]
every month	elke maand	['ɛlkə mānt]
twice a month	twee keer per maand	[twē ker per mānt]

year	jaar (het)	[jār]
this year	dit jaar	[dit jār]
next year	volgend jaar	['vɔlxənt jār]
last year	vorig jaar	['vɔrəx jār]

a year ago	een jaar geleden	[en jār xə'ledən]
in a year	over een jaar	['ɔvər en jār]
in two years	over twee jaar	['ɔvər twē jār]
the whole year	het hele jaar	[ət 'helə jār]

all year long	een vol jaar	[en vɔl jār]
every year	elk jaar	[ɛlk jār]
annual (adj)	jaar-, jaarlijks	[jār], ['jārləks]
annually (adv)	jaarlijks	['jārləks]
4 times a year	4 keer per jaar	[vir kēr per 'jār]

date (e.g., today's ~)	datum (de)	['datʉm]
date (e.g., ~ of birth)	datum (de)	['datʉm]
calendar	kalender (de)	[ka'lɛndər]

half a year	een half jaar	[en half jār]
six months	zes maanden	[zɛs 'māndən]
season (summer, etc.)	seizoen (het)	[sɛj'zun]
century	eeuw (de)	[ēw]

22. Time. Miscellaneous

time	tijd (de)	[tɛjt]
moment	ogenblik (het)	['ɔxənblik]
instant (n)	moment (het)	[mɔ'mɛnt]
instant (adj)	ogenblikkelijk	['ɔxən'blikələk]
lapse (of time)	tijdsbestek (het)	['tɛjts·bɛstək]
life	leven (het)	['levən]
eternity	eeuwigheid (de)	['ēwəxhɛjt]

epoch	epoche (de),	[ɛ'pɔxə],
	tijdperk (het)	['tɛjtpɛrk]
era	era (de), tijdperk (het)	['ɛra], ['tɛjtpɛrk]
cycle	cyclus (de)	['siklʉs]
period	periode (de)	[peri'ɔdə]
term (short-~)	termijn (de)	[tɛr'mɛjn]

the future	toekomst (de)	['tukɔmst]
future (as adj)	toekomstig	[tu'kɔmstəx]
next time	de volgende keer	[də 'vɔlxəndə kēr]
the past	verleden (het)	[vər'ledən]
past (recent)	vorig	['vɔrəx]
last time	de vorige keer	[də 'vɔrixə kēr]

later (adv)	later	['latər]
after (prep.)	na	[na]
nowadays (adv)	tegenwoordig	['texən·'wōrdəx]
now (adv)	nu	[nʉ]
immediately (adv)	onmiddellijk	[ɔn'midələk]
soon (adv)	snel	[snɛl]
in advance (beforehand)	bij voorbaat	[bɛj vōr'bāt]

a long time ago	lang geleden	[laŋ xə'ledən]
recently (adv)	kort geleden	[kɔrt xə'ledən]
destiny	noodlot (het)	['nōtlɔt]

| memories (childhood ~) | herinneringen | [hɛ'rinəriŋ] |
| archives | archief (het) | [ar'xif] |

during ...	tijdens ...	['tɛjdəns]
long, a long time (adv)	lang	[laŋ]
not long (adv)	niet lang	[nit laŋ]
early (in the morning)	vroeg	[vrux]
late (not early)	laat	[lāt]

forever (for good)	voor altijd	[vōr al'tɛjt]
to start (begin)	beginnen	[bə'xinən]
to postpone (vt)	uitstellen	['œytstɛlən]

at the same time	tegelijkertijd	[təxəlɛjkər'tɛjt]
permanently (adv)	voortdurend	[vōr'dɯrənt]
constant (noise, pain)	voortdurend	[vōr'dɯrənt]
temporary (adj)	tijdelijk	['tɛjdələk]

sometimes (adv)	soms	[sɔms]
rarely (adv)	zelden	['zɛldən]
often (adv)	vaak	[vāk]

23. Opposites

| rich (adj) | rijk | [rɛjk] |
| poor (adj) | arm | [arm] |

| ill, sick (adj) | ziek | [zik] |
| well (not sick) | gezond | [xə'zɔnt] |

| big (adj) | groot | [xrōt] |
| small (adj) | klein | [klɛjn] |

| quickly (adv) | snel | [snɛl] |
| slowly (adv) | langzaam | ['laŋzām] |

| fast (adj) | snel | [snɛl] |
| slow (adj) | langzaam | ['laŋzām] |

| glad (adj) | vrolijk | ['vrɔlək] |
| sad (adj) | treurig | ['trørəx] |

| together (adv) | samen | ['samən] |
| separately (adv) | apart | [a'part] |

| aloud (to read) | hardop | ['hartɔp] |
| silently (to oneself) | stil | [stil] |

| tall (adj) | hoog | [hōx] |
| low (adj) | laag | [lāx] |

| deep (adj) | diep | [dip] |
| shallow (adj) | ondiep | [ɔn'dip] |

| yes | ja | [ja] |
| no | nee | [nē] |

| distant (in space) | ver | [vɛr] |
| nearby (adj) | dicht | [dixt] |

| far (adv) | ver | [vɛr] |
| nearby (adv) | dichtbij | [dix'bɛj] |

| long (adj) | lang | [laŋ] |
| short (adj) | kort | [kɔrt] |

| good (kindhearted) | vriendelijk | ['vrindələk] |
| evil (adj) | kwaad | ['kwãt] |

| married (adj) | gehuwd | [xə'hʉwt] |
| single (adj) | ongehuwd | [ɔnhə'hʉwt] |

| to forbid (vt) | verbieden | [vər'bidən] |
| to permit (vt) | toestaan | ['tustãn] |

| end | einde (het) | ['ɛjndə] |
| beginning | begin (het) | [bə'xin] |

| left (adj) | linker | ['linkər] |
| right (adj) | rechter | ['rɛxtər] |

| first (adj) | eerste | ['ērstə] |
| last (adj) | laatste | ['lãtstə] |

| crime | misdaad (de) | ['misdãt] |
| punishment | bestraffing (de) | [bə'strafiŋ] |

| to order (vt) | bevelen | [bə'velən] |
| to obey (vi, vt) | gehoorzamen | [xə'hōrzamən] |

| straight (adj) | recht | [rɛxt] |
| curved (adj) | krom | [krɔm] |

| paradise | paradijs (het) | [para'dajs] |
| hell | hel (de) | [hɛl] |

| to be born | geboren worden | [xə'bɔrən 'wɔrdən] |
| to die (vi) | sterven | ['stɛrvən] |

strong (adj)	sterk	[stɛrk]
weak (adj)	zwak	[zwak]
old (adj)	oud	['aut]
young (adj)	jong	[jɔŋ]

| old (adj) | oud | ['aut] |
| new (adj) | nieuw | [niu] |

| hard (adj) | hard | [hart] |
| soft (adj) | zacht | [zaxt] |

| warm (tepid) | warm | [warm] |
| cold (adj) | koud | ['kaut] |

| fat (adj) | dik | [dik] |
| thin (adj) | dun | [dʉn] |

| narrow (adj) | smal | [smal] |
| wide (adj) | breed | [brēt] |

| good (adj) | goed | [xut] |
| bad (adj) | slecht | [slɛxt] |

| brave (adj) | moedig | ['mudəx] |
| cowardly (adj) | laf | [laf] |

24. Lines and shapes

square	vierkant (het)	['virkant]
square (as adj)	vierkant	['virkant]
circle	cirkel (de)	['sirkəl]
round (adj)	rond	[ront]
triangle	driehoek (de)	['drihuk]
triangular (adj)	driehoekig	[dri'hukəx]

oval	ovaal (het)	[ɔ'vāl]
oval (as adj)	ovaal	[ɔ'vāl]
rectangle	rechthoek (de)	['rɛxthuk]
rectangular (adj)	rechthoekig	[rɛht'hukəx]

pyramid	piramide (de)	[pira'midə]
rhombus	ruit (de)	['rœyt]
trapezoid	trapezium (het)	[tra'pezijum]
cube	kubus (de)	['kʉbʉs]
prism	prisma (het)	['prizma]

circumference	omtrek (de)	['ɔmtrɛk]
sphere	bol, sfeer (de)	[bɔl], [sfēr]
ball (solid sphere)	bal (de)	[bal]
diameter	diameter (de)	['diametər]
radius	straal (de)	[strāl]
perimeter (circle's ~)	omtrek (de)	['ɔmtrɛk]
center	middelpunt (het)	['midəl·pʉnt]
horizontal (adj)	horizontaal	[hɔrizɔn'tāl]
vertical (adj)	verticaal	[vərti'kāl]

| parallel (n) | parallel (de) | [para'lɛl] |
| parallel (as adj) | parallel | [para'lɛl] |

line	lijn (de)	[lɛjn]
stroke	streep (de)	[strēp]
straight line	rechte lijn (de)	['rɛxtə lɛjn]
curve (curved line)	kromme (de)	['krɔmə]
thin (line, etc.)	dun	[dʉn]
contour (outline)	omlijning (de)	[ɔm'lɛjniŋ]

intersection	snijpunt (het)	['snɛj·punt]
right angle	rechte hoek (de)	['rɛxtə huk]
segment	segment (het)	[sɛx'mɛnt]
sector	sector (de)	['sɛktɔr]
side (of triangle)	zijde (de)	['zɛjdə]
angle	hoek (de)	[huk]

25. Units of measurement

weight	gewicht (het)	[xə'wixt]
length	lengte (de)	['lɛŋtə]
width	breedte (de)	['brētə]
height	hoogte (de)	['hõxtə]
depth	diepte (de)	['diptə]
volume	volume (het)	[vɔ'lʉmə]
area	oppervlakte (de)	['ɔpərvlaktə]

gram	gram (het)	[xram]
milligram	milligram (het)	['milixram]
kilogram	kilogram (het)	[kilɔxram]
ton	ton (de)	[tɔn]
pound	pond (het)	[pɔnt]
ounce	ons (het)	[ɔns]

meter	meter (de)	['metər]
millimeter	millimeter (de)	['milimetər]
centimeter	centimeter (de)	['sɛnti'metər]
kilometer	kilometer (de)	[kilɔmetər]
mile	mijl (de)	[mɛjl]

inch	duim (de)	['dœɤm]
foot	voet (de)	[vut]
yard	yard (de)	[jart]

| square meter | vierkante meter (de) | ['virkantə 'metər] |
| hectare | hectare (de) | [hɛk'tarə] |

liter	liter (de)	['litər]
degree	graad (de)	[xrãt]
volt	volt (de)	[vɔlt]

| ampere | ampère (de) | [am'pɛrə] |
| horsepower | paardenkracht (de) | ['pārdən·kraxt] |

quantity	hoeveelheid (de)	[hu'vēlhɛjt]
a little bit of ...	een beetje ...	[en 'bētʃə]
half	helft (de)	[hɛlft]
dozen	dozijn (het)	[dɔ'zɛjn]
piece (item)	stuk (het)	[stʉk]

| size | afmeting (de) | ['afmetiŋ] |
| scale (map ~) | schaal (de) | [sxāl] |

minimal (adj)	minimaal	[mini'māl]
the smallest (adj)	minste	['minstə]
medium (adj)	medium	['medijum]
maximal (adj)	maximaal	[maksi'māl]
the largest (adj)	grootste	['xrōtstə]

26. Containers

canning jar (glass ~)	glazen pot (de)	['xlazən pɔt]
can	blik (het)	[blik]
bucket	emmer (de)	['ɛmər]
barrel	ton (de)	[tɔn]

wash basin (e.g., plastic ~)	ronde waterbak (de)	['watər·bak]
tank (100L water ~)	tank (de)	[tank]
hip flask	heupfles (de)	['hʉp·flɛs]
jerrycan	jerrycan (de)	['dʒɛrikən]
tank (e.g., tank car)	tank (de)	[tank]

mug	beker (de)	['bekər]
cup (of coffee, etc.)	kopje (het)	['kɔpjə]
saucer	schoteltje (het)	['sxɔteltʃə]
glass (tumbler)	glas (het)	[xlas]
wine glass	wijnglas (het)	['wɛjn·xlas]
stock pot (soup pot)	pan (de)	[pan]

| bottle (~ of wine) | fles (de) | [fles] |
| neck (of the bottle, etc.) | flessenhals (de) | ['flesən·hals] |

carafe (decanter)	karaf (de)	[ka'raf]
pitcher	kruik (de)	['krœɤk]
vessel (container)	vat (het)	[vat]
pot (crock, stoneware ~)	pot (de)	[pɔt]
vase	vaas (de)	[vās]

bottle (perfume ~)	flacon (de)	[fla'kɔn]
vial, small bottle	flesje (het)	['fleçə]
tube (of toothpaste)	tube (de)	['tʉbə]

sack (bag)	zak (de)	[zak]
bag (paper ~, plastic ~)	tasje (het)	['taɕə]
pack (of cigarettes, etc.)	pakje (het)	['pakjə]

box (e.g., shoebox)	doos (de)	[dōs]
crate	kist (de)	[kist]
basket	mand (de)	[mant]

27. Materials

material	materiaal (het)	[materi'āl]
wood (n)	hout (het)	['haut]
wood-, wooden (adj)	houten	['hautən]

| glass (n) | glas (het) | [xlas] |
| glass (as adj) | glazen | ['xlazən] |

| stone (n) | steen (de) | [stēn] |
| stone (as adj) | stenen | ['stenən] |

plastic (n)	plastic (het)	['plastik]
plastic (as adj)	plastic	['plastik]
rubber (n)	rubber (het)	['rʉbər]
rubber (as adj)	rubber-, rubberen	['rʉbər], ['rʉbərən]

| cloth, fabric (n) | stof (de) | [stɔf] |
| fabric (as adj) | van stof | [van 'stɔf] |

paper (n)	papier (het)	[pa'pir]
paper (as adj)	papieren	[pa'pirən]
cardboard (n)	karton (het)	[kar'tɔn]
cardboard (as adj)	kartonnen	[kar'tɔnən]

polyethylene	polyethyleen (het)	[pɔlieti'lēn]
cellophane	cellofaan (het)	[sɛlɔ'fān]
plywood	multiplex (het)	['mʉltiplɛks]

porcelain (n)	porselein (het)	[pɔrsə'lɛjn]
porcelain (as adj)	porseleinen	[pɔrsə'lɛjnən]
clay (n)	klei (de)	[klɛj]
clay (as adj)	klei-, van klei	[klɛj], [van klɛj]
ceramic (n)	keramiek (de)	[kera'mik]
ceramic (as adj)	keramieken	[ke'ramikən]

28. Metals

| metal (n) | metaal (het) | [me'tāl] |
| metal (as adj) | metalen | [me'talən] |

alloy (n)	legering (de)	[le'xɛriŋ]
gold (n)	goud (het)	['xaut]
gold, golden (adj)	gouden	['xaudən]
silver (n)	zilver (het)	['zilvər]
silver (as adj)	zilveren	['zilvərən]

iron (n)	ijzer (het)	['ɛjzər]
iron-, made of iron (adj)	ijzeren	['ɛjzərən]
steel (n)	staal (het)	[stāl]
steel (as adj)	stalen	['stalən]
copper (n)	koper (het)	['kɔpər]
copper (as adj)	koperen	['kɔpərən]

aluminum (n)	aluminium (het)	[alʉ'minijum]
aluminum (as adj)	aluminium	[alʉ'minijum]
bronze (n)	brons (het)	[brɔns]
bronze (as adj)	bronzen	['brɔnzən], [van brɔns]

brass	messing (het)	['mesiŋ]
nickel	nikkel (het)	['nikəl]
platinum	platina (het)	['platina]
mercury	kwik (het)	['kwik]
tin	tin (het)	[tin]
lead	lood (het)	[lōt]
zinc	zink (het)	[zink]

HUMAN BEING

Human being. The body

29. Humans. Basic concepts

human being	mens (de)	[mɛns]
man (adult male)	man (de)	[man]
woman	vrouw (de)	['vrau]
child	kind (het)	[kint]
girl	meisje (het)	['mɛjɕə]
boy	jongen (de)	['jɔŋən]
teenager	tiener, adolescent (de)	['tinər], [adɔlɛ'sɛnt]
old man	oude man (de)	['audə man]
old woman	oude vrouw (de)	['audə 'vrau]

30. Human anatomy

organism (body)	organisme (het)	[ɔrxa'nismə]
heart	hart (het)	[hart]
blood	bloed (het)	[blut]
artery	slagader (de)	['slaxadər]
vein	ader (de)	['adər]
brain	hersenen	['hɛrsənən]
nerve	zenuw (de)	['zenʉw]
nerves	zenuwen	['zenʉwən]
vertebra	wervel (de)	['wɛrvəl]
spine (backbone)	ruggengraat (de)	['rʉxə·xrāt]
stomach (organ)	maag (de)	[māx]
intestines, bowels	darmen	['darmən]
intestine (e.g., large ~)	darm (de)	[darm]
liver	lever (de)	['levər]
kidney	nier (de)	[nir]
bone	been (het)	[bēn]
skeleton	skelet (het)	[ske'lɛt]
rib	rib (de)	[rib]
skull	schedel (de)	['sxedəl]
muscle	spier (de)	[spir]
biceps	biceps (de)	['bisɛps]

triceps	triceps (de)	['trisɛps]
tendon	pees (de)	[pēs]
joint	gewricht (het)	[xə'wriht]
lungs	longen	['lɔŋən]
genitals	geslachtsorganen	[xə'slahts·ɔr'xanən]
skin	huid (de)	['hœyt]

31. Head

head	hoofd (het)	[hōft]
face	gezicht (het)	[xə'ziht]
nose	neus (de)	['nøs]
mouth	mond (de)	[mɔnt]

eye	oog (het)	[ōx]
eyes	ogen	['ɔxən]
pupil	pupil (de)	[pʉ'pil]
eyebrow	wenkbrauw (de)	['wɛnk·brau]
eyelash	wimper (de)	['wimpər]
eyelid	ooglid (het)	['ōx·lit]

tongue	tong (de)	[tɔŋ]
tooth	tand (de)	[tant]
lips	lippen	['lipən]
cheekbones	jukbeenderen	[juk'·bēndərən]
gum	tandvlees (het)	['tand·vlēs]
palate	gehemelte (het)	[xə'heməltə]

nostrils	neusgaten	['nøsxatən]
chin	kin (de)	[kin]
jaw	kaak (de)	[kāk]
cheek	wang (de)	[waŋ]

forehead	voorhoofd (het)	['vōrhōft]
temple	slaap (de)	[slāp]
ear	oor (het)	[ōr]
back of the head	achterhoofd (het)	['axtər·hōft]
neck	hals (de)	[hals]
throat	keel (de)	[kēl]

hair	haren	['harən]
hairstyle	kapsel (het)	['kapsəl]
haircut	haarsnit (de)	['hārsnit]
wig	pruik (de)	['prœyk]

mustache	snor (de)	[snɔr]
beard	baard (de)	[bārt]
to have (a beard, etc.)	dragen	['draxən]
braid	vlecht (de)	[vlɛxt]
sideburns	bakkebaarden	[bakə'bārtən]

red-haired (adj)	ros	[rɔs]
gray (hair)	grijs	[xrɛjs]
bald (adj)	kaal	[kāl]
bald patch	kale plek (de)	['kalə plɛk]
ponytail	paardenstaart (de)	['pārdən·stārt]
bangs	pony (de)	['pɔni]

32. Human body

hand	hand (de)	[hant]
arm	arm (de)	[arm]
finger	vinger (de)	['viŋər]
toe	teen (de)	[tēn]
thumb	duim (de)	['dœʏm]
little finger	pink (de)	[pink]
nail	nagel (de)	['naxəl]
fist	vuist (de)	['vœʏst]
palm	handpalm (de)	['hantpalm]
wrist	pols (de)	[pɔls]
forearm	voorarm (de)	['vōrarm]
elbow	elleboog (de)	['ɛləbōx]
shoulder	schouder (de)	['sxaudər]
leg	been (het)	[bēn]
foot	voet (de)	[vut]
knee	knie (de)	[kni]
calf (part of leg)	kuit (de)	['kœʏt]
hip	heup (de)	['høp]
heel	hiel (de)	[hil]
body	lichaam (het)	['lixām]
stomach	buik (de)	['bœʏk]
chest	borst (de)	[bɔrst]
breast	borst (de)	[bɔrst]
flank	zijde (de)	['zɛjdə]
back	rug (de)	[rʉx]
lower back	lage rug (de)	[laxə rʉx]
waist	taille (de)	['tajə]
navel (belly button)	navel (de)	['navəl]
buttocks	billen	['bilən]
bottom	achterwerk (het)	['axtərwɛrk]
beauty mark	huidvlek (de)	['hœʏt·vlɛk]
birthmark	moedervlek (de)	['mudər·vlɛk]
(café au lait spot)		
tattoo	tatoeage (de)	[tatu'aʒə]
scar	litteken (het)	['litekən]

Clothing & Accessories

33. Outerwear. Coats

clothes	kleren (mv.)	['klerən]
outerwear	bovenkleding (de)	['bovən·'kledɪŋ]
winter clothing	winterkleding (de)	['wɪntər·'kledɪŋ]
coat (overcoat)	jas (de)	[jas]
fur coat	bontjas (de)	[bɔnt jas]
fur jacket	bontjasje (het)	[bɔnt 'jaɕə]
down coat	donzen jas (de)	['dɔnzən jas]
jacket (e.g., leather ~)	jasje (het)	['jaɕə]
raincoat (trenchcoat, etc.)	regenjas (de)	['rexən jas]
waterproof (adj)	waterdicht	['watərdɪxt]

34. Men's & women's clothing

shirt (button shirt)	overhemd (het)	['ɔvərhɛmt]
pants	broek (de)	[bruk]
jeans	jeans (de)	[dʒins]
suit jacket	colbert (de)	['kɔlbər]
suit	kostuum (het)	[kɔs'tūm]
dress (frock)	jurk (de)	[jurk]
skirt	rok (de)	[rɔk]
blouse	blouse (de)	['blus]
knitted jacket (cardigan, etc.)	wollen vest (de)	['wɔlən vɛst]
jacket (of woman's suit)	blazer (de)	['blezər]
T-shirt	T-shirt (het)	['tiʃøt]
shorts (short trousers)	shorts	[ʃɔrts]
tracksuit	trainingspak (het)	['trɛjnɪŋs·pak]
bathrobe	badjas (de)	['batjas]
pajamas	pyjama (de)	[pi'jama]
sweater	sweater (de)	['swetər]
pullover	pullover (de)	[pʉ'lovər]
vest	gilet (het)	[ʒi'lɛt]
tailcoat	rokkostuum (het)	[rɔk·kɔs'tūm]
tuxedo	smoking (de)	['smɔkɪŋ]

uniform	uniform (het)	['junifɔrm]
workwear	werkkleding (de)	['wɛrk·'kledɪŋ]
overalls	overall (de)	[ovə'ral]
coat (e.g., doctor's smock)	doktersjas (de)	['dɔktərs jas]

35. Clothing. Underwear

underwear	ondergoed (het)	['ɔndərxut]
boxers, briefs	herenslip (de)	['herən·slip]
panties	slipjes	['slipjes]
undershirt (A-shirt)	onderhemd (het)	['ɔndərhɛmt]
socks	sokken	['sɔkən]
nightgown	nachthemd (het)	['naxthɛmt]
bra	beha (de)	[be'ha]
knee highs (knee-high socks)	kniekousen	[kni·'kausən]
pantyhose	panty (de)	['pɛnti]
stockings (thigh highs)	nylonkousen	['nɛjlɔn·'kausən]
bathing suit	badpak (het)	['bad·pak]

36. Headwear

hat	hoed (de)	[hut]
fedora	deukhoed (de)	['døkhut]
baseball cap	honkbalpet (de)	['hɔnkbal·'pɛt]
flatcap	kleppet (de)	['klɛpɛt]
beret	baret (de)	[ba'rɛt]
hood	kap (de)	[kap]
panama hat	panamahoed (de)	[pa'nama·hut]
knit cap (knitted hat)	gebreide muts (de)	[xəb'rɛjdə mʉts]
headscarf	hoofddoek (de)	['hõftduk]
women's hat	dameshoed (de)	['daməs·hut]
hard hat	veiligheidshelm (de)	['vɛjləxhɛjts·hɛlm]
garrison cap	veldmuts (de)	['vɛlt·mʉts]
helmet	helm, valhelm (de)	[hɛlm], ['valhɛlm]
derby	bolhoed (de)	['bɔlhut]
top hat	hoge hoed (de)	['hɔxə hut]

37. Footwear

| footwear | schoeisel (het) | ['sxuisəl] |
| shoes (men's shoes) | schoenen | ['sxunən] |

shoes (women's shoes)	**vrouwenschoenen**	['vrauwən·'sxunən]
boots (e.g., cowboy ~)	**laarzen**	['lārzən]
slippers	**pantoffels**	[pan'tɔfəls]
tennis shoes (e.g., Nike ~)	**sportschoenen**	['spɔrt·'sxunən]
sneakers (e.g., Converse ~)	**sneakers**	['snikərs]
sandals	**sandalen**	[san'dalən]
cobbler (shoe repairer)	**schoenlapper (de)**	['sxun·'lapər]
heel	**hiel (de)**	[hil]
pair (of shoes)	**paar (het)**	[pār]
shoestring	**veter (de)**	['vetər]
to lace (vt)	**rijgen**	['rɛjxən]
shoehorn	**schoenlepel (de)**	['sxun·'lepəl]
shoe polish	**schoensmeer (de/het)**	['sxun·smēr]

38. Textile. Fabrics

cotton (n)	**katoen (de/het)**	[ka'tun]
cotton (as adj)	**katoenen**	[ka'tunən]
flax (n)	**vlas (het)**	[vlas]
flax (as adj)	**vlas-, van vlas**	[vlas], [van vlas]
silk (n)	**zijde (de)**	['zɛjdə]
silk (as adj)	**zijden**	['zɛjdən]
wool (n)	**wol (de)**	[wɔl]
wool (as adj)	**wollen**	['wɔlən]
velvet	**fluweel (het)**	[flʉ'wēl]
suede	**suède (de)**	['svɛdə]
corduroy	**ribfluweel (het)**	['rib·flʉ'wēl]
nylon (n)	**nylon (de/het)**	['nɛjlɔn]
nylon (as adj)	**nylon-, van nylon**	['nɛjlɔn], [van 'nɛjlɔn]
polyester (n)	**polyester (het)**	[pɔli'ɛstər]
polyester (as adj)	**polyester-**	[pɔli'ɛstər]
leather (n)	**leer (het)**	[lēr]
leather (as adj)	**leren**	['lerən]
fur (n)	**bont (het)**	[bɔnt]
fur (e.g., ~ coat)	**bont-**	[bɔnt]

39. Personal accessories

gloves	**handschoenen**	['xand 'sxunən]
mittens	**wanten**	['wantən]

scarf (muffler)	sjaal (de)	[çāl]
glasses (eyeglasses)	bril (de)	[bril]
frame (eyeglass ~)	brilmontuur (het)	[bril·mɔn'tūr]
umbrella	paraplu (de)	[parap'lʉ]
walking stick	wandelstok (de)	['wandəl·stɔk]
hairbrush	haarborstel (de)	[hār·'bɔrstəl]
fan	waaier (de)	['wājər]

tie (necktie)	das (de)	[das]
bow tie	strikje (het)	['strikjə]
suspenders	bretels	[brə'tɛls]
handkerchief	zakdoek (de)	['zagduk]

comb	kam (de)	[kam]
barrette	haarspeldje (het)	[hār·'spɛldjə]
hairpin	schuifspeldje (het)	['sxœʏf·'spɛldjə]
buckle	gesp (de)	[xɛsp]

| belt | broekriem (de) | ['bruk·rim] |
| shoulder strap | draagriem (de) | ['drāx·rim] |

bag (handbag)	handtas (de)	['hand·tas]
purse	damestas (de)	['daməs·tas]
backpack	rugzak (de)	['rʉxzak]

40. Clothing. Miscellaneous

fashion	mode (de)	['mɔdə]
in vogue (adj)	de mode	[də 'mɔdə]
fashion designer	kledingstilist (de)	['kledɪŋ·sti'list]

collar	kraag (de)	[krāx]
pocket	zak (de)	[zak]
pocket (as adj)	zak-	[zak]
sleeve	mouw (de)	['mau]
hanging loop	lusje (het)	['lʉçə]
fly (on trousers)	gulp (de)	[xjulp]

zipper (fastener)	rits (de)	[rits]
fastener	sluiting (de)	['slœʏtɪŋ]
button	knoop (de)	[knōp]
buttonhole	knoopsgat (het)	['knōps·xat]
to come off (ab. button)	losraken	[lɔs'rakən]

to sew (vi, vt)	naaien	['nājən]
to embroider (vi, vt)	borduren	[bɔr'dʉrən]
embroidery	borduursel (het)	[bɔr'dūrsəl]
sewing needle	naald (de)	[nālt]
thread	draad (de)	[drāt]
seam	naad (de)	[nāt]

to get dirty (vi)	vies worden	[vis 'wɔrdən]
stain (mark, spot)	vlek (de)	[vlɛk]
to crease, crumple (vi)	gekreukt raken	[xə'krøkt 'rakən]
to tear, to rip (vt)	scheuren	['sxørən]
clothes moth	mot (de)	[mɔt]

41. Personal care. Cosmetics

toothpaste	tandpasta (de)	['tand·pasta]
toothbrush	tandenborstel (de)	['tandən·'bɔrstəl]
to brush one's teeth	tanden poetsen	['tandən 'putsən]

razor	scheermes (het)	['sxēr·mɛs]
shaving cream	scheerschuim (het)	[sxēr·sxœʏm]
to shave (vi)	zich scheren	[zix 'sxerən]

| soap | zeep (de) | [zēp] |
| shampoo | shampoo (de) | ['ʃʌmpõ] |

scissors	schaar (de)	[sxār]
nail file	nagelvijl (de)	['naxəl·vɛjl]
nail clippers	nagelknipper (de)	['naxəl·'knipər]
tweezers	pincet (het)	[pin'sɛt]

cosmetics	cosmetica (mv.)	[kɔs'metika]
face mask	masker (het)	['maskər]
manicure	manicure (de)	[mani'kʉrə]
to have a manicure	manicure doen	[mani'kʉrə dun]
pedicure	pedicure (de)	[pedi'kʉrə]

make-up bag	cosmetica tasje (het)	[kɔs'metika 'taçə]
face powder	poeder (de/het)	['pudər]
powder compact	poederdoos (de)	['pudər·dōs]
blusher	rouge (de)	['ruʒə]

perfume (bottled)	parfum (de/het)	[par'fʉm]
toilet water (lotion)	eau de toilet (de)	[ɔ də tua'lɛt]
lotion	lotion (de)	[lɔt'ʃon]
cologne	eau de cologne (de)	[ɔ də kɔ'lɔnjə]

eyeshadow	oogschaduw (de)	['ōx·sxadʉw]
eyeliner	oogpotlood (het)	['ōx·'pɔtlɔt]
mascara	mascara (de)	[mas'kara]

lipstick	lippenstift (de)	['lipən·stift]
nail polish, enamel	nagellak (de)	['naxəl·lak]
hair spray	haarlak (de)	['hār·lak]
deodorant	deodorant (de)	[deodɔ'rant]
cream	crème (de)	[krɛ:m]
face cream	gezichtscrème (de)	[xə'zihts·krɛ:m]

hand cream	handcrème (de)	[hant·krɛ:m]
anti-wrinkle cream	antirimpelcrème (de)	[anti'rimpəl·krɛ:m]
day cream	dagcrème (de)	['dax·krɛ:m]
night cream	nachtcrème (de)	['naxt·krɛ:m]
day (as adj)	dag-	[dax]
night (as adj)	nacht-	[naxt]

tampon	tampon (de)	[tam'pɔn]
toilet paper (toilet roll)	toiletpapier (het)	[tua'lɛt·pa'pir]
hair dryer	föhn (de)	['føn]

42. Jewelry

jewelry	sieraden	['siradən]
precious (e.g., ~ stone)	edel	['edɛl]
hallmark stamp	keurmerk (het)	['kørmɛrk]

ring	ring (de)	[riŋ]
wedding ring	trouwring (de)	['trauwriŋ]
bracelet	armband (de)	['armbant]

earrings	oorringen	['ōr·riŋən]
necklace (~ of pearls)	halssnoer (het)	['hals·snur]
crown	kroon (de)	[krōn]
bead necklace	kralen snoer (het)	['kralən 'snur]

diamond	diamant (de)	[dia'mant]
emerald	smaragd (de)	[sma'raxt]
ruby	robijn (de)	[rɔ'bɛjn]
sapphire	saffier (de)	[sa'fir]
pearl	parel (de)	['parəl]
amber	barnsteen (de)	['barn·stēn]

43. Watches. Clocks

watch (wristwatch)	polshorloge (het)	['pɔls·hɔr'lɔʒə]
dial	wijzerplaat (de)	['wɛjzər·plāt]
hand (of clock, watch)	wijzer (de)	['wɛjzər]
metal watch band	metalen horlogeband (de)	[me'talən hɔr'lɔʒə·bant]
watch strap	horlogebandje (het)	[hɔr'lɔʒə·'bandjə]

battery	batterij (de)	[batə'rɛj]
to be dead (battery)	leeg zijn	[lēx zɛjn]
to change a battery	batterij vervangen	[batə'rɛj vər'vaŋən]
to run fast	voorlopen	['vōrlopən]
to run slow	achterlopen	['axtərlopən]
wall clock	wandklok (de)	['want·klɔk]

hourglass	**zandloper (de)**	['zant·lopər]
sundial	**zonnewijzer (de)**	['zɔnə·wɛjzər]
alarm clock	**wekker (de)**	['wɛkər]
watchmaker	**horlogemaker (de)**	[hɔr'lɔʒə·'makər]
to repair (vt)	**repareren**	[repa'rerən]

Food. Nutricion

44. Food

meat	vlees (het)	[vlēs]
chicken	kip (de)	[kip]
Rock Cornish hen (poussin)	kuiken (het)	['kœʏkən]
duck	eend (de)	[ēnt]
goose	gans (de)	[xans]
game	wild (het)	[wilt]
turkey	kalkoen (de)	[kal'kun]
pork	varkensvlees (het)	['varkəns·vlēs]
veal	kalfsvlees (het)	['kalfs·vlēs]
lamb	schapenvlees (het)	['sxapən·vlēs]
beef	rundvlees (het)	['rʉnt·vlēs]
rabbit	konijnenvlees (het)	[kɔ'nɛjnən·vlēs]
sausage (bologna, pepperoni, etc.)	worst (de)	[wɔrst]
vienna sausage (frankfurter)	saucijs (de)	['sɔsɛjs]
bacon	spek (het)	[spɛk]
ham	ham (de)	[ham]
gammon	gerookte achterham (de)	[xə'rōktə 'ahtərham]
pâté	paté (de)	[pa'tɛ]
liver	lever (de)	['levər]
hamburger (ground beef)	gehakt (het)	[xə'hakt]
tongue	tong (de)	[tɔŋ]
egg	ei (het)	[ɛj]
eggs	eieren	['ɛjerən]
egg white	eiwit (het)	['ɛjwit]
egg yolk	eigeel (het)	['ɛjxēl]
fish	vis (de)	[vis]
seafood	zeevruchten	[zē·'vrʉxtən]
crustaceans	schaaldieren	['sxal·dīrən]
caviar	kaviaar (de)	[ka'vjār]
crab	krab (de)	[krab]
shrimp	garnaal (de)	[xar'nāl]
oyster	oester (de)	['ustər]
spiny lobster	langoest (de)	[lan'xust]

octopus	octopus (de)	['ɔktɔpʉs]
squid	inktvis (de)	['inktvis]
sturgeon	steur (de)	['stør]
salmon	zalm (de)	[zalm]
halibut	heilbot (de)	['hɛjlbɔt]
cod	kabeljauw (de)	[kabə'ljau]
mackerel	makreel (de)	[ma'krēl]
tuna	tonijn (de)	[tɔ'nɛjn]
eel	paling (de)	[pa'liŋ]
trout	forel (de)	[fɔ'rɛl]
sardine	sardine (de)	[sar'dinə]
pike	snoek (de)	[snuk]
herring	haring (de)	['hariŋ]
bread	brood (het)	[brõt]
cheese	kaas (de)	[kās]
sugar	suiker (de)	[sœʏkər]
salt	zout (het)	['zaut]
rice	rijst (de)	[rɛjst]
pasta (macaroni)	pasta (de)	['pasta]
noodles	noedels	['nudɛls]
butter	boter (de)	['botər]
vegetable oil	plantaardige olie (de)	[plant'ārdixə 'ɔli]
sunflower oil	zonnebloemolie (de)	['zɔnəblum·'ɔli]
margarine	margarine (de)	[marxa'rinə]
olives	olijven	[ɔ'lɛjvən]
olive oil	olijfolie (de)	[ɔ'lɛjf·'ɔli]
milk	melk (de)	[mɛlk]
condensed milk	gecondenseerde melk (de)	[xəkɔnsən'sērdə mɛlk]
yogurt	yoghurt (de)	['jogʉrt]
sour cream	zure room (de)	['zʉrə rõm]
cream (of milk)	room (de)	[rõm]
mayonnaise	mayonaise (de)	[majo'nɛzə]
buttercream	crème (de)	[krɛːm]
cereal grains (wheat, etc.)	graan (het)	[xrān]
flour	meel (het), bloem (de)	[mēl], [blum]
canned food	conserven	[kɔn'sɛrvən]
cornflakes	maïsvlokken	[majs·'vlɔkən]
honey	honing (de)	['hɔniŋ]
jam	jam (de)	[ʃɛm]
chewing gum	kauwgom (de)	['kauxɔm]

45. Drinks

water	water (het)	['watər]
drinking water	drinkwater (het)	['drink·'watər]
mineral water	mineraalwater (het)	[minə'rāl·'watər]
still (adj)	zonder gas	['zɔndər xas]
carbonated (adj)	koolzuurhoudend	[kōlzūr·'haudənt]
sparkling (adj)	bruisend	['brœysənt]
ice	ijs (het)	[ɛjs]
with ice	met ijs	[mɛt ɛjs]
non-alcoholic (adj)	alcohol vrij	['alkɔhɔl vrɛj]
soft drink	alcohol vrije drank (de)	['alkɔhɔl 'vrɛjə drank]
refreshing drink	frisdrank (de)	['fris·drank]
lemonade	limonade (de)	[limɔ'nadə]
liquors	alcoholische dranken	[alkɔ'holisə 'drankən]
wine	wijn (de)	[wɛjn]
white wine	witte wijn (de)	['witə wɛjn]
red wine	rode wijn (de)	['rɔdə wɛjn]
liqueur	likeur (de)	[li'kør]
champagne	champagne (de)	[ʃʌm'panjə]
vermouth	vermout (de)	['vɛrmut]
whiskey	whisky (de)	['wiski]
vodka	wodka (de)	['wɔdka]
gin	gin (de)	[dʒin]
cognac	cognac (de)	[kɔ'njak]
rum	rum (de)	[rʉm]
coffee	koffie (de)	['kɔfi]
black coffee	zwarte koffie (de)	['zwartə 'kɔfi]
coffee with milk	koffie (de) met melk	['kɔfi mɛt mɛlk]
cappuccino	cappuccino (de)	[kapu'tʃinɔ]
instant coffee	oploskoffie (de)	['ɔplɔs·'kɔfi]
milk	melk (de)	[mɛlk]
cocktail	cocktail (de)	['kɔktəl]
milkshake	milkshake (de)	['milk·ʃɛjk]
juice	sap (het)	[sap]
tomato juice	tomatensap (het)	[tɔ'matən·sap]
orange juice	sinaasappelsap (het)	['sināsapəl·sap]
freshly squeezed juice	vers geperst sap (het)	[vɛrs xə'pɛrst sap]
beer	bier (het)	[bir]
light beer	licht bier (het)	[lixt bir]
dark beer	donker bier (het)	['dɔnkər bir]

tea	thee (de)	[tē]
black tea	zwarte thee (de)	['zwartə tē]
green tea	groene thee (de)	['xrunə tē]

46. Vegetables

vegetables	groenten	['xruntən]
greens	verse kruiden	['vɛrsə 'krœydən]
tomato	tomaat (de)	[tɔ'māt]
cucumber	augurk (de)	[au'xʉrk]
carrot	wortel (de)	['wɔrtəl]
potato	aardappel (de)	['ārd·apəl]
onion	ui (de)	['œy]
garlic	knoflook (de)	['knõflɔk]
cabbage	kool (de)	[kōl]
cauliflower	bloemkool (de)	['blum·kōl]
Brussels sprouts	spruitkool (de)	['sprœyt·kōl]
broccoli	broccoli (de)	['brɔkɔli]
beetroot	rode biet (de)	['rɔdə bit]
eggplant	aubergine (de)	[ɔbɛr'ʒinə]
zucchini	courgette (de)	[kur'ʒɛt]
pumpkin	pompoen (de)	[pɔm'pun]
turnip	raap (de)	[rāp]
parsley	peterselie (de)	[petər'sɛli]
dill	dille (de)	['dilə]
lettuce	sla (de)	[sla]
celery	selderij (de)	['sɛldɛrɛj]
asparagus	asperge (de)	[as'pɛrʒə]
spinach	spinazie (de)	[spi'nazi]
pea	erwt (de)	[ɛrt]
beans	bonen	['bɔnən]
corn (maize)	maïs (de)	[majs]
kidney bean	boon (de)	[bõn]
bell pepper	peper (de)	['pepər]
radish	radijs (de)	[ra'dɛjs]
artichoke	artisjok (de)	[arti'ɕɔk]

47. Fruits. Nuts

fruit	vrucht (de)	[vrʉxt]
apple	appel (de)	['apəl]
pear	peer (de)	[pēr]

lemon	citroen (de)	[si'trun]
orange	sinaasappel (de)	['sināsapəl]
strawberry (garden ~)	aardbei (de)	['ārd·bɛj]

mandarin	mandarijn (de)	[manda'rɛjn]
plum	pruim (de)	['prœʏm]
peach	perzik (de)	['pɛrzik]
apricot	abrikoos (de)	[abri'kōs]
raspberry	framboos (de)	[fram'bōs]
pineapple	ananas (de)	['ananas]

banana	banaan (de)	[ba'nān]
watermelon	watermeloen (de)	['watərmɛ'lun]
grape	druif (de)	[drœʏf]
sour cherry	zure kers (de)	['zʉrə kɛrs]
sweet cherry	zoete kers (de)	['zutə kɛrs]
melon	meloen (de)	[mə'lun]

grapefruit	grapefruit (de)	['grepfrut]
avocado	avocado (de)	[avɔ'kadɔ]
papaya	papaja (de)	[pa'paja]
mango	mango (de)	['mangɔ]
pomegranate	granaatappel (de)	[xra'nāt·'apəl]

redcurrant	rode bes (de)	['rɔdə bɛs]
blackcurrant	zwarte bes (de)	['zwartə bɛs]
gooseberry	kruisbes (de)	['krœʏsbɛs]
bilberry	bosbes (de)	['bɔsbɛs]
blackberry	braambes (de)	['brāmbɛs]

raisin	rozijn (de)	[rɔ'zɛjn]
fig	vijg (de)	[vɛjx]
date	dadel (de)	['dadəl]

peanut	pinda (de)	['pinda]
almond	amandel (de)	[a'mandəl]
walnut	walnoot (de)	['walnōt]
hazelnut	hazelnoot (de)	['hazəl·nōt]
coconut	kokosnoot (de)	['kokɔs·nōt]
pistachios	pistaches	[pi'staʃəs]

48. Bread. Candy

bakers' confectionery (pastry)	suikerbakkerij (de)	[sœʏkər bakə'rɛj]
bread	brood (het)	[brōt]
cookies	koekje (het)	['kukjə]

| chocolate (n) | chocolade (de) | [ʃɔkɔ'ladə] |
| chocolate (as adj) | chocolade- | [ʃɔkɔ'ladə] |

candy (wrapped)	snoepje (het)	['snupjə]
cake (e.g., cupcake)	cakeje (het)	['kɛjkjə]
cake (e.g., birthday ~)	taart (de)	[tārt]

| pie (e.g., apple ~) | pastei (de) | [pas'tɛj] |
| filling (for cake, pie) | vulling (de) | ['vʉliŋ] |

jam (whole fruit jam)	confituur (de)	[kɔnfi'tūr]
marmalade	marmelade (de)	[marmə'ladə]
waffles	wafel (de)	['wafəl]
ice-cream	ijsje (het)	['ɛisjə], ['ɛiʃə]
pudding	pudding (de)	['pʉdiŋ]

49. Cooked dishes

course, dish	gerecht (het)	[xe'rɛht]
cuisine	keuken (de)	['køkən]
recipe	recept (het)	[re'sɛpt]
portion	portie (de)	['pɔrsi]

| salad | salade (de) | [sa'ladə] |
| soup | soep (de) | [sup] |

clear soup (broth)	bouillon (de)	[bu'jon]
sandwich (bread)	boterham (de)	['botərham]
fried eggs	spiegelei (het)	['spixəl·ɛj]

| hamburger (beefburger) | hamburger (de) | ['hambʉrxər] |
| beefsteak | biefstuk (de) | ['bifstʉk] |

side dish	garnering (de)	[xar'neriŋ]
spaghetti	spaghetti (de)	[spa'xeti]
mashed potatoes	aardappelpuree (de)	['ārdapəl·pʉ'rē]
pizza	pizza (de)	['pitsa]
porridge (oatmeal, etc.)	pap (de)	[pap]
omelet	omelet (de)	[ɔmə'lɛt]

boiled (e.g., ~ beef)	gekookt	[xə'kōkt]
smoked (adj)	gerookt	[xə'rōkt]
fried (adj)	gebakken	[xə'bakən]
dried (adj)	gedroogd	[xə'drōxt]
frozen (adj)	diepvries	['dip·vris]
pickled (adj)	gemarineerd	[xəmari'nērt]

sweet (sugary)	zoet	[zut]
salty (adj)	gezouten	[xə'zautən]
cold (adj)	koud	['kaut]
hot (adj)	heet	[hēt]
bitter (adj)	bitter	['bitər]
tasty (adj)	lekker	['lɛkər]

to cook in boiling water	koken	['kɔkən]
to cook (dinner)	bereiden	[bə'rɛjdən]
to fry (vt)	bakken	['bakən]
to heat up (food)	opwarmen	['ɔpwarmən]

to salt (vt)	zouten	['zautən]
to pepper (vt)	peperen	['pepərən]
to grate (vt)	raspen	['raspən]
peel (n)	schil (de)	[sxil]
to peel (vt)	schillen	['sxilən]

50. Spices

salt	zout (het)	['zaut]
salty (adj)	gezouten	[xə'zautən]
to salt (vt)	zouten	['zautən]

black pepper	zwarte peper (de)	['zwartə 'pepər]
red pepper (milled ~)	rode peper (de)	['rɔdə 'pepər]
mustard	mosterd (de)	['mɔstərt]
horseradish	mierikswortel (de)	['miriks·'wɔrtəl]

condiment	condiment (het)	[kɔndi'mɛnt]
spice	specerij , kruiderij (de)	[spesə'rɛj], [krœydə'rɛj]
sauce	saus (de)	['saus]
vinegar	azijn (de)	[a'zɛjn]

anise	anijs (de)	[a'nɛjs]
basil	basilicum (de)	[ba'silikəm]
cloves	kruidnagel (de)	['krœytnaxəl]

ginger	gember (de)	['xɛmbər]
coriander	koriander (de)	[kɔri'andər]
cinnamon	kaneel (de/het)	[ka'nēl]

sesame	sesamzaad (het)	['sɛzam·zāt]
bay leaf	laurierblad (het)	[lau'rir·blat]
paprika	paprika (de)	['paprika]
caraway	komijn (de)	[kɔ'mɛjn]
saffron	saffraan (de)	[saf'rān]

51. Meals

| food | eten (het) | ['etən] |
| to eat (vi, vt) | eten | ['etən] |

| breakfast | ontbijt (het) | [ɔn'bɛjt] |
| to have breakfast | ontbijten | [ɔn'bɛjtən] |

lunch	lunch (de)	['lʉnʃ]
to have lunch	lunchen	['lʉnʃən]
dinner	avondeten (het)	['avɔntetən]
to have dinner	souperen	[su'perən]

| appetite | eetlust (de) | ['ētlʉst] |
| Enjoy your meal! | Eet smakelijk! | [ēt 'smakələk] |

to open (~ a bottle)	openen	['ɔpənən]
to spill (liquid)	morsen	['mɔrsən]
to spill out (vi)	zijn gemorst	[zɛjn xɛ'mɔrst]

to boil (vi)	koken	['kɔkən]
to boil (vt)	koken	['kɔkən]
boiled (~ water)	gekookt	[xə'kōkt]
to chill, cool down (vt)	afkoelen	['afkulən]
to chill (vi)	afkoelen	['afkulən]

| taste, flavor | smaak (de) | [smāk] |
| aftertaste | nasmaak (de) | ['nasmāk] |

to slim down (lose weight)	volgen een dieet	['vɔlxə en di'ēt]
diet	dieet (het)	[di'ēt]
vitamin	vitamine (de)	[vita'minə]
calorie	calorie (de)	[kalɔ'ri]

| vegetarian (n) | vegetariër (de) | [vəxɛ'tarier] |
| vegetarian (adj) | vegetarisch | [vəxɛ'taris] |

fats (nutrient)	vetten	['vɛtən]
proteins	eiwitten	['ɛjwitən]
carbohydrates	koolhydraten	[kōlhi'dratən]

slice (of lemon, ham)	snede (de)	['snedə]
piece (of cake, pie)	stuk (het)	[stʉk]
crumb (of bread, cake, etc.)	kruimel (de)	['krœʏməl]

52. Table setting

spoon	lepel (de)	['lepəl]
knife	mes (het)	[mɛs]
fork	vork (de)	[vɔrk]

| cup (e.g., coffee ~) | kopje (het) | ['kɔpjə] |
| plate (dinner ~) | bord (het) | [bɔrt] |

saucer	schoteltje (het)	['sxɔtɛltʃə]
napkin (on table)	servet (het)	[sɛr'vɛt]
toothpick	tandenstoker (de)	['tandən·'stɔkər]

53. Restaurant

restaurant	**restaurant (het)**	[rɛsto'rant]
coffee house	**koffiehuis (het)**	['kɔfi·hœys]
pub, bar	**bar (de)**	[bar]
tearoom	**tearoom (de)**	['ti·rõm]
waiter	**kelner, ober (de)**	['kɛlnər], ['ɔbər]
waitress	**serveerster (de)**	[sɛr'vɛ̃rstər]
bartender	**barman (de)**	['barman]
menu	**menu (het)**	[me'nʉ]
wine list	**wijnkaart (de)**	['wɛjn·kãrt]
to book a table	**een tafel reserveren**	[en 'tafəl rezər'verən]
course, dish	**gerecht (het)**	[xe'rɛht]
to order (meal)	**bestellen**	[bə'stɛlən]
to make an order	**een bestelling maken**	[en bə'stɛliŋ 'makən]
aperitif	**aperitief (de/het)**	[aperi'tif]
appetizer	**voorgerecht (het)**	['võrxərɛht]
dessert	**dessert (het)**	[dɛ'sɛːr]
check	**rekening (de)**	['rekəniŋ]
to pay the check	**de rekening betalen**	[də 'rekəniŋ bə'talən]
to give change	**wisselgeld teruggeven**	['wisəl·xɛlt tɛ'rʉxevən]
tip	**fooi (de)**	[fõj]

Family, relatives and friends

54. Personal information. Forms

name (first name)	naam (de)	[nām]
surname (last name)	achternaam (de)	['axtər·nām]
date of birth	geboortedatum (de)	[xə'bōrtə·datʉm]
place of birth	geboorteplaats (de)	[xə'bōrtə·plāts]
nationality	nationaliteit (de)	[natsjɔnali'tɛjt]
place of residence	woonplaats (de)	['wōm·plāts]
country	land (het)	[lant]
profession (occupation)	beroep (het)	[bə'rup]
gender, sex	geslacht (het)	[xə'slaht]
height	lengte (de)	['lɛŋtə]
weight	gewicht (het)	[xə'wixt]

55. Family members. Relatives

mother	moeder (de)	['mudər]
father	vader (de)	['vadər]
son	zoon (de)	[zōn]
daughter	dochter (de)	['dɔxtər]
younger daughter	jongste dochter (de)	['jɔŋstə 'dɔxtər]
younger son	jongste zoon (de)	['jɔŋstə zōn]
eldest daughter	oudste dochter (de)	['audstə 'dɔxtər]
eldest son	oudste zoon (de)	['audstə zōn]
brother	broer (de)	[brur]
elder brother	oudere broer (de)	['audərə brur]
younger brother	jongere broer (de)	['jɔŋərə brur]
sister	zuster (de)	['zʉstər]
elder sister	oudere zuster (de)	['audərə 'zʉstər]
younger sister	jongere zuster (de)	['jɔŋərə 'zʉstər]
cousin (masc.)	neef (de)	[nēf]
cousin (fem.)	nicht (de)	[nixt]
mom, mommy	mama (de)	['mama]
dad, daddy	papa (de)	['papa]
parents	ouders	['audərs]
child	kind (het)	[kint]
children	kinderen	['kindərən]

grandmother	oma (de)	['ɔma]
grandfather	opa (de)	['ɔpa]
grandson	kleinzoon (de)	[klɛjn·zōn]
granddaughter	kleindochter (de)	[klɛjn·'dɔxtər]
grandchildren	kleinkinderen	[klɛjn·'kinderən]
uncle	oom (de)	[ōm]
aunt	tante (de)	['tantə]
nephew	neef (de)	[nēf]
niece	nicht (de)	[nixt]

mother-in-law (wife's mother)	schoonmoeder (de)	['sxōn·mudər]
father-in-law (husband's father)	schoonvader (de)	['sxōn·vadər]
son-in-law (daughter's husband)	schoonzoon (de)	['sxōn·zōn]
stepmother	stiefmoeder (de)	['stif·mudər]
stepfather	stiefvader (de)	['stif·vadər]

infant	zuigeling (de)	['zœɣəliŋ]
baby (infant)	wiegenkind (het)	['wixən·kint]
little boy, kid	kleuter (de)	['kløtər]
wife	vrouw (de)	['vrau]
husband	man (de)	[man]
spouse (husband)	echtgenoot (de)	['ɛhtxənōt]
spouse (wife)	echtgenote (de)	['ɛhtxənotə]

married (masc.)	gehuwd	[xə'huwt]
married (fem.)	gehuwd	[xə'huwt]
single (unmarried)	ongehuwd	[ɔnhə'huwt]
bachelor	vrijgezel (de)	[vrɛjxə'zɛl]
divorced (masc.)	gescheiden	[xə'sxɛjdən]
widow	weduwe (de)	['weduwə]
widower	weduwnaar (de)	['weduwnār]

relative	familielid (het)	[fa'mililit]
close relative	dichte familielid (het)	['dixtə fa'mililit]
distant relative	verre familielid (het)	['vɛrə fa'mililit]
relatives	familieleden	[fa'mili'ledən]

orphan (boy or girl)	wees (de), weeskind (het)	[wēs], ['wēskint]
guardian (of a minor)	voogd (de)	[vōxt]
to adopt (a boy)	adopteren	[adɔp'terən]
to adopt (a girl)	adopteren	[adɔp'terən]

56. Friends. Coworkers

| friend (masc.) | vriend (de) | [vrint] |
| friend (fem.) | vriendin (de) | [vrin'din] |

| friendship | vriendschap (de) | ['vrintsxap] |
| to be friends | bevriend zijn | [bə'vrint zɛjn] |

buddy (masc.)	makker (de)	['makər]
buddy (fem.)	vriendin (de)	[vrin'din]
partner	partner (de)	['partnər]

chief (boss)	chef (de)	[ʃɛf]
superior (n)	baas (de)	[bãs]
owner, proprietor	eigenaar (de)	['ɛjxənãr]
subordinate (n)	ondergeschikte (de)	['ɔndərxə'sxiktə]
colleague	collega (de)	[kɔ'lexa]

acquaintance (person)	kennis (de)	['kɛnis]
fellow traveler	medereiziger (de)	['medə·'rɛjzixər]
classmate	klasgenoot (de)	['klas·xənõt]

neighbor (masc.)	buurman (de)	['bũrman]
neighbor (fem.)	buurvrouw (de)	['bũrvrau]
neighbors	buren	['bʉrən]

57. Man. Woman

woman	vrouw (de)	['vrau]
girl (young woman)	meisje (het)	['mɛjɕə]
bride	bruid (de)	['brœyd]

beautiful (adj)	mooi, mooie	[mõj], ['mõjə]
tall (adj)	groot, grote	[xrõt], ['xrotə]
slender (adj)	slank, slanke	[slaŋk], ['slaŋkə]
short (adj)	korte, kleine	['kortə], ['klɛjnə]

| blonde (n) | blondine (de) | [blɔn'dinə] |
| brunette (n) | brunette (de) | [brʉ'netə] |

ladies' (adj)	dames-	['daməs]
virgin (girl)	maagd (de)	[mãxt]
pregnant (adj)	zwanger	['zwaŋər]

man (adult male)	man (de)	[man]
blond (n)	blonde man (de)	['blondə man]
brunet (n)	bruinharige man (de)	['brœyn 'harixə man]
tall (adj)	groot	[xrõt]
short (adj)	klein	[klɛjn]

rude (rough)	onbeleefd	[ɔnbə'lẽft]
stocky (adj)	gedrongen	[xə'drɔŋə]
robust (adj)	robuust	[rɔ'bũst]
strong (adj)	sterk	[stɛrk]
strength	sterkte (de)	['stɛrktə]

stout, fat (adj)	**mollig**	['mɔləx]
swarthy (adj)	**getaand**	[xə'tānt]
slender (well-built)	**slank**	[slaŋk]
elegant (adj)	**elegant**	[ɛle'xant]

58. Age

age	**leeftijd (de)**	['lēftɛjt]
youth (young age)	**jeugd (de)**	[øxt]
young (adj)	**jong**	[joŋ]
younger (adj)	**jonger**	['joŋər]
older (adj)	**ouder**	['audər]
young man	**jongen (de)**	['joŋən]
teenager	**tiener, adolescent (de)**	['tinər], [adɔlɛ'sɛnt]
guy, fellow	**kerel (de)**	['kerɛl]
old man	**oude man (de)**	['audə man]
old woman	**oude vrouw (de)**	['audə 'vrau]
adult (adj)	**volwassen**	[vɔl'wasən]
middle-aged (adj)	**van middelbare leeftijd**	[van 'midəlbarə 'lēftɛjt]
elderly (adj)	**bejaard**	[bɛ'jārt]
old (adj)	**oud**	['aut]
retirement	**pensioen (het)**	[pɛn'ʃun]
to retire (from job)	**met pensioen gaan**	[mɛt pɛn'ʃun xān]
retiree	**gepensioneerde (de)**	[xəpɛnʃə'nērdə]

59. Children

child	**kind (het)**	[kint]
children	**kinderen**	['kindərən]
twins	**tweeling (de)**	['twēliŋ]
cradle	**wieg (de)**	[wix]
rattle	**rammelaar (de)**	['ramɛlār]
diaper	**luier (de)**	['lœyər]
pacifier	**speen (de)**	[spēn]
baby carriage	**kinderwagen (de)**	['kindər·'waxən]
kindergarten	**kleuterschool (de)**	['kløtər·sxōl]
babysitter	**babysitter (de)**	['bɛjbisitər]
childhood	**kindertijd (de)**	['kindər·tɛjt]
doll	**pop (de)**	[pɔp]
toy	**speelgoed (het)**	['spēl·xut]

construction set (toy)	bouwspeelgoed (het)	['bau·'spēlxut]
well-bred (adj)	welopgevoed	[wɛl'ɔpxəvut]
ill-bred (adj)	onopgevoed	[ɔn'ɔpxəvut]
spoiled (adj)	verwend	[vər'wɛnt]
to be naughty	stout zijn	['staut zɛjn]
mischievous (adj)	stout	['staut]
mischievousness	stoutheid (de)	['stauthɛjt]
mischievous child	stouterd (de)	['stautərt]
obedient (adj)	gehoorzaam	[xə'hōrzām]
disobedient (adj)	ongehoorzaam	[ɔnxə'hōrzām]
docile (adj)	braaf	[brāf]
clever (smart)	slim	[slim]
child prodigy	wonderkind (het)	['wɔndərkint]

60. Married couples. Family life

to kiss (vt)	kussen	['kʉsən]
to kiss (vi)	elkaar kussen	[ɛl'kār 'kʉsən]
family (n)	gezin (het)	[xə'zin]
family (as adj)	gezins-	[xə'zins]
couple	paar (het)	[pār]
marriage (state)	huwelijk (het)	['hʉwələk]
hearth (home)	thuis (het)	['tœys]
dynasty	dynastie (de)	[dinas'ti]
date	date (de)	[dɛt]
kiss	zoen (de)	[zun]
love (for sb)	liefde (de)	['lifdə]
to love (sb)	liefhebben	['lifhɛbən]
beloved	geliefde	[xə'lifdə]
tenderness	tederheid (de)	['tedərhɛjt]
tender (affectionate)	teder	['tedər]
faithfulness	trouw (de)	['trau]
faithful (adj)	trouw	['trau]
care (attention)	zorg (de)	[zɔrx]
caring (~ father)	zorgzaam	['zɔrxzām]
newlyweds	jonggehuwden	[jɔŋhə·'hʉwdən]
honeymoon	wittebroodsweken	['witəbrōts·'wekən]
to get married (ab. woman)	trouwen	['trauən]
to get married (ab. man)	trouwen	['trauən]
wedding	bruiloft (de)	['brœylɔft]
golden wedding	gouden bruiloft (de)	['xaudən 'brœylɔft]

anniversary	**verjaardag (de)**	[vər'jār·dax]
lover (masc.)	**minnaar (de)**	['minār]
mistress (lover)	**minnares (de)**	['minarɛs]
adultery	**overspel (het)**	['ɔvərspɛl]
to cheat on … (commit adultery)	**overspel plegen**	['ɔvərspɛl 'plexən]
jealous (adj)	**jaloers**	[ja'lurs]
to be jealous	**jaloers zijn**	[ja'lurs zɛjn]
divorce	**echtscheiding (de)**	['ɛxtsxɛjdiŋ]
to divorce (vi)	**scheiden**	['sxɛjdən]
to quarrel (vi)	**ruzie hebben**	['rʉzi 'hɛbən]
to be reconciled (after an argument)	**vrede sluiten**	['vredə 'slœʏtən]
together (adv)	**samen**	['samən]
sex	**seks (de)**	[sɛks]
happiness	**geluk (het)**	[xə'lʉk]
happy (adj)	**gelukkig**	[xə'lʉkəx]
misfortune (accident)	**ongeluk (het)**	['ɔnxəlʉk]
unhappy (adj)	**ongelukkig**	[ɔnxə'lʉkəx]

Character. Feelings. Emotions

61. Feelings. Emotions

feeling (emotion)	gevoel (het)	['xə'vul]
feelings	gevoelens	[xə'vuləns]
to feel (vt)	voelen	['vulən]
hunger	honger (de)	['hɔŋər]
to be hungry	honger hebben	['hɔŋər 'hɛbən]
thirst	dorst (de)	[dɔrst]
to be thirsty	dorst hebben	[dɔrst 'hɛbən]
sleepiness	slaperigheid (de)	['slapərəxhɛjt]
to feel sleepy	willen slapen	['wilən 'slapən]
tiredness	moeheid (de)	['muhɛjt]
tired (adj)	moe	[mu]
to get tired	vermoeid raken	[vər'mujt 'rakən]
mood (humor)	stemming (de)	['stɛmiŋ]
boredom	verveling (de)	[vər'veliŋ]
to be bored	zich vervelen	[zix vər'velən]
seclusion	afzondering (de)	['afsɔndəriŋ]
to seclude oneself	zich afzonderen	[zix 'afsɔndərən]
to worry (make anxious)	bezorgd maken	[bə'zɔrxt 'makən]
to be worried	bezorgd zijn	[bə'zɔrxt zɛjn]
worrying (n)	zorg (de)	[zɔrx]
anxiety	ongerustheid (de)	[ɔnxə'rʉsthɛjt]
preoccupied (adj)	ongerust	[ɔnxə'rʉst]
to be nervous	zenuwachtig zijn	['zenʉw·ahtəx zɛjn]
to panic (vi)	in paniek raken	[in pa'nik 'rakən]
hope	hoop (de)	[hōp]
to hope (vi, vt)	hopen	['hɔpən]
certainty	zekerheid (de)	['zekərhɛjt]
certain, sure (adj)	zeker	['zekər]
uncertainty	onzekerheid (de)	[ɔn'zekərhɛjt]
uncertain (adj)	onzeker	[ɔn'zekər]
drunk (adj)	dronken	['drɔnkən]
sober (adj)	nuchter	['nʉxtər]
weak (adj)	zwak	[zwak]
happy (adj)	gelukkig	[xə'lʉkəx]
to scare (vt)	doen schrikken	[dun 'sxrikən]

fury (madness)	toorn (de)	[tōrn]
rage (fury)	woede (de)	['wudə]
depression	depressie (de)	[dep'rɛsi]
discomfort (unease)	ongemak (het)	[ɔnxə'mak]
comfort	gemak, comfort (het)	[xə'mak], [kɔm'fɔr]
to regret (be sorry)	spijt hebben	[spɛjt 'hɛbən]
regret	spijt (de)	[spɛjt]
bad luck	pech (de)	[pɛx]
sadness	bedroefdheid (de)	[bə'druft hɛjt]
shame (remorse)	schaamte (de)	['sxāmtə]
gladness	pret (de), plezier (het)	[prɛt], [plə'zir]
enthusiasm, zeal	enthousiasme (het)	[ɛntusi'asmə]
enthusiast	enthousiasteling (de)	[ɛntusi'astəliŋ]
to show enthusiasm	enthousiasme vertonen	[ɛntusi'asmə vər'tɔnən]

62. Character. Personality

character	karakter (het)	[ka'raktər]
character flaw	karakterfout (de)	[ka'raktər·'faut]
mind	verstand (het)	[vər'stant]
reason	rede (de)	['redə]
conscience	geweten (het)	[xə'wetən]
habit (custom)	gewoonte (de)	[xə'wōntə]
ability (talent)	bekwaamheid (de)	[bək'wāmhɛjt]
can (e.g., ~ swim)	kunnen	['kʉnən]
patient (adj)	geduldig	[xə'dʉldəx]
impatient (adj)	ongeduldig	[ɔnxə'dʉldəx]
curious (inquisitive)	nieuwsgierig	[niu'sxirəx]
curiosity	nieuwsgierigheid (de)	[niu'sxirəxɛjt]
modesty	bescheidenheid (de)	[bə'sxɛjdənhɛjt]
modest (adj)	bescheiden	[bə'sxɛjdən]
immodest (adj)	onbescheiden	[ɔnbə'sxɛjdən]
laziness	luiheid (de)	['lœyhɛjt]
lazy (adj)	lui	['lœy]
lazy person (masc.)	luiwammes (de)	['lœywaməs]
cunning (n)	sluwheid (de)	['slʉwhɛjt]
cunning (as adj)	sluw	[slʉw]
distrust	wantrouwen (het)	['wantrauvən]
distrustful (adj)	wantrouwig	['wantrauvəx]
generosity	gulheid (de)	['xʉlhɛjt]
generous (adj)	gul	[xjul]
talented (adj)	talentrijk	[ta'lɛntrɛjk]

talent	**talent (het)**	[ta'lɛnt]
courageous (adj)	**moedig**	['mudəx]
courage	**moed (de)**	[mut]
honest (adj)	**eerlijk**	['ērlək]
honesty	**eerlijkheid (de)**	['ērləkhɛjt]
careful (cautious)	**voorzichtig**	[vōr'zihtəx]
brave (courageous)	**manhaftig**	[man'xaftəh]
serious (adj)	**ernstig**	['ɛrnstəx]
strict (severe, stern)	**streng**	[strɛŋ]
decisive (adj)	**resoluut**	[rezɔ'lūt]
indecisive (adj)	**onzeker, irresoluut**	[ɔn'zekər], [irezɔ'lūt]
shy, timid (adj)	**schuchter**	['sxʉxtər]
shyness, timidity	**schuchterheid (de)**	['sxʉxtərxɛjt]
confidence (trust)	**vertrouwen (het)**	[vər'trauwən]
to believe (trust)	**vertrouwen**	[vər'trauwən]
trusting (credulous)	**goedgelovig**	[xutxə'lovəx]
sincerely (adv)	**oprecht**	[ɔp'rɛxt]
sincere (adj)	**oprecht**	[ɔp'rɛxt]
sincerity	**oprechtheid (de)**	[ɔp'rɛxtxɛjt]
open (person)	**open**	['ɔpən]
calm (adj)	**rustig**	['rʉstəx]
frank (sincere)	**openhartig**	[ɔpən'hartəx]
naïve (adj)	**naïef**	[na'if]
absent-minded (adj)	**verstrooid**	[vər'strōjt]
funny (odd)	**leuk, grappig**	['løk], ['xrapəx]
greed	**gierigheid (de)**	['xirəxhɛjt]
greedy (adj)	**gierig**	['xirəx]
stingy (adj)	**inhalig**	[in'haləx]
evil (adj)	**kwaad**	['kwāt]
stubborn (adj)	**koppig**	['kɔpəx]
unpleasant (adj)	**onaangenaam**	[ɔ'nānxənām]
selfish person (masc.)	**egoïst (de)**	[ɛxɔ'ist]
selfish (adj)	**egoïstisch**	[ɛxɔ'istis]
coward	**lafaard (de)**	['lafārt]
cowardly (adj)	**laf**	[laf]

63. Sleep. Dreams

to sleep (vi)	**slapen**	['slapən]
sleep, sleeping	**slaap (de)**	[slāp]
dream	**droom (de)**	[drōm]
to dream (in sleep)	**dromen**	['drɔmən]
sleepy (adj)	**slaperig**	['slapərəx]

bed	bed (het)	[bɛt]
mattress	matras (de)	[ma'tras]
blanket (comforter)	deken (de)	['dekən]
pillow	kussen (het)	['kʉsən]
sheet	laken (het)	['lakən]

insomnia	slapeloosheid (de)	['slapəlōshɛjt]
sleepless (adj)	slapeloos	['slapəlōs]
sleeping pill	slaapmiddel (het)	['slāp·midəl]
to take a sleeping pill	slaapmiddel innemen	['slāpmidəl 'innemən]

to feel sleepy	willen slapen	['wilən 'slapən]
to yawn (vi)	geeuwen	['xēuwən]
to go to bed	gaan slapen	[xān 'slapən]
to make up the bed	het bed opmaken	[ət bɛt 'ɔpmakən]
to fall asleep	inslapen	['inslapən]

nightmare	nachtmerrie (de)	['naxtmɛri]
snore, snoring	gesnurk (het)	[xə'snurk]
to snore (vi)	snurken	['snurkən]

alarm clock	wekker (de)	['wɛkər]
to wake (vt)	wekken	['wɛkən]
to wake up	wakker worden	['wakər 'vɔrdən]
to get up (vi)	opstaan	['ɔpstān]
to wash up (wash face)	zich wassen	[zix 'wasən]

64. Humour. Laughter. Gladness

humor (wit, fun)	humor (de)	['hʉmɔr]
sense of humor	gevoel (het) voor humor	[xə'vul vōr 'hʉmɔr]
to enjoy oneself	plezier hebben	[plɛ'zir 'hɛbən]
cheerful (merry)	vrolijk	['vrɔlək]
merriment (gaiety)	pret (de), plezier (het)	[prɛt], [plə'zir]

smile	glimlach (de)	['xlimlah]
to smile (vi)	glimlachen	['xlimlahən]
to start laughing	beginnen te lachen	[bə'xinən tə 'lahən]
to laugh (vi)	lachen	['laxən]
laugh, laughter	lach (de)	[lax]

anecdote	mop (de)	[mɔp]
funny (anecdote, etc.)	grappig	['xrapəx]
funny (odd)	grappig	['xrapəx]

to joke (vi)	grappen maken	['xrapən 'makən]
joke (verbal)	grap (de)	[xrap]
joy (emotion)	blijheid (de)	['blɛjhɛjt]
to rejoice (vi)	blij zijn	[blɛj zɛjn]
joyful (adj)	blij	[blɛj]

65. Discussion, conversation. Part 1

| communication | communicatie (de) | [kɔmuni'katsi] |
| to communicate | communiceren | [kɔmuni'serən] |

conversation	conversatie (de)	[kɔnvər'satsi]
dialog	dialoog (de)	[dia'lōx]
discussion (discourse)	discussie (de)	[dis'kusi]
dispute (debate)	debat (het)	[de'bat]
to dispute	debatteren, twisten	[deba'terən], ['twistən]

interlocutor	gesprekspartner (de)	[xə'sprɛks·'partnər]
topic (theme)	thema (het)	['tema]
point of view	standpunt (het)	['stant·punt]
opinion (point of view)	mening (de)	['meniŋ]
speech (talk)	toespraak (de)	['tusprāk]

discussion (of report, etc.)	bespreking (de)	[bə'sprekiŋ]
to discuss (vt)	bespreken	[bə'sprekən]
talk (conversation)	gesprek (het)	[xə'sprɛk]
to talk (to chat)	spreken	['sprekən]
meeting	ontmoeting (de)	[ɔnt'mutiŋ]
to meet (vi, vt)	ontmoeten	[ɔnt'mutən]

proverb	spreekwoord (het)	['sprēk·wōrt]
saying	gezegde (het)	[xə'zɛxdə]
riddle (poser)	raadsel (het)	['rātsəl]
to pose a riddle	een raadsel opgeven	[en 'rātsəl 'ɔpxevən]
password	wachtwoord (het)	['waxt·wōrt]
secret	geheim (het)	[xə'hɛjm]

oath (vow)	eed (de)	[ēd]
to swear (an oath)	zweren	['zwerən]
promise	belofte (de)	[bə'lɔftə]
to promise (vt)	beloven	[bə'lovən]

advice (counsel)	advies (het)	[at'vis]
to advise (vt)	adviseren	[atvi'zirən]
to follow one's advice	advies volgen	[at'vis 'vɔlxən]
to listen to … (obey)	luisteren	['lœysterən]

news	nieuws (het)	['nius]
sensation (news)	sensatie (de)	[sɛn'satsi]
information (data)	informatie (de)	[infɔr'matsi]
conclusion (decision)	conclusie (de)	[kɔn'kluzi]
voice	stem (de)	[stɛm]
compliment	compliment (het)	[kɔmpli'mɛnt]
kind (nice)	vriendelijk	['vrindələk]

| word | woord (het) | [wōrt] |
| phrase | zin (de), zinsdeel (het) | [zin], ['zinsdēl] |

answer	antwoord (het)	['antwõrt]
truth	waarheid (de)	['wārhɛjt]
lie	leugen (de)	['løxən]

thought	gedachte (de)	[xə'dahtə]
idea (inspiration)	idee (de/het)	[i'dē]
fantasy	fantasie (de)	[fanta'zi]

66. Discussion, conversation. Part 2

respected (adj)	gerespecteerd	[xərɛspɛk'tẽrt]
to respect (vt)	respecteren	[rɛspɛk'terən]
respect	respect (het)	[rɛ'spɛkt]
Dear ... (letter)	Geachte ...	[xe'ahtə]

to introduce (sb to sb)	voorstellen	['võrstɛlən]
to make acquaintance	kennismaken	['kɛnis·makən]
intention	intentie (de)	[in'tɛntsi]
to intend (have in mind)	intentie hebben	[in'tɛntsi 'hɛbən]
wish	wens (de)	[wɛns]
to wish (~ good luck)	wensen	['wɛnsən]

surprise (astonishment)	verbazing (de)	[vər'baziŋ]
to surprise (amaze)	verbazen	[vər'bazən]
to be surprised	verbaasd zijn	[vər'bāst zɛjn]

to give (vt)	geven	['xevən]
to take (get hold of)	nemen	['nemən]
to give back	teruggeven	[te'rux·xevən]
to return (give back)	retourneren	[retur'nerən]

to apologize (vi)	zich verontschuldigen	[zih vərɔnt'sxuldəxən]
apology	verontschuldiging (de)	[vərɔnt'sxuldəxiŋ]
to forgive (vt)	vergeven	[vər'xevən]

to talk (speak)	spreken	['sprekən]
to listen (vi)	luisteren	['lœystərən]
to hear out	aanhoren	['ānhɔrən]
to understand (vt)	begrijpen	[bə'xrɛjpən]

to show (to display)	tonen	['tɔnən]
to look at ...	kijken naar ...	['kɛjkən nār]
to call (yell for sb)	roepen	['rupən]
to distract (disturb)	afleiden	['aflɛjdən]
to disturb (vt)	storen	['stɔrən]
to pass (to hand sth)	doorgeven	[dõr'xevən]

demand (request)	verzoek (het)	[vər'zuk]
to request (ask)	verzoeken	[vər'zukən]
demand (firm request)	eis (de)	[ɛjs]

to demand (request firmly)	eisen	['ɛjsən]
to tease (call names)	beledigen	[bə'ledəxən]
to mock (make fun of)	uitlachen	['œʏtlaxən]
mockery, derision	spot (de)	[spɔt]
nickname	bijnaam (de)	['bɛjnãm]

insinuation	zinspeling (de)	['zinspeliŋ]
to insinuate (imply)	zinspelen	['zinspelən]
to mean (vt)	impliceren	[impli'serən]

description	beschrijving (de)	[bəsx'rɛjviŋ]
to describe (vt)	beschrijven	[bəsx'rɛjvən]
praise (compliments)	lof (de)	[lɔf]
to praise (vt)	loven	['lovən]

disappointment	teleurstelling (de)	[tə'lørstɛliŋ]
to disappoint (vt)	teleurstellen	[tə'lørstɛlən]
to be disappointed	teleurgesteld zijn	[tə'lørxɛstəlt zɛjn]

supposition	veronderstelling (de)	[verɔndər'stɛliŋ]
to suppose (assume)	veronderstellen	[verɔndər'stɛlən]
warning (caution)	waarschuwing (de)	['wãrsxjuviŋ]
to warn (vt)	waarschuwen	['wãrsxjuvən]

67. Discussion, conversation. Part 3

to talk into (convince)	aanpraten	['ãnpratən]
to calm down (vt)	kalmeren	[kal'merən]

silence (~ is golden)	stilte (de)	['stiltə]
to be silent (not speaking)	zwijgen	['zwɛjxən]
to whisper (vi, vt)	fluisteren	['flœʏstərən]
whisper	gefluister (het)	[xə'flœʏstər]

frankly, sincerely (adv)	open, eerlijk	['ɔpən], ['ērlək]
in my opinion ...	volgens mij ...	['vɔlxəns mɛj]

detail (of the story)	detail (het)	[de'taj]
detailed (adj)	gedetailleerd	[xədeta'jērt]
in detail (adv)	gedetailleerd	[xədeta'jērt]

hint, clue	hint (de)	[hint]
to give a hint	een hint geven	[en hint 'xevən]

look (glance)	blik (de)	[blik]
to have a look	een kijkje nemen	[en 'kɛjkje 'nemən]
fixed (look)	strak	[strak]
to blink (vi)	knipperen	['kniperən]
to wink (vi)	knipogen	['knipɔxən]
to nod (in assent)	knikken	['knikən]

sigh	zucht (de)	[zʉxt]
to sigh (vi)	zuchten	['zʉxtən]
to shudder (vi)	huiveren	['hœyvərən]
gesture	gebaar (het)	[xə'bār]
to touch (one's arm, etc.)	aanraken	['ānrakən]
to seize	grijpen	['xrɛjpən]
(e.g., ~ by the arm)		
to tap (on the shoulder)	een schouderklopje geven	[en 'shaudər·'klɔpje 'xevən]

Look out!	Kijk uit!	[kɛjk œyt]
Really?	Echt?	[ɛxt]
Good luck!	Succes!	[sʉk'sɛs]
I see!	Juist, ja!	[jœyst ja]
What a pity!	Wat jammer!	[wat 'jamə]

68. Agreement. Refusal

consent	instemming (het)	['instɛmiŋ]
to consent (vi)	instemmen	['instɛmən]
approval	goedkeuring (de)	[xut'køriŋ]
to approve (vt)	goedkeuren	[xut'kørən]
refusal	weigering (de)	['wɛjxəriŋ]
to refuse (vi, vt)	weigeren	['wɛjxərən]

Great!	Geweldig!	[xə'wɛldəx]
All right!	Goed!	[xut]
Okay! (I agree)	Akkoord!	[a'kōrt]

forbidden (adj)	verboden	[vər'bɔdən]
it's forbidden	het is verboden	[ət is vər'bɔdən]
it's impossible	het is onmogelijk	[ət is ɔn'mɔxələk]
incorrect (adj)	onjuist	['ɔnjœyst]

to reject (~ a demand)	afwijzen	['afwɛjzən]
to support (cause, idea)	steunen	['stønən]
to accept (~ an apology)	aanvaarden	['ānvārdən]

to confirm (vt)	bevestigen	[bə'vɛstixən]
confirmation	bevestiging (de)	[bə'vɛstixiŋ]
permission	toestemming (de)	['tustɛmiŋ]
to permit (vt)	toestaan	['tustān]
decision	beslissing (de)	[bə'slisiŋ]
to say nothing (hold one's tongue)	z'n mond houden	[zən mɔnt 'haudən]

condition (term)	voorwaarde (de)	['vōrwārdə]
excuse (pretext)	smoes (de)	[smus]
praise (compliments)	lof (de)	[lɔf]
to praise (vt)	loven	['lɔvən]

69. Success. Good luck. Failure

success	succes (het)	[sʉk'sɛs]
successfully (adv)	succesvol	[sʉk'sɛsvɔl]
successful (adj)	succesvol	[sʉk'sɛsvɔl]
luck (good luck)	geluk (het)	[xə'lʉk]
Good luck!	Succes!	[sʉk'sɛs]
lucky (e.g., ~ day)	geluks-	[xə'lʉks]
lucky (fortunate)	gelukkig	[xə'lʉkəx]
failure	mislukking (de)	[mis'lʉkiŋ]
misfortune	tegenslag (de)	['texənslax]
bad luck	pech (de)	[pɛx]
unsuccessful (adj)	zonder succes	['zɔndər sʉk'sɛs]
catastrophe	catastrofe (de)	[kata'strɔfə]
pride	fierheid (de)	['firhɛjt]
proud (adj)	fier	[fir]
to be proud	fier zijn	[fir zɛjn]
winner	winnaar (de)	['winãr]
to win (vi)	winnen	['winən]
to lose (not win)	verliezen	[vər'lizən]
try	poging (de)	['pɔxiŋ]
to try (vi)	pogen, proberen	['pɔxən], [prɔ'berən]
chance (opportunity)	kans (de)	[kans]

70. Quarrels. Negative emotions

shout (scream)	schreeuw (de)	[sxrẽw]
to shout (vi)	schreeuwen	['sxrẽwən]
to start to cry out	beginnen te schreeuwen	[bə'xinən tə 'sxrẽwən]
quarrel	ruzie (de)	['rʉzi]
to quarrel (vi)	ruzie hebben	['rʉzi 'hɛbən]
fight (squabble)	schandaal (het)	[sxan'dãl]
to make a scene	schandaal maken	[sxan'dãl 'makən]
conflict	conflict (het)	[kɔn'flikt]
misunderstanding	misverstand (het)	['misvərstant]
insult	belediging (de)	[bə'ledəxiŋ]
to insult (vt)	beledigen	[bə'ledəxən]
insulted (adj)	beledigd	[bə'ledəxt]
resentment	krenking (de)	['krenkiŋ]
to offend (vt)	krenken	['krenkən]
to take offense	gekwetst worden	[xə'kwɛtst 'wordən]
indignation	verontwaardiging (de)	[vərɔnt'wãrdixiŋ]
to be indignant	verontwaardigd zijn	[vərɔnt'wãrdixt zɛjn]

| complaint | klacht (de) | [klaxt] |
| to complain (vi, vt) | klagen | ['klaxən] |

apology	verontschuldiging (de)	[vərɔnt'sxʉldəxiŋ]
to apologize (vi)	zich verontschuldigen	[zih vərɔnt'sxʉldəxən]
to beg pardon	excuus vragen	[ɛks'kûs 'vraxən]

criticism	kritiek (de)	[kri'tik]
to criticize (vt)	bekritiseren	[bəkriti'zerən]
accusation	beschuldiging (de)	[bə'sxʉldəxiŋ]
to accuse (vt)	beschuldigen	[bə'sxʉldəxən]

revenge	wraak (de)	[wrãk]
to avenge (get revenge)	wreken	['wrekən]
to pay back	wraak nemen	[wrãk 'nemən]

disdain	minachting (de)	['minaxtiŋ]
to despise (vt)	minachten	['minaxtən]
hatred, hate	haat (de)	[hãt]
to hate (vt)	haten	['hatən]

nervous (adj)	zenuwachtig	['zenʉw·ahtəx]
to be nervous	zenuwachtig zijn	['zenʉw·ahtəx zɛjn]
angry (mad)	boos	[bõs]
to make angry	boos maken	[bõs 'makən]

humiliation	vernedering (de)	[vər'nedəriŋ]
to humiliate (vt)	vernederen	[vər'nedərən]
to humiliate oneself	zich vernederen	[zix vər'nedərən]

| shock | schok (de) | [sxɔk] |
| to shock (vt) | schokken | ['sxɔkən] |

| trouble (e.g., serious ~) | onaangenaamheid (de) | [ɔ'nãnxənãmhɛjt] |
| unpleasant (adj) | onaangenaam | [ɔ'nãnxənãm] |

fear (dread)	vrees (de)	[vrẽs]
terrible (storm, heat)	vreselijk	['vresələk]
scary (e.g., ~ story)	eng	[ɛŋ]
horror	gruwel (de)	['xrʉwəl]
awful (crime, news)	vreselijk	['vresələk]

to begin to tremble	beginnen te beven	[bə'xinən tə 'bevən]
to cry (weep)	huilen	['hœylən]
to start crying	beginnen te huilen	[bə'xinən tə 'hœylən]
tear	traan (de)	[trãn]

fault	schuld (de)	[sxʉlt]
guilt (feeling)	schuldgevoel (het)	['sxʉlt·xəvul]
dishonor (disgrace)	schande (de)	['sxandə]
protest	protest (het)	[pro'tɛst]
stress	stress (de)	[strɛs]

to disturb (vt)	**storen**	['stɔrən]
to be furious	**kwaad zijn**	['kwāt zɛjn]
mad, angry (adj)	**kwaad**	['kwāt]
to end (~ a relationship)	**beëindigen**	[be'ɛjndəxən]
to swear (at sb)	**vloeken**	['vlukən]
to scare (become afraid)	**schrikken**	['sxrikən]
to hit (strike with hand)	**slaan**	[slān]
to fight (street fight, etc.)	**vechten**	['vɛxtən]
to settle (a conflict)	**regelen**	['rexələn]
discontented (adj)	**ontevreden**	[ɔntə'vredən]
furious (adj)	**woedend**	['wudənt]
It's not good!	**Dat is niet goed!**	[dat is 'nit xut]
It's bad!	**Dat is slecht!**	[dat is 'slɛxt]

Medicine

71. Diseases

sickness	ziekte (de)	['ziktə]
to be sick	ziek zijn	[zik zɛjn]
health	gezondheid (de)	[xə'zɔnthɛjt]
runny nose (coryza)	snotneus (de)	[snɔt'nøs]
tonsillitis	angina (de)	[an'xina]
cold (illness)	verkoudheid (de)	[vər'kauthɛjt]
to catch a cold	verkouden raken	[vər'kaudən 'rakən]
bronchitis	bronchitis (de)	[brɔn'xitis]
pneumonia	longontsteking (de)	['lɔŋ·ɔntstekiŋ]
flu, influenza	griep (de)	[xrip]
nearsighted (adj)	bijziend	[bɛj'zint]
farsighted (adj)	verziend	['vɛrzint]
strabismus (crossed eyes)	scheelheid (de)	['sxēlxɛjt]
cross-eyed (adj)	scheel	[sxēl]
cataract	grauwe staar (de)	['xrauə stār]
glaucoma	glaucoom (het)	[xlau'kōm]
stroke	beroerte (de)	[bə'rurtə]
heart attack	hartinfarct (het)	['hart·in'farkt]
myocardial infarction	myocardiaal infarct (het)	[miɔkardi'āl in'farkt]
paralysis	verlamming (de)	[vər'lamiŋ]
to paralyze (vt)	verlammen	[vər'lamən]
allergy	allergie (de)	[alɛr'xi]
asthma	astma (de/het)	['astma]
diabetes	diabetes (de)	[dia'betəs]
toothache	tandpijn (de)	['tand·pɛjn]
caries	tandbederf (het)	['tand·bə'dɛrf]
diarrhea	diarree (de)	[dia'rē]
constipation	constipatie (de)	[kɔnsti'patsi]
stomach upset	maagstoornis (de)	['māx·stōrnis]
food poisoning	voedselvergiftiging (de)	['vudsəl·vər'xiftəxiŋ]
to get food poisoning	voedselvergiftiging oplopen	['vudsəl·vər'xiftəxiŋ 'ɔplɔpən]
arthritis	artritis (de)	[ar'tritis]
rickets	rachitis (de)	[ra'xitis]

rheumatism	reuma (het)	['røma]
atherosclerosis	arteriosclerose (de)	[artɛriɔskle'rɔzə]
gastritis	gastritis (de)	[xas'tritis]
appendicitis	blindedar- montsteking (de)	[blində'darm ɔntstɛkiŋ]
cholecystitis	galblaasontsteking (de)	['xalblaxāns·ɔnt'stɛkiŋ]
ulcer	zweer (de)	[zwēr]
measles	mazelen	['mazelən]
rubella (German measles)	rodehond (de)	['rɔdəhɔnt]
jaundice	geelzucht (de)	['xēlzʉht]
hepatitis	leverontsteking (de)	['levər ɔnt'stekiŋ]
schizophrenia	schizofrenie (de)	[sxitsɔfrə'ni]
rabies (hydrophobia)	dolheid (de)	['dɔlhɛjt]
neurosis	neurose (de)	['nø'rɔzə]
concussion	hersenschudding (de)	['hɛrsən·sxjudiŋ]
cancer	kanker (de)	['kankər]
sclerosis	sclerose (de)	[skle'rɔzə]
multiple sclerosis	multiple sclerose (de)	['mʉltiplə skle'rɔzə]
alcoholism	alcoholisme (het)	[alkɔhɔ'lismə]
alcoholic (n)	alcoholicus (de)	[alkɔ'hɔlikʉs]
syphilis	syfilis (de)	['sifilis]
AIDS	AIDS (de)	[ets]
tumor	tumor (de)	['tʉmɔr]
malignant (adj)	kwaadaardig	['kwāt·'ārdəx]
benign (adj)	goedaardig	[xu'tārdəx]
fever	koorts (de)	[kōrts]
malaria	malaria (de)	[ma'laria]
gangrene	gangreen (het)	[xanx'rēn]
seasickness	zeeziekte (de)	[zē·'ziktə]
epilepsy	epilepsie (de)	[ɛpilɛp'si]
epidemic	epidemie (de)	[ɛpidə'mi]
typhus	tyfus (de)	['tifʉs]
tuberculosis	tuberculose (de)	[tʉbərkʉ'lozə]
cholera	cholera (de)	['xɔlera]
plague (bubonic ~)	pest (de)	[pɛst]

72. Symptoms. Treatments. Part 1

symptom	symptoom (het)	[simp'tōm]
temperature	temperatuur (de)	[tɛmpəra'tūr]
high temperature (fever)	verhoogde temperatuur (de)	[vər'hōxtə tɛmpəra'tūr]

pulse	polsslag (de)	['pɔls·slax]
dizziness (vertigo)	duizeling (de)	['dœyzəliŋ]
hot (adj)	heet	[hēt]
shivering	koude rillingen	['kaudə 'riliŋən]
pale (e.g., ~ face)	bleek	[blēk]

cough	hoest (de)	[hust]
to cough (vi)	hoesten	['hustən]
to sneeze (vi)	niezen	['nizən]
faint	flauwte (de)	['flautə]
to faint (vi)	flauwvallen	['flauvalən]

bruise (hématome)	blauwe plek (de)	['blauə plɛk]
bump (lump)	buil (de)	['bœyl]
to bang (bump)	zich stoten	[zix 'stɔtən]
contusion (bruise)	kneuzing (de)	['knøziŋ]
to get a bruise	kneuzen	['knøzən]

to limp (vi)	hinken	['hinkən]
dislocation	verstuiking (de)	[vər'stœɣkiŋ]
to dislocate (vt)	verstuiken	[vər'stœɣkən]
fracture	breuk (de)	['brøk]
to have a fracture	een breuk oplopen	[en 'brøk 'ɔplɔpən]

cut (e.g., paper ~)	snijwond (de)	['snɛj·wɔnt]
to cut oneself	zich snijden	[zix snɛjdən]
bleeding	bloeding (de)	['bludiŋ]

| burn (injury) | brandwond (de) | ['brant·wɔnt] |
| to get burned | zich branden | [zix 'brandən] |

to prick (vt)	prikken	['prikən]
to prick oneself	zich prikken	[zix 'prikən]
to injure (vt)	blesseren	[blɛ'serən]
injury	blessure (de)	[blɛ'sʉrə]
wound	wond (de)	[wɔnt]
trauma	trauma (het)	['trauma]

to be delirious	ijlen	['ɛjlən]
to stutter (vi)	stotteren	['stɔtɛrən]
sunstroke	zonnesteek (de)	['zɔnə·stēk]

73. Symptoms. Treatments. Part 2

| pain, ache | pijn (de) | [pɛjn] |
| splinter (in foot, etc.) | splinter (de) | ['splintər] |

sweat (perspiration)	zweet (het)	['zwēt]
to sweat (perspire)	zweten	['zwetən]
vomiting	braking (de)	['brakiŋ]

convulsions	stuiptrekkingen	['stœɐp·'trɛkiŋən]
pregnant (adj)	zwanger	['zwaŋər]
to be born	geboren worden	[xə'borən 'wɔrdən]
delivery, labor	geboorte (de)	[xə'bõrtə]
to deliver (~ a baby)	baren	['barən]
abortion	abortus (de)	[a'bɔrtʉs]

breathing, respiration	ademhaling (de)	['adəmhaliŋ]
in-breath (inhalation)	inademing (de)	['inademiŋ]
out-breath (exhalation)	uitademing (de)	['œɐtademiŋ]
to exhale (breathe out)	uitademen	['œɐtademən]
to inhale (vi)	inademen	['inademən]

disabled person	invalide (de)	[inva'lidə]
cripple	gehandicapte (de)	[hə'handikaptə]
drug addict	drugsverslaafde (de)	['drʉks·vər'slãfdə]

deaf (adj)	doof	[dõf]
mute (adj)	stom	[stɔm]
deaf mute (adj)	doofstom	[dõf·'stɔm]

mad, insane (adj)	krankzinnig	[kraŋk'sinəx]
madman (demented person)	krankzinnige (de)	[kraŋk'sinəxə]
madwoman	krankzinnige (de)	[kraŋk'sinəxə]
to go insane	krankzinnig worden	[kraŋk'sinəx 'wɔrdən]

gene	gen (het)	[xen]
immunity	immuniteit (de)	[imʉni'tɛjt]
hereditary (adj)	erfelijk	['ɛrfələk]
congenital (adj)	aangeboren	['ãnxəborən]

virus	virus (het)	['virʉs]
microbe	microbe (de)	[mik'rɔbə]
bacterium	bacterie (de)	[bak'teri]
infection	infectie (de)	[in'fɛksi]

74. Symptoms. Treatments. Part 3

hospital	ziekenhuis (het)	['zikən·hœɐs]
patient	patiënt (de)	[pasi'ent]
diagnosis	diagnose (de)	[diax'nɔzə]
cure	genezing (de)	[xə'neziŋ]
medical treatment	medische behandeling (de)	['mɛdisə bə'handəliŋ]
to get treatment	onder behandeling zijn	['ɔndər bə'handəliŋ zɛjn]
to treat (~ a patient)	behandelen	[bə'handələn]
to nurse (look after)	zorgen	['zɔrxən]
care (nursing ~)	ziekenzorg (de)	['zikən·zɔrx]
operation, surgery	operatie (de)	[ɔpe'ratsi]

to bandage (head, limb)	**verbinden**	[vər'bindən]
bandaging	**verband (het)**	[vər'bant]
vaccination	**vaccin (het)**	[vaksən]
to vaccinate (vt)	**inenten**	['inɛntən]
injection, shot	**injectie (de)**	[inj'eksi]
to give an injection	**een injectie geven**	[ɛn inj'eksi 'xɛvən]
attack	**aanval (de)**	['ānval]
amputation	**amputatie (de)**	[ampʉ'tatsi]
to amputate (vt)	**amputeren**	[ampʉ'terən]
coma	**coma (het)**	['kɔma]
to be in a coma	**in coma liggen**	[in 'kɔma 'lixən]
intensive care	**intensieve zorg, ICU (de)**	[intən'sivə zɔrx], [isɛ'ju]
to recover (~ from flu)	**zich herstellen**	[zix hɛr'ʃtɛlən]
condition (patient's ~)	**toestand (de)**	['tustant]
consciousness	**bewustzijn (het)**	[bə'wʉstsɛjn]
memory (faculty)	**geheugen (het)**	[xə'høxən]
to pull out (tooth)	**trekken**	['trɛkən]
filling	**vulling (de)**	['vʉliŋ]
to fill (a tooth)	**vullen**	['vʉlən]
hypnosis	**hypnose (de)**	['hipnɔzə]
to hypnotize (vt)	**hypnotiseren**	[hipnɔti'zerən]

75. Doctors

doctor	**dokter, arts (de)**	['dɔktər], [arts]
nurse	**ziekenzuster (de)**	['zikən·zʉstər]
personal doctor	**lijfarts (de)**	['lɛjf·arts]
dentist	**tandarts (de)**	['tand·arts]
eye doctor	**oogarts (de)**	['ōx·arts]
internist	**therapeut (de)**	[tera'pøt]
surgeon	**chirurg (de)**	[ʃi'rʉrx]
psychiatrist	**psychiater (de)**	[psixi'atər]
pediatrician	**pediater (de)**	[pedi'atər]
psychologist	**psycholoog (de)**	[psihɔ'lōx]
gynecologist	**gynaecoloog (de)**	[xinekɔ'lōx]
cardiologist	**cardioloog (de)**	[kardiɔ'lōx]

76. Medicine. Drugs. Accessories

medicine, drug	**geneesmiddel (het)**	[xə'nēsmidəl]
remedy	**middel (het)**	['midəl]

| to prescribe (vt) | voorschrijven | ['võrsxrɛjvən] |
| prescription | recept (het) | [re'sɛpt] |

tablet, pill	tablet (de/het)	[tab'lɛt]
ointment	zalf (de)	[zalf]
ampule	ampul (de)	[am'pʉl]
mixture	drank (de)	[drank]
syrup	siroop (de)	[si'rõp]
pill	pil (de)	[pil]
powder	poeder (de/het)	['pudər]

gauze bandage	verband (het)	[vər'bant]
cotton wool	watten	['watən]
iodine	jodium (het)	['jodijum]

Band-Aid	pleister (de)	['plɛjstər]
eyedropper	pipet (de)	[pi'pɛt]
thermometer	thermometer (de)	['tɛrmɔmetər]
syringe	spuit (de)	['spœyt]

| wheelchair | rolstoel (de) | ['rɔl·stul] |
| crutches | krukken | ['krʉkən] |

painkiller	pijnstiller (de)	['pɛjn·stilər]
laxative	laxeermiddel (het)	[la'ksẽr·midəl]
spirits (ethanol)	spiritus (de)	['spiritʉs]
medicinal herbs	medicinale kruiden	[mɛdisi'nalə krœydən]
herbal (~ tea)	kruiden-	['krœydən]

77. Smoking. Tobacco products

tobacco	tabak (de)	[ta'bak]
cigarette	sigaret (de)	[sixa'rɛt]
cigar	sigaar (de)	[si'xãr]
pipe	pijp (de)	[pɛjp]
pack (of cigarettes)	pakje (het)	['pakjə]

matches	lucifers	['lʉsifərs]
matchbox	luciferdoosje (het)	['lʉsifər·'dõçə]
lighter	aansteker (de)	['ãnstekər]
ashtray	asbak (de)	['asbak]
cigarette case	sigarettendoosje (het)	[sixa'rɛtən·'dõçə]

| cigarette holder | sigarettenpijpje (het) | [sixa'rɛtən·'pɛjpjə] |
| filter (cigarette tip) | filter (de/het) | ['filtər] |

to smoke (vi, vt)	roken	['rɔkən]
to light a cigarette	een sigaret opsteken	[en sixa'rɛt 'ɔpstekən]
smoking	roken (het)	['rɔkən]
smoker	roker (de)	['rɔkər]

stub, butt (of cigarette)	**peuk (de)**	['pøk]
smoke, fumes	**rook (de)**	[rōk]
ash	**as (de)**	[as]

HUMAN HABITAT

City

78. City. Life in the city

city, town	**stad (de)**	[stat]
capital city	**hoofdstad (de)**	['hōft·stat]
village	**dorp (het)**	[dɔrp]
city map	**plattegrond (de)**	['platə·xrɔnt]
downtown	**centrum (het)**	['sɛntrʉm]
suburb	**voorstad (de)**	['vōrstat]
suburban (adj)	**voorstads-**	['vōrstats]
outskirts	**randgemeente (de)**	['rant·xəmēntə]
environs (suburbs)	**omgeving (de)**	[ɔm'xeviŋ]
city block	**blok (het)**	[blɔk]
residential block (area)	**woonwijk (de)**	['wōnvɛjk]
traffic	**verkeer (het)**	[vər'kēr]
traffic lights	**verkeerslicht (het)**	[vər'kērs·lixt]
public transportation	**openbaar vervoer (het)**	[ɔpən'bār vər'vur]
intersection	**kruispunt (het)**	['krœys·pynt]
crosswalk	**zebrapad (het)**	['zɛbra·pat]
pedestrian underpass	**onderdoorgang (de)**	['ɔndər·'dōrxaŋ]
to cross (~ the street)	**oversteken**	[ɔvər'stekən]
pedestrian	**voetganger (de)**	['vutxaŋər]
sidewalk	**trottoir (het)**	[trɔtu'ar]
bridge	**brug (de)**	[brʉx]
embankment (river walk)	**dijk (de)**	[dɛjk]
fountain	**fontein (de)**	[fɔn'tɛjn]
allée (garden walkway)	**allee (de)**	[a'lē]
park	**park (het)**	[park]
boulevard	**boulevard (de)**	[bulə'var]
square	**plein (het)**	[plɛjn]
avenue (wide street)	**laan (de)**	[lān]
street	**straat (de)**	[strāt]
side street	**zijstraat (de)**	['zɛj·strāt]
dead end	**doodlopende straat (de)**	[dōd'lɔpəndə strāt]
house	**huis (het)**	['hœys]
building	**gebouw (het)**	[xə'bau]

skyscraper	wolkenkrabber (de)	['wɔlkən·'krabər]
facade	gevel (de)	['xevəl]
roof	dak (het)	[dak]
window	venster (het)	['vɛnstər]
arch	boog (de)	[bõx]
column	pilaar (de)	[pi'lãr]
corner	hoek (de)	[huk]

store window	vitrine (de)	[vit'rinə]
signboard (store sign, etc.)	gevelreclame (de)	['xevəl·re'klamə]
poster	affiche (de/het)	[a'fiʃə]
advertising poster	reclameposter (de)	[re'klamə·'postər]
billboard	aanplakbord (het)	['ãnplak·'bɔrt]

garbage, trash	vuilnis (de/het)	['vœylnis]
trashcan (public ~)	vuilnisbak (de)	['vœylnis·bak]
to litter (vi)	afval weggooien	['afval 'wɛxõjən]
garbage dump	stortplaats (de)	['stɔrt·plãts]

phone booth	telefooncel (de)	[telə'fõn·səl]
lamppost	straatlicht (het)	['strãt·lixt]
bench (park ~)	bank (de)	[bank]

police officer	politieagent (de)	[pɔ'litsi·a'xɛnt]
police	politie (de)	[pɔ'litsi]
beggar	zwerver (de)	['zwɛrvər]
homeless (n)	dakloze (de)	[dak'lɔzə]

79. Urban institutions

store	winkel (de)	['winkəl]
drugstore, pharmacy	apotheek (de)	[apɔ'tẽk]
eyeglass store	optiek (de)	[ɔp'tik]
shopping mall	winkelcentrum (het)	['winkəl·'sɛntrʉm]
supermarket	supermarkt (de)	['sʉpərmarkt]

bakery	bakkerij (de)	['bakərɛj]
baker	bakker (de)	['bakər]
pastry shop	banketbakkerij (de)	[ban'ket·bakə'rɛj]
grocery store	kruidenier (de)	[krœydə'nir]
butcher shop	slagerij (de)	[slaxə'rɛj]

| produce store | groentewinkel (de) | ['xrunte·'winkəl] |
| market | markt (de) | [markt] |

coffee house	koffiehuis (het)	['kɔfi·hœys]
restaurant	restaurant (het)	[rɛstɔ'rant]
pub, bar	bar (de)	[bar]
pizzeria	pizzeria (de)	[pitsə'rija]
hair salon	kapperssalon (de/het)	['kapərs·sa'lɔn]

post office	postkantoor (het)	[pɔst·kan'tõr]
dry cleaners	stomerij (de)	[stɔmɛ'rɛj]
photo studio	fotostudio (de)	[fɔtɔ·'stʉdiɔ]
shoe store	schoenwinkel (de)	['sxʉn·'winkəl]
bookstore	boekhandel (de)	['bukən·'handəl]
sporting goods store	sportwinkel (de)	['spɔrt·'winkəl]
clothes repair shop	kledingreparatie (de)	['klediŋ·repa'ratsi]
formal wear rental	kledingverhuur (de)	['klediŋ·vər'hūr]
video rental store	videotheek (de)	[video'tẽk]
circus	circus (de/het)	['sirkʉs]
zoo	dierentuin (de)	['dĩrən·tœʏn]
movie theater	bioscoop (de)	[biɔ'skõp]
museum	museum (het)	[mʉ'zejum]
library	bibliotheek (de)	[bibliɔ'tẽk]
theater	theater (het)	[te'atər]
opera (opera house)	opera (de)	['ɔpera]
nightclub	nachtclub (de)	['naxt·klʉp]
casino	casino (het)	[ka'sinɔ]
mosque	moskee (de)	[mɔs'kẽ]
synagogue	synagoge (de)	[sina'xɔxə]
cathedral	kathedraal (de)	[kate'drāl]
temple	tempel (de)	['tɛmpəl]
church	kerk (de)	[kɛrk]
college	instituut (het)	[insti'tūt]
university	universiteit (de)	[junivɛrsi'tɛjt]
school	school (de)	[sxõl]
prefecture	gemeentehuis (het)	[xə'mẽntə·hœʏs]
city hall	stadhuis (het)	['stat·hœʏs]
hotel	hotel (het)	[hɔ'tɛl]
bank	bank (de)	[bank]
embassy	ambassade (de)	[amba'sadə]
travel agency	reisbureau (het)	[rɛjs·bʉ'rɔ]
information office	informatieloket (het)	[infor'matsi·lɔ'kɛt]
currency exchange	wisselkantoor (het)	['wisəl·kan'tõr]
subway	metro (de)	['metrɔ]
hospital	ziekenhuis (het)	['zikən·hœʏs]
gas station	benzinestation (het)	[bɛn'zinə·sta'tsjɔn]
parking lot	parking (de)	['parkiŋ]

80. Signs

signboard (store sign, etc.)	gevelreclame (de)	['xevəl·re'klamə]
notice (door sign, etc.)	opschrift (het)	['ɔpsxrift]
poster	poster (de)	['pɔstər]
direction sign	wegwijzer (de)	['wɛx·wɛjzər]
arrow (sign)	pijl (de)	[pɛjl]
caution	waarschuwing (de)	['wãrsxjuviŋ]
warning sign	waarschuwings- bord (het)	['wãrsxjuviŋs bɔrt]
to warn (vt)	waarschuwen	['wãrsxjuvən]
rest day (weekly ~)	vrije dag (de)	['vrɛjə dax]
timetable (schedule)	dienstregeling (de)	[dinst·'rexəliŋ]
opening hours	openingsuren	['ɔpəniŋs·ʉrən]
WELCOME!	WELKOM!	['wɛlkɔm]
ENTRANCE	INGANG	['inxaŋ]
EXIT	UITGANG	['œʏtxaŋ]
PUSH	DUWEN	['dʉwən]
PULL	TREKKEN	['trɛkən]
OPEN	OPEN	['ɔpən]
CLOSED	GESLOTEN	[xə'slotən]
WOMEN	DAMES	['daməs]
MEN	HEREN	['herən]
DISCOUNTS	KORTING	['kortiŋ]
SALE	UITVERKOOP	['œʏtverkõp]
NEW!	NIEUW!	[niu]
FREE	GRATIS	['xratis]
ATTENTION!	PAS OP!	[pas 'ɔp]
NO VACANCIES	VOLGEBOEKT	['vɔlxəbukt]
RESERVED	GERESERVEERD	[xərezər'vẽrt]
ADMINISTRATION	ADMINISTRATIE	[atminist'ratsi]
STAFF ONLY	ALLEEN VOOR PERSONEEL	[a'lẽn võr pərsɔ'nẽl]
BEWARE OF THE DOG!	GEVAARLIJKE HOND	[xe'vãrləkə hɔnt]
NO SMOKING	VERBODEN TE ROKEN!	[vər'bodən tə 'rɔkən]
DO NOT TOUCH!	NIET AANRAKEN!	[nit ãn'rakən]
DANGEROUS	GEVAARLIJK	[xe'vãrlək]
DANGER	GEVAAR	[xe'vãr]
HIGH VOLTAGE	HOOGSPANNING	[hõh·'spaniŋ]
NO SWIMMING!	VERBODEN TE ZWEMMEN	[vər'bodən tə 'zwɛmən]

OUT OF ORDER	BUITEN GEBRUIK	['bœytən xəbrœʏk]
FLAMMABLE	ONTVLAMBAAR	[ɔnt'flambār]
FORBIDDEN	VERBODEN	[vər'bodən]
NO TRESPASSING!	DOORGANG VERBODEN	['dōrxaŋ vər'bɔdən]
WET PAINT	OPGELET	[ɔpxe'lɛt
	PAS GEVERFD	pas xə'verft]

81. Urban transportation

bus	bus, autobus (de)	[bʉs], ['autobʉs]
streetcar	tram (de)	[trɛm]
trolley bus	trolleybus (de)	['trɔlibʉs]
route (of bus, etc.)	route (de)	['rutə]
number (e.g., bus ~)	nummer (het)	['nʉmər]
to go by ...	rijden met ...	['rɛjdən mɛt]
to get on (~ the bus)	stappen	['stapən]
to get off ...	afstappen	['afstapən]
stop (e.g., bus ~)	halte (de)	['haltə]
next stop	volgende halte (de)	['vɔlxəndə 'haltə]
terminus	eindpunt (het)	['ɛjnt·pʉnt]
schedule	dienstregeling (de)	[dinst·'rexəliŋ]
to wait (vt)	wachten	['waxtən]
ticket	kaartje (het)	['kārtʃə]
fare	reiskosten (de)	['rɛjs·kɔstən]
cashier (ticket seller)	kassier (de)	[ka'sir]
ticket inspection	kaartcontrole (de)	['kārt·kɔn'trɔlə]
ticket inspector	controleur (de)	[kɔntrɔ'lør]
to be late (for ...)	te laat zijn	[tə 'lāt zɛjn]
to miss (~ the train, etc.)	missen (de bus ~)	['misən]
to be in a hurry	zich haasten	[zix 'hāstən]
taxi, cab	taxi (de)	['taksi]
taxi driver	taxichauffeur (de)	['taksi·ʃo'før]
by taxi	met de taxi	[mɛt də 'taksi]
taxi stand	taxistandplaats (de)	['taksi·'stant·plāts]
to call a taxi	een taxi bestellen	[en 'taksi bə'stɛlən]
to take a taxi	een taxi nemen	[en 'taksi 'nemən]
traffic	verkeer (het)	[vər'kēr]
traffic jam	file (de)	['filə]
rush hour	spitsuur (het)	['spits·ūr]
to park (vi)	parkeren	[par'kerən]
to park (vt)	parkeren	[par'kerən]
parking lot	parking (de)	['parkiŋ]
subway	metro (de)	['metrɔ]

station	halte (de)	['haltə]
to take the subway	de metro nemen	[də 'metrɔ 'nemən]
train	trein (de)	[trɛjn]
train station	station (het)	[sta'tsjɔn]

82. Sightseeing

monument	monument (het)	[mɔnʉ'mɛnt]
fortress	vesting (de)	['vɛstiŋ]
palace	paleis (het)	[pa'lɛjs]
castle	kasteel (het)	[kas'tēl]
tower	toren (de)	['tɔrən]
mausoleum	mausoleum (het)	[mauzɔ'leum]

architecture	architectuur (de)	[arʃitək'tūr]
medieval (adj)	middeleeuws	['midəlēws]
ancient (adj)	oud	['aut]
national (adj)	nationaal	[natsjɔ'nāl]
famous (monument, etc.)	bekend	[bə'kɛnt]

tourist	toerist (de)	[tu'rist]
guide (person)	gids (de)	[xits]
excursion, sightseeing tour	rondleiding (de)	['rɔntlɛjdiŋ]
to show (vt)	tonen	['tɔnən]
to tell (vt)	vertellen	[vər'tɛlən]

to find (vt)	vinden	['vindən]
to get lost (lose one's way)	verdwalen	[vərd'walən]
map (e.g., subway ~)	plattegrond (de)	['platə·xrɔnt]
map (e.g., city ~)	plattegrond (de)	['platə·xrɔnt]

souvenir, gift	souvenir (het)	[suve'nir]
gift shop	souvenirwinkel (de)	[suve'nir·'winkəl]
to take pictures	foto's maken	['fotɔs 'makən]
to have one's picture taken	zich laten fotograferen	[zih 'latən fɔtɔxra'ferən]

83. Shopping

to buy (purchase)	kopen	['kɔpən]
purchase	aankoop (de)	['ānkɔp]
to go shopping	winkelen	['winkelən]
shopping	winkelen (het)	['winkelən]

| to be open (ab. store) | open zijn | ['ɔpən zɛjn] |
| to be closed | gesloten zijn | [xə'slotən zɛjn] |

| footwear, shoes | schoeisel (het) | ['sxuisəl] |
| clothes, clothing | kleren (mv.) | ['klerən] |

cosmetics	cosmetica (mv.)	[kɔs'metika]
food products	voedingswaren	['vudiŋs·warən]
gift, present	geschenk (het)	[xə'sxɛnk]

| salesman | verkoper (de) | [vər'kɔpər] |
| saleswoman | verkoopster (de) | [vər'kõpstər] |

check out, cash desk	kassa (de)	['kasa]
mirror	spiegel (de)	['spixəl]
counter (store ~)	toonbank (de)	['tõn·bank]
fitting room	paskamer (de)	['pas·kamər]

to try on	aanpassen	['ānpasən]
to fit (ab. dress, etc.)	passen	['pasən]
to like (I like …)	bevallen	[bə'valən]

price	prijs (de)	[prɛjs]
price tag	prijskaartje (het)	['prɛjs·'kārtʃə]
to cost (vt)	kosten	['kɔstən]
How much?	Hoeveel?	[hu'vēl]
discount	korting (de)	['kɔrtiŋ]

inexpensive (adj)	niet duur	[nit dūr]
cheap (adj)	goedkoop	[xut'kõp]
expensive (adj)	duur	[dūr]
It's expensive	Dat is duur.	[dat is 'dūr]

rental (n)	verhuur (de)	[vər'hūr]
to rent (~ a tuxedo)	huren	['hʉrən]
credit (trade credit)	krediet (het)	[kre'dit]
on credit (adv)	op krediet	[ɔp kre'dit]

84. Money

money	geld (het)	[xɛlt]
currency exchange	ruil (de)	[rœyl]
exchange rate	koers (de)	[kurs]
ATM	geldautomaat (de)	[xɛlt·auto'māt]
coin	muntstuk (de)	['mʉntstʉk]

| dollar | dollar (de) | ['dɔlar] |
| euro | euro (de) | [ørɔ] |

lira	lire (de)	['lirə]
Deutschmark	Duitse mark (de)	['dœytsə mark]
franc	frank (de)	[frank]
pound sterling	pond sterling (het)	[pɔnt 'stɛrliŋ]
yen	yen (de)	[jen]
debt	schuld (de)	[sxʉlt]
debtor	schuldenaar (de)	['sxʉldənār]

| to lend (money) | uitlenen | ['œytlənən] |
| to borrow (vi, vt) | lenen | ['lenən] |

bank	bank (de)	[bank]
account	bankrekening (de)	[bank·'rekəniŋ]
to deposit (vt)	storten	['stɔrtən]
to deposit into the account	op rekening storten	[ɔp 'rekəniŋ 'stɔrtən]
to withdraw (vt)	opnemen	['ɔpnemən]

credit card	kredietkaart (de)	[kre'dit·kārt]
cash	baar geld (het)	[bār 'xɛlt]
check	cheque (de)	[ʃɛk]
to write a check	een cheque uitschrijven	[en ʃɛk œyt'sxrɛjvən]
checkbook	chequeboekje (het)	[ʃɛk·'bukjə]

wallet	portefeuille (de)	[pɔrtə'fœyə]
change purse	geldbeugel (de)	[xɛlt·'bøxəl]
safe	safe (de)	[sef]

heir	erfgenaam (de)	['ɛrfxənām]
inheritance	erfenis (de)	['ɛrfənis]
fortune (wealth)	fortuin (het)	[fɔr'tœyn]

lease	huur (de)	[hūr]
rent (money)	huurprijs (de)	['hūr·prɛjs]
to rent (sth from sb)	huren	['hʉrən]

price	prijs (de)	[prɛjs]
cost	kostprijs (de)	['kɔstprɛjs]
sum	som (de)	[sɔm]

to spend (vt)	uitgeven	['œytxevən]
expenses	kosten	['kɔstən]
to economize (vi, vt)	bezuinigen	[bə'zœynəxən]
economical	zuinig	['zœynəx]

to pay (vi, vt)	betalen	[bə'talən]
payment	betaling (de)	[bə'taliŋ]
change (give the ~)	wisselgeld (het)	['wisəl·xɛlt]

tax	belasting (de)	[bə'lastiŋ]
fine	boete (de)	['butə]
to fine (vt)	beboeten	[bə'butən]

85. Post. Postal service

post office	postkantoor (het)	[pɔst·kan'tōr]
mail (letters, etc.)	post (de)	[pɔst]
mailman	postbode (de)	['pɔst·bodə]
opening hours	openingsuren	['ɔpəniŋs·ʉrən]

letter	**brief (de)**	[brif]
registered letter	**aangetekende brief (de)**	['ānxə'tekəndə brif]
postcard	**briefkaart (de)**	['brif·kārt]
telegram	**telegram (het)**	[teləx'ram]
package (parcel)	**postpakket (het)**	[pɔstpa'ket]
money transfer	**overschrijving (de)**	[ɔvər'sxrɛjviŋ]
to receive (vt)	**ontvangen**	[ɔnt'faŋən]
to send (vt)	**sturen**	['stʉrən]
sending	**verzending (de)**	[vər'zɛndiŋ]
address	**adres (het)**	[ad'rɛs]
ZIP code	**postcode (de)**	['pɔst·kɔdə]
sender	**verzender (de)**	[vər'zɛndər]
receiver	**ontvanger (de)**	[ɔnt'faŋər]
name (first name)	**naam (de)**	[nām]
surname (last name)	**achternaam (de)**	['axtər·nām]
postage rate	**tarief (het)**	[ta'rif]
standard (adj)	**standaard**	['standārt]
economical (adj)	**zuinig**	['zœʏnəx]
weight	**gewicht (het)**	[xə'wixt]
to weigh (~ letters)	**afwegen**	['afwexən]
envelope	**envelop (de)**	[ɛnve'lɔp]
postage stamp	**postzegel (de)**	['pɔst·zexəl]
to stamp an envelope	**een postzegel plakken op**	[en pɔst'zexəl 'plakən ɔp]

Dwelling. House. Home

86. House. Dwelling

house	huis (het)	['hœys]
at home (adv)	thuis	['tœys]
yard	cour (de)	[kur]
fence (iron ~)	omheining (de)	[ɔm'hɛjniŋ]
brick (n)	baksteen (de)	['bakstēn]
brick (as adj)	van bakstenen	[van 'bakstənən]
stone (n)	steen (de)	[stēn]
stone (as adj)	stenen	['stenən]
concrete (n)	beton (het)	[bə'tɔn]
concrete (as adj)	van beton	[van bə'tɔn]
new (new-built)	nieuw	[niu]
old (adj)	oud	['aut]
decrepit (house)	vervallen	[vər'valən]
modern (adj)	modern	[mɔ'dɛrn]
multistory (adj)	met veel verdiepingen	[mɛt vēl vɛr'dipiŋən]
tall (~ building)	hoog	[hōx]
floor, story	verdieping (de)	[vər'dipiŋ]
single-story (adj)	met een verdieping	[mɛt en vər'dipiŋ]
1st floor	laagste verdieping (de)	['lāxstə vər'dipiŋ]
top floor	bovenverdieping (de)	['bɔvən·vər'dipiŋ]
roof	dak (het)	[dak]
chimney	schoorsteen (de)	['sxōr·stēn]
roof tiles	dakpan (de)	['dakpan]
tiled (adj)	pannen-	['panən]
attic (storage place)	zolder (de)	['zɔldər]
window	venster (het)	['vɛnstər]
glass	glas (het)	[xlas]
window ledge	vensterbank (de)	['vɛnstər·bank]
shutters	luiken	['lœykən]
wall	muur (de)	[mūr]
balcony	balkon (het)	[bal'kɔn]
downspout	regenpijp (de)	['rexən·pɛjp]
upstairs (to be ~)	boven	['bɔvən]
to go upstairs	naar boven gaan	[nār 'bɔvən xān]

| to come down (the stairs) | **afdalen** | ['afdalən] |
| to move (to new premises) | **verhuizen** | [vər'hœyzən] |

87. House. Entrance. Lift

entrance	**ingang (de)**	['inxaŋ]
stairs (stairway)	**trap (de)**	[trap]
steps	**treden**	['tredən]
banister	**trapleuning (de)**	['trap·'løniŋ]
lobby (hotel ~)	**hal (de)**	[hal]

mailbox	**postbus (de)**	['post·bʉs]
garbage can	**vuilnisbak (de)**	['vœylnis·bak]
trash chute	**vuilniskoker (de)**	['vœylnis·'kokər]

elevator	**lift (de)**	[lift]
freight elevator	**goederenlift (de)**	['xudərən·lift]
elevator cage	**liftcabine (de)**	[lift·ka'binə]
to take the elevator	**de lift nemen**	[də lift 'nemən]

apartment	**appartement (het)**	[apartə'mɛnt]
residents (~ of a building)	**bewoners**	[bə'wonərs]
neighbor (masc.)	**buurman (de)**	['bʉrman]
neighbor (fem.)	**buurvrouw (de)**	['bʉrvrau]
neighbors	**buren**	['bʉrən]

88. House. Electricity

electricity	**elektriciteit (de)**	[ɛlɛktrisi'tɛjt]
light bulb	**lamp (de)**	[lamp]
switch	**schakelaar (de)**	['sxakəlār]
fuse (plug fuse)	**zekering (de)**	['zekəriŋ]

cable, wire (electric ~)	**draad (de)**	[drāt]
wiring	**bedrading (de)**	[bə'dradiŋ]
electricity meter	**elektriciteitsmeter (de)**	[ɛlɛktrisi'tɛjt·'metər]
readings	**gegevens**	[xə'xevəns]

89. House. Doors. Locks

door	**deur (de)**	['dør]
gate (vehicle ~)	**toegangspoort (de)**	['tuxaŋs·pōrt]
handle, doorknob	**deurkruk (de)**	['dør·krʉk]
to unlock (unbolt)	**ontsluiten**	[on'slœytən]
to open (vt)	**openen**	['opənən]
to close (vt)	**sluiten**	['slœytən]

key	sleutel (de)	['sløtəl]
bunch (of keys)	sleutelbos (de)	['sløtəl·bɔs]
to creak (door, etc.)	knarsen	['knarsən]
creak	knarsgeluid (het)	['knarsxəlœyt]
hinge (door ~)	scharnier (het)	[sxar'nir]
doormat	deurmat (de)	['dør·mat]

door lock	slot (het)	[slɔt]
keyhole	sleutelgat (het)	['sløtəl·xat]
crossbar (sliding bar)	grendel (de)	['xrɛndəl]
door latch	schuif (de)	['sxœyf]
padlock	hangslot (het)	['haŋ·slɔt]

to ring (~ the door bell)	aanbellen	['ãmbɛlən]
ringing (sound)	bel (de)	[bel]
doorbell	deurbel (de)	['dør·bel]
doorbell button	belknop (de)	['bel·knɔp]
knock (at the door)	geklop (het)	[xə'klɔp]
to knock (vi)	kloppen	['klɔpən]

code	code (de)	['kɔdə]
combination lock	cijferslot (het)	['sɛjfər·slɔt]
intercom	parlofoon (de)	['parlɔfõn]
number (on the door)	nummer (het)	['nʉmər]
doorplate	naambordje (het)	['nãm·'bɔrdjə]
peephole	deurspion (de)	['dør·spiɔn]

90. Country house

village	dorp (het)	[dɔrp]
vegetable garden	moestuin (de)	['mus·tœyn]
fence	hek (het)	[hɛk]
picket fence	houten hekwerk (het)	['hautən 'hɛkwɛrk]
wicket gate	tuinpoortje (het)	['tœyn·'põrtʃe]

granary	graanschuur (de)	['xrãn·sxūr]
root cellar	wortelkelder (de)	['wɔrtəl·'kɛldər]
shed (garden ~)	schuur (de)	[sxūr]
well (water)	waterput (de)	['watər·pʉt]

| stove (wood-fired ~) | kachel (de) | ['kaxəl] |
| to stoke the stove | de kachel stoken | [də 'kaxəl 'stɔkən] |

| firewood | brandhout (het) | ['brant·haut] |
| log (firewood) | houtblok (het) | ['hautblɔk] |

veranda	veranda (de)	[və'randa]
deck (terrace)	terras (het)	[tɛ'ras]
stoop (front steps)	bordes (het)	[bɔr'dɛs]
swing (hanging seat)	schommel (de)	['sxɔmɛl]

91. Villa. Mansion

country house	landhuisje (het)	['lant·hœʏɕə]
villa (seaside ~)	villa (de)	['vila]
wing (~ of a building)	vleugel (de)	['vløxəl]
garden	tuin (de)	['tœʏn]
park	park (het)	[park]
tropical greenhouse	oranjerie (de)	[ɔranʒɛ'ri]
to look after (garden, etc.)	onderhouden	['ɔndər'haudən]
swimming pool	zwembad (het)	['zwɛm·bat]
gym (home gym)	gym (het)	[ʒim]
tennis court	tennisveld (het)	['tɛnis·vɛlt]
home theater (room)	bioscoopkamer (de)	[biɔ'skōp·'kamər]
garage	garage (de)	[xa'raʒə]
private property	privé-eigendom (het)	[pri've-'ɛjxəndɔm]
private land	eigen terrein (het)	['ɛjxən te'rɛjn]
warning (caution)	waarschuwing (de)	['wārsxjuviŋ]
warning sign	waarschuwings-bord (het)	['wārsxjuviŋs bɔrt]
security	bewaking (de)	[bə'wakiŋ]
security guard	bewaker (de)	[bə'wakər]
burglar alarm	inbraakalarm (het)	['inbrāk·a'larm]

92. Castle. Palace

castle	kasteel (het)	[kas'tēl]
palace	paleis (het)	[pa'lɛjs]
fortress	vesting (de)	['vɛstiŋ]
wall (round castle)	ringmuur (de)	['riŋ·mūr]
tower	toren (de)	['tɔrən]
keep, donjon	donjon (de)	[dɔn'ʒɔn]
portcullis	valhek (het)	['valhək]
underground passage	onderaardse gang (de)	[ɔndər'ārdsə xaŋ]
moat	slotgracht (de)	['slɔt·xraht]
chain	ketting (de)	['kɛtiŋ]
arrow loop	schietgat (het)	['sxitxat]
magnificent (adj)	prachtig	['prahtəx]
majestic (adj)	majestueus	[mahəstʉ'øz]
impregnable (adj)	onneembaar	[ɔ'nēmbār]
medieval (adj)	middeleeuws	['midəlēws]

93. Apartment

apartment	appartement (het)	[apartə'mɛnt]
room	kamer (de)	['kamər]
bedroom	slaapkamer (de)	['slāp·kamər]
dining room	eetkamer (de)	[ēt·'kamər]
living room	salon (de)	[sa'lɔn]
study (home office)	studeerkamer (de)	[stu'dēr·'kamər]
entry room	gang (de)	[xaŋ]
bathroom (room with a bath or shower)	badkamer (de)	['bat·kamər]
half bath	toilet (het)	[tua'lɛt]
ceiling	plafond (het)	[pla'fɔnt]
floor	vloer (de)	[vlur]
corner	hoek (de)	[huk]

94. Apartment. Cleaning

to clean (vi, vt)	schoonmaken	['sxōn·makən]
to put away (to stow)	opbergen	['ɔpbɛrxən]
dust	stof (het)	[stɔf]
dusty (adj)	stoffig	['stɔfəx]
to dust (vt)	stoffen	['stɔfən]
vacuum cleaner	stofzuiger (de)	['stɔf·zœyxər]
to vacuum (vt)	stofzuigen	['stɔf·zœyxən]
to sweep (vi, vt)	vegen	['vexən]
sweepings	veegsel (het)	['vēxsəl]
order	orde (de)	['ɔrdə]
disorder, mess	wanorde (de)	['wanɔrdə]
mop	zwabber (de)	['zwabər]
dust cloth	poetsdoek (de)	['putsduk]
short broom	veger (de)	['vexər]
dustpan	stofblik (het)	['stɔf·blik]

95. Furniture. Interior

furniture	meubels	['møbəl]
table	tafel (de)	['tafəl]
chair	stoel (de)	[stul]
bed	bed (het)	[bɛt]
couch, sofa	bankstel (het)	['bankstəl]
armchair	fauteuil (de)	[fo'tøj]
bookcase	boekenkast (de)	['bukən·kast]

shelf	boekenrek (het)	['bukən·rɛk]
wardrobe	kledingkast (de)	['klediŋ·kast]
coat rack (wall-mounted ~)	kapstok (de)	['kapstɔk]
coat stand	staande kapstok (de)	['stāndə 'kapstɔk]

| bureau, dresser | commode (de) | [kɔ'mɔdə] |
| coffee table | salontafeltje (het) | [sa'lɔn·'tafəltʃə] |

mirror	spiegel (de)	['spixəl]
carpet	tapijt (het)	[ta'pɛjt]
rug, small carpet	tapijtje (het)	[ta'pɛjtʃə]

fireplace	haard (de)	[hārt]
candle	kaars (de)	[kārs]
candlestick	kandelaar (de)	['kandəlār]

drapes	gordijnen	[xɔr'dɛjnən]
wallpaper	behang (het)	[bə'haŋ]
blinds (jalousie)	jaloezie (de)	[jalu'zi]

table lamp	bureaulamp (de)	[bʉ'ro·lamp]
wall lamp (sconce)	wandlamp (de)	['want·lamp]
floor lamp	staande lamp (de)	['stāndə lamp]
chandelier	luchter (de)	['lʉxtər]

leg (of chair, table)	poot (de)	[pōt]
armrest	armleuning (de)	[arm·'løniŋ]
back (backrest)	rugleuning (de)	['rʉx·'løniŋ]
drawer	la (de)	[la]

96. Bedding

bedclothes	beddengoed (het)	['bɛdən·xut]
pillow	kussen (het)	['kʉsən]
pillowcase	kussenovertrek (de)	['kʉsən·'ɔvərtrɛk]
duvet, comforter	deken (de)	['dekən]
sheet	laken (het)	['lakən]
bedspread	sprei (de)	[sprɛj]

97. Kitchen

kitchen	keuken (de)	['køkən]
gas	gas (het)	[xas]
gas stove (range)	gasfornuis (het)	[xas·for'nœys]
electric stove	elektrisch fornuis (het)	[ɛ'lɛktris for'nœys]
oven	oven (de)	['ɔvən]
microwave oven	magnetronoven (de)	['mahnətrɔn·'ɔvən]
refrigerator	koelkast (de)	['kul·kast]

freezer	diepvriezer (de)	[dip·'vrizər]
dishwasher	vaatwasmachine (de)	['vātwas·ma'ʃinə]
meat grinder	vleesmolen (de)	['vlēs·mɔlən]
juicer	vruchtenpers (de)	['vrʉxtən·pɛrs]
toaster	toaster (de)	['tōstər]
mixer	mixer (de)	['miksər]
coffee machine	koffiemachine (de)	['kɔfi·ma'ʃinə]
coffee pot	koffiepot (de)	['kɔfi·pɔt]
coffee grinder	koffiemolen (de)	['kɔfi·mɔlən]
kettle	fluitketel (de)	['flœʏt·'ketəl]
teapot	theepot (de)	['tē·pɔt]
lid	deksel (de/het)	['dɛksəl]
tea strainer	theezeefje (het)	['tē·zefjə]
spoon	lepel (de)	['lepəl]
teaspoon	theelepeltje (het)	[tē·'lepəltʃə]
soup spoon	eetlepel (de)	[ēt·'lepəl]
fork	vork (de)	[vɔrk]
knife	mes (het)	[mɛs]
tableware (dishes)	vaatwerk (het)	['vātwɛrk]
plate (dinner ~)	bord (het)	[bɔrt]
saucer	schoteltje (het)	['sxɔteltʃə]
shot glass	likeurglas (het)	[li'kør·xlas]
glass (tumbler)	glas (het)	[xlas]
cup	kopje (het)	['kɔpjə]
sugar bowl	suikerpot (de)	[sœʏkər·pɔt]
salt shaker	zoutvat (het)	['zaut·vat]
pepper shaker	pepervat (het)	['pepər·vat]
butter dish	boterschaaltje (het)	['botər·'sxāltʃə]
stock pot (soup pot)	pan (de)	[pan]
frying pan (skillet)	bakpan (de)	['bak·pan]
ladle	pollepel (de)	[pɔl·'lepəl]
colander	vergiet (de/het)	[vər'xit]
tray (serving ~)	dienblad (het)	['dinblat]
bottle	fles (de)	[fles]
jar (glass)	glazen pot (de)	['xlazən pɔt]
can	blik (het)	[blik]
bottle opener	flesopener (de)	[fles·'ɔpənər]
can opener	blikopener (de)	[blik·'ɔpənər]
corkscrew	kurkentrekker (de)	['kʉrkən·'trɛkər]
filter	filter (de/het)	['filtər]
to filter (vt)	filteren	['filtərən]
trash, garbage (food waste, etc.)	huisvuil (het)	['hœʏsvœʏl]
trash can (kitchen ~)	vuilnisemmer (de)	['vœʏlnis·'ɛmər]

98. Bathroom

bathroom	**badkamer (de)**	['bat·kamər]
water	**water (het)**	['watər]
faucet	**kraan (de)**	[krān]
hot water	**warm water (het)**	[warm 'watər]
cold water	**koud water (het)**	['kaut 'watər]
toothpaste	**tandpasta (de)**	['tand·pasta]
to brush one's teeth	**tanden poetsen**	['tandən 'putsən]
toothbrush	**tandenborstel (de)**	['tandən·'bɔrstəl]
to shave (vi)	**zich scheren**	[zix 'sxerən]
shaving foam	**scheercrème (de)**	[sxēr·krɛ:m]
razor	**scheermes (het)**	['sxēr·mɛs]
to wash (one's hands, etc.)	**wassen**	['wasən]
to take a bath	**een bad nemen**	[en bat 'nemən]
shower	**douche (de)**	[duʃ]
to take a shower	**een douche nemen**	[en duʃ 'nemən]
bathtub	**bad (het)**	[bat]
toilet (toilet bowl)	**toiletpot (de)**	[tua'lɛt·pɔt]
sink (washbasin)	**wastafel (de)**	['was·tafəl]
soap	**zeep (de)**	[zēp]
soap dish	**zeepbakje (het)**	['zēp·bakjə]
sponge	**spons (de)**	[spɔns]
shampoo	**shampoo (de)**	['ʃampō]
towel	**handdoek (de)**	['handuk]
bathrobe	**badjas (de)**	['batjas]
laundry (process)	**was (de)**	[was]
washing machine	**wasmachine (de)**	['was·ma'ʃinə]
to do the laundry	**de was doen**	[də was dun]
laundry detergent	**waspoeder (de)**	['was·'pudər]

99. Household appliances

TV set	**televisie (de)**	[telə'vizi]
tape recorder	**cassettespeler (de)**	[ka'sɛtə·'spelər]
VCR (video recorder)	**videorecorder (de)**	['videɔ·re'kɔrdər]
radio	**radio (de)**	['radiɔ]
player (CD, MP3, etc.)	**speler (de)**	['spelər]
video projector	**videoprojector (de)**	['videɔ·prɔ'jektɔr]
home movie theater	**home theater systeem (het)**	[hɔm te'jater si'stēm]

DVD player	DVD-speler (de)	[deve'de-'speler]
amplifier	versterker (de)	[ver'sterker]
video game console	spelconsole (de)	['spɛl·kɔn'sɔle]

video camera	videocamera (de)	['video·'kamera]
camera (photo)	fotocamera (de)	['fotɔ·'kamera]
digital camera	digitale camera (de)	[dixi'tale 'kamera]

vacuum cleaner	stofzuiger (de)	['stɔf·zœyxer]
iron (e.g., steam ~)	strijkijzer (het)	['strɛjk·ɛjzer]
ironing board	strijkplank (de)	['strɛjk·plank]

telephone	telefoon (de)	[tele'fõn]
cell phone	mobieltje (het)	[mɔ'biltʃe]
typewriter	schrijfmachine (de)	['sxrɛjf·ma'ʃine]
sewing machine	naaimachine (de)	['nãj·ma'ʃine]

microphone	microfoon (de)	[mikrɔ'fõn]
headphones	koptelefoon (de)	['kɔp·tele'fõn]
remote control (TV)	afstandsbediening (de)	['afstants·be'diniŋ]

CD, compact disc	CD (de)	[se'de]
cassette, tape	cassette (de)	[ka'sɛte]
vinyl record	vinylplaat (de)	[vi'nil·plãt]

100. Repairs. Renovation

renovations	renovatie (de)	[renɔ'vatsi]
to renovate (vt)	renoveren	[renɔ'viren]
to repair, to fix (vt)	repareren	[repa'reren]
to put in order	op orde brengen	[ɔp 'ɔrde 'brɛŋen]
to redo (do again)	overdoen	['ɔverdun]

paint	verf (de)	[vɛrf]
to paint (~ a wall)	verven	['vɛrven]
house painter	schilder (de)	['sxilder]
paintbrush	kwast (de)	['kwast]
whitewash	kalk (de)	[kalk]
to whitewash (vt)	kalken	['kalken]
wallpaper	behang (het)	[be'haŋ]
to wallpaper (vt)	behangen	[be'haŋen]
varnish	lak (de/het)	[lak]
to varnish (vt)	lakken	['laken]

101. Plumbing

water	water (het)	['water]
hot water	warm water (het)	[warm 'water]

cold water	koud water (het)	['kaut 'watər]
faucet	kraan (de)	[krān]

drop (of water)	druppel (de)	['drʉpəl]
to drip (vi)	druppelen	['drʉpələn]
to leak (ab. pipe)	lekken	['lɛkən]
leak (pipe ~)	lekkage (de)	[lɛ'kaʒə]
puddle	plasje (het)	[plaɕə]

pipe	buis, leiding (de)	['bœys], ['lɛjdiŋ]
valve (e.g., ball ~)	stopkraan (de)	['stɔp·krān]
to be clogged up	verstopt raken	[vər'stɔpt 'rakən]

tools	gereedschap (het)	[xə'rētsxap]
adjustable wrench	Engelse sleutel (de)	['ɛŋɛlsə 'sløtəl]
to unscrew (lid, filter, etc.)	losschroeven	[lɔs'sxruvən]
to screw (tighten)	aanschroeven	['ānsxruvən]

to unclog (vt)	ontstoppen	[ɔnt'stɔpən]
plumber	loodgieter (de)	['lōtxitər]
basement	kelder (de)	['kɛldər]
sewerage (system)	riolering (de)	[rio'lɛriŋ]

102. Fire. Conflagration

fire (accident)	brand (de)	[brant]
flame	vlam (de)	[vlam]
spark	vonk (de)	[vɔnk]
smoke (from fire)	rook (de)	[rōk]
torch (flaming stick)	fakkel (de)	['fakəl]
campfire	kampvuur (het)	['kampvūr]

gas, gasoline	benzine (de)	[bɛn'zinə]
kerosene (type of fuel)	kerosine (de)	[kerə'zinə]
flammable (adj)	brandbaar	['brandbār]
explosive (adj)	ontplofbaar	[ɔnt'plɔfbār]
NO SMOKING	VERBODEN TE ROKEN!	[vər'bodən tə 'rɔkən]

safety	veiligheid (de)	['vɛjləxhɛjt]
danger	gevaar (het)	[xe'vār]
dangerous (adj)	gevaarlijk	[xe'vārlək]

to catch fire	in brand vliegen	[in brant 'vlixən]
explosion	explosie (de)	[ɛks'plɔzi]
to set fire	in brand steken	[in brant 'stekən]
arsonist	brandstichter (de)	['brant·stixtər]
arson	brandstichting (de)	['brant·stixtiŋ]

to blaze (vi)	vlammen	['vlamən]
to burn (be on fire)	branden	['brandən]

to burn down	afbranden	['afbrandən]
to call the fire department	de brandweer bellen	[də 'brantwēr 'bɛlən]
firefighter, fireman	brandweerman (de)	['brantwēr·man]
fire truck	brandweerwagen (de)	['brantwēr·'waxən]
fire department	brandweer (de)	['brantwēr]
fire truck ladder	uitschuifbare ladder (de)	['œʏtsxœʏfbarə 'ladər]

fire hose	brandslang (de)	['brant·slaŋ]
fire extinguisher	brandblusser (de)	['brant·blɵsər]
helmet	helm (de)	[hɛlm]
siren	sirene (de)	[si'renə]

to cry (for help)	roepen	['rupən]
to call for help	hulp roepen	[hɵlp 'rupən]
rescuer	redder (de)	['rɛdər]
to rescue (vt)	redden	['rɛdən]

to arrive (vi)	aankomen	['ānkɔmən]
to extinguish (vt)	blussen	['blɵsən]
water	water (het)	['watər]
sand	zand (het)	[zant]

ruins (destruction)	ruïnes	[rɵ'inəs]
to collapse (building, etc.)	instorten	['instɔrtən]
to fall down (vi)	ineenstorten	['inēnstɔrtən]
to cave in (ceiling, floor)	inzakken	[inzakən]

| piece of debris | brokstuk (het) | ['brɔk·stɵk] |
| ash | as (de) | [as] |

| to suffocate (die) | verstikken | [vər'stikən] |
| to be killed (perish) | omkomen | [ɔmkɔmən] |

HUMAN ACTIVITIES

Job. Business. Part 1

103. Office. Working in the office

office (company ~)	kantoor (het)	[kan'tōr]
office (of director, etc.)	kamer (de)	['kamər]
reception desk	receptie (de)	[re'sɛpsi]
secretary	secretaris (de)	[sekre'taris]
secretary (fem.)	secretaresse (de)	[sekreta'rɛsə]
director	directeur (de)	[dirɛk'tør]
manager	manager (de)	['mɛnədʒər]
accountant	boekhouder (de)	[buk 'haudər]
employee	werknemer (de)	['wɛrknemər]
furniture	meubilair (het)	['møbi'lɛr]
desk	tafel (de)	['tafəl]
desk chair	bureaustoel (de)	[bʉ'ro·stul]
drawer unit	ladeblok (het)	['ladə·blɔk]
coat stand	kapstok (de)	['kapstɔk]
computer	computer (de)	[kɔm'pjutər]
printer	printer (de)	['printər]
fax machine	fax (de)	[faks]
photocopier	kopieerapparaat (het)	[kɔpi'ēr·apa'rāt]
paper	papier (het)	[pa'pir]
office supplies	kantoorartikelen	[kan'tōr·ar'tikelən]
mouse pad	muismat (de)	['mœʏs·mat]
sheet (of paper)	blad (het)	[blat]
binder	ordner (de)	['ɔrdnər]
catalog	catalogus (de)	[ka'talogʉs]
phone directory	telefoongids (de)	[telə'fōn·xits]
documentation	documentatie (de)	[dɔkʉmen'tatsi]
brochure	brochure (de)	[brɔ'ʃʉrə]
(e.g., 12 pages ~)		
leaflet (promotional ~)	flyer (de)	['flajər]
sample	monster (het), staal (de)	['mɔnstər], [stāl]
training meeting	training (de)	['trɛjniŋ]
meeting (of managers)	vergadering (de)	[vər'xadəriŋ]
lunch time	lunchpauze (de)	['lʉnʃ·'pauzə]

to make a copy	een kopie maken	[en kɔ'pi 'makən]
to make multiple copies	de kopieën maken	[de kɔ'piɛn makən]
to receive a fax	een fax ontvangen	[en faks ɔnt'vaŋən]
to send a fax	een fax versturen	[en faks vər'stʉrən]

to call (by phone)	opbellen	['ɔpbelən]
to answer (vt)	antwoorden	['antwõrdən]
to put through	doorverbinden	['dõrvər'bindən]

to arrange, to set up	afspreken	['afsprekən]
to demonstrate (vt)	demonstreren	[demɔn'strerən]
to be absent	absent zijn	[ap'sɛnt zɛjn]
absence	afwezigheid (de)	['afwezəxhɛjt]

104. Business processes. Part 1

business	bedrijf (het)	[bə'drɛjf]
occupation	zaak (de), beroep (het)	[zāk], [bə'rup]
firm	firma (de)	['firma]
company	bedrijf (het)	[bə'drɛjf]
corporation	corporatie (de)	[kɔrpo'ratsi]
enterprise	onderneming (de)	['ɔndər'nemiŋ]
agency	agentschap (het)	[a'xɛntsxap]

agreement (contract)	overeenkomst (de)	[ɔvər'ēnkomst]
contract	contract (het)	[kɔn'trakt]
deal	transactie (de)	[tran'saksi]
order (to place an ~)	bestelling (de)	[bə'stɛliŋ]
terms (of the contract)	voorwaarde (de)	['võrwārdə]

wholesale (adv)	in het groot	[in ət xrõt]
wholesale (adj)	groothandels-	[xrõt·'handəls]
wholesale (n)	groothandel (de)	[xrõt·'handəl]
retail (adj)	kleinhandels-	[klɛjn·'handəls]
retail (n)	kleinhandel (de)	[klɛjn·'handəl]

competitor	concurrent (de)	[kɔnkju'rɛnt]
competition	concurrentie (de)	[kɔnkju'rɛntsi]
to compete (vi)	concurreren	[kɔnkju'rerən]

| partner (associate) | partner (de) | ['partnər] |
| partnership | partnerschap (het) | ['partnərsxap] |

crisis	crisis (de)	['krisis]
bankruptcy	bankroet (het)	[bank'rut]
to go bankrupt	bankroet gaan	[bank'rut xān]
difficulty	moeilijkheid (de)	['mujləkhɛjt]
problem	probleem (het)	[prɔ'blēm]
catastrophe	catastrofe (de)	[kata'strɔfə]
economy	economie (de)	[ɛkɔnɔ'mi]

economic (~ growth)	**economisch**	[ɛkɔ'nɔmis]
economic recession	**economische recessie (de)**	[ɛkɔ'nɔmisə rɛ'sɛsi]
goal (aim)	**doel (het)**	[dul]
task	**taak (de)**	[tāk]
to trade (vi)	**handelen**	['handələn]
network (distribution ~)	**netwerk (het)**	['nɛtwɛrk]
inventory (stock)	**voorraad (de)**	['vōr·rāt]
range (assortment)	**assortiment (het)**	[asɔrti'mɛnt]
leader (leading company)	**leider (de)**	['lɛjdər]
large (~ company)	**groot**	[xrōt]
monopoly	**monopolie (het)**	[mɔnɔ'pɔli]
theory	**theorie (de)**	[teɔ'ri]
practice	**praktijk (de)**	[prak'tɛjk]
experience (in my ~)	**ervaring (de)**	[ɛr'variŋ]
trend (tendency)	**tendentie (de)**	[ten'dɛnsi]
development	**ontwikkeling (de)**	[ɔnt'wikəliŋ]

105. Business processes. Part 2

profit (foregone ~)	**voordeel (het)**	['vōrdēl]
profitable (~ deal)	**voordelig**	[vōr'deləx]
delegation (group)	**delegatie (de)**	[dele'xatsi]
salary	**salaris (het)**	[sa'laris]
to correct (an error)	**corrigeren**	[kɔri'dʒɛrən]
business trip	**zakenreis (de)**	['zakən·rɛjs]
commission	**commissie (de)**	[kɔ'misi]
to control (vt)	**controleren**	[kɔntrɔ'lerən]
conference	**conferentie (de)**	[kɔnfə'rɛntsi]
license	**licentie (de)**	[li'sɛntsi]
reliable (~ partner)	**betrouwbaar**	[bə'traubār]
initiative (undertaking)	**aanzet (de)**	['ānzɛt]
norm (standard)	**norm (de)**	[nɔrm]
circumstance	**omstandigheid (de)**	[ɔm'standəxhɛjt]
duty (of employee)	**taak, plicht (de)**	[tāk], [plixt]
organization (company)	**organisatie (de)**	[ɔrxani'zatsi]
organization (process)	**organisatie (de)**	[ɔrxani'zatsi]
organized (adj)	**georganiseerd**	[xeɔrxani'zērt]
cancellation	**afzegging (de)**	['afzɛxiŋ]
to cancel (call off)	**afzeggen**	['afzɛxən]
report (official ~)	**verslag (het)**	[vər'slax]
patent	**patent (het)**	[pa'tɛnt]

| to patent (obtain patent) | patenteren | [patɛn'terən] |
| to plan (vt) | plannen | ['planən] |

bonus (money)	premie (de)	['premi]
professional (adj)	professioneel	[prɔfesiɔ'nēl]
procedure	procedure (de)	[prɔsə'dɵrə]

to examine (contract, etc.)	onderzoeken	['ɔndər'zukən]
calculation	berekening (de)	[bə'rekəniŋ]
reputation	reputatie (de)	[repɵ'tatsi]
risk	risico (het)	['riziko]

to manage, to run	beheren	[bə'herən]
information	informatie (de)	[infɔr'matsi]
property	eigendom (het)	['ɛjxəndɔm]
union	unie (de)	['juni]

life insurance	levensverzekering (de)	['levəns·vər'zekəriŋ]
to insure (vt)	verzekeren	[vər'zekərən]
insurance	verzekering (de)	[vər'zekəriŋ]

auction (~ sale)	veiling (de)	['vɛjliŋ]
to notify (inform)	verwittigen	[vər'witixən]
management (process)	beheer (het)	[bə'hēr]
service (~ industry)	dienst (de)	[dinst]

forum	forum (het)	['forɵm]
to function (vi)	functioneren	[fɵnktsiɔ'nerən]
stage (phase)	stap, etappe (de)	[stap], [e'tapə]
legal (~ services)	juridisch	[ju'ridis]
lawyer (legal advisor)	jurist (de)	[ju'rist]

106. Production. Works

plant	fabriek (de)	[fab'rik]
factory	fabriek (de)	[fab'rik]
workshop	werkplaatsruimte (de)	['wɛrkplāts·'rœɤmtə]
works, production site	productielocatie (de)	[prɔ'dɵktsi·lɔ'katsi]

industry (manufacturing)	industrie (de)	[indɵs'tri]
industrial (adj)	industrieel	[indɵstri'ēl]
heavy industry	zware industrie (de)	['zwarə indɵs'tri]
light industry	lichte industrie (de)	['lixtə indɵs'tri]

products	productie (de)	[prɔ'dɵksi]
to produce (vt)	produceren	[prɔdɵ'serən]
raw materials	grondstof (de)	['xrɔnt·stɔf]

| foreman (construction ~) | voorman, ploegbaas (de) | ['vōrman], ['pluxbās] |
| workers team (crew) | ploeg (de) | [plux] |

worker	arbeider (de)	['arbɛjdər]
working day	werkdag (de)	['wɛrk·dax]
pause (rest break)	pauze (de)	['pauzə]
meeting	samenkomst (de)	['samənkɔmst]
to discuss (vt)	bespreken	[bə'sprekən]

plan	plan (het)	[plan]
to fulfill the plan	het plan uitvoeren	[ət plan œyt'vurən]
rate of output	productienorm (de)	[prɔ'dʉktsi·nɔrm]
quality	kwaliteit (de)	[kwali'tɛjt]
control (checking)	controle (de)	[kɔn'trɔlə]
quality control	kwaliteitscontrole (de)	['kwali'tɛjts·kɔn'trɔlə]

workplace safety	arbeidsveiligheid (de)	['arbɛjds·'vɛjləxhɛjt]
discipline	discipline (de)	[disip'linə]
violation (of safety rules, etc.)	overtreding (de)	[ɔvər'tredɪŋ]
to violate (rules)	overtreden	[ɔvər'tredən]

strike	staking (de)	['stakɪŋ]
striker	staker (de)	['stakər]
to be on strike	staken	['stakən]
labor union	vakbond (de)	['vakbɔnt]

to invent (machine, etc.)	uitvinden	['œytvindən]
invention	uitvinding (de)	['œytvindɪŋ]
research	onderzoek (het)	['ɔndərzuk]
to improve (make better)	verbeteren	[vər'betərən]
technology	technologie (de)	[tɛxnɔlɔ'ʒi]
technical drawing	technische tekening (de)	['tɛxnisə 'tekənɪŋ]

load, cargo	vracht (de)	[vraxt]
loader (person)	lader (de)	['ladər]
to load (vehicle, etc.)	laden	['ladən]
loading (process)	laden (het)	['ladən]
to unload (vi, vt)	lossen	['lɔsən]
unloading	lossen (het)	['lɔsən]

transportation	transport (het)	[trans'pɔrt]
transportation company	transportbedrijf (de)	[trans'pɔrt·bəd'rɛjf]
to transport (vt)	transporteren	[transpɔr'terən]

freight car	goederenwagon (de)	['xudərən·wa'xɔn]
tank (e.g., oil ~)	tank (de)	[tank]
truck	vrachtwagen (de)	['vraht·'waxən]

| machine tool | machine (de) | [ma'ʃinə] |
| mechanism | mechanisme (het) | [mexa'nismə] |

industrial waste	industrieel afval (het)	[indʉstri'ēl 'afval]
packing (process)	verpakking (de)	[vər'pakɪŋ]
to pack (vt)	verpakken	[vər'pakən]

107. Contract. Agreement

contract	**contract (het)**	[kɔn'trakt]
agreement	**overeenkomst (de)**	[ɔvər'ēnkɔmst]
addendum	**bijlage (de)**	['bɛjlaxə]
to sign a contract	**een contract sluiten**	[ən kɔn'trakt 'slœytən]
signature	**handtekening (de)**	['hand·'tekəniŋ]
to sign (vt)	**ondertekenen**	['ɔndər'tekənən]
seal (stamp)	**stempel (de)**	['stɛmpəl]
subject of contract	**voorwerp (het)** **van de overeenkomst**	['vōrwərp van də ɔvə'rēnkɔmst]
clause	**clausule (de)**	[klau'zʉlə]
parties (in contract)	**partijen**	[par'tɛjən]
legal address	**vestigingsadres (het)**	['vɛstəhiŋs·a'drɛs]
to violate the contract	**het contract verbreken**	[ət kɔn'trakt vər'brekən]
commitment (obligation)	**verplichting (de)**	[vər'plixtiŋ]
responsibility	**verantwoordelijk-** **heid (de)**	[vərant·'wōrdələk 'hɛjt]
force majeure	**overmacht (de)**	['ɔvərmaxt]
dispute	**geschil (het)**	[xə'sxil]
penalties	**sancties**	['sanksis]

108. Import & Export

import	**import (de)**	['impɔrt]
importer	**importeur (de)**	[impɔr'tør]
to import (vt)	**importeren**	[impɔr'terən]
import (as adj.)	**import-**	['impɔrt]
export (exportation)	**uitvoer (de)**	['œytvur]
exporter	**exporteur (de)**	[ɛkspɔr'tør]
to export (vi, vt)	**exporteren**	[ɛkspɔr'terən]
export (as adj.)	**uitvoer-**	['œytvur]
goods (merchandise)	**goederen**	['xudərən]
consignment, lot	**partij (de)**	[par'tɛj]
weight	**gewicht (het)**	[xə'wixt]
volume	**volume (het)**	[vɔ'lʉmə]
cubic meter	**kubieke meter (de)**	[kʉ'bikə 'metər]
manufacturer	**producent (de)**	[prodʉ'sɛnt]
transportation company	**transportbedrijf (de)**	[trans'pɔrt·bəd'rɛjf]
container	**container (de)**	[kɔn'tenər]
border	**grens (de)**	[xrɛns]
customs	**douane (de)**	[du'anə]

customs duty	douanerecht (het)	[du'anə·rɛxt]
customs officer	douanier (de)	[dua'njē]
smuggling	smokkelen (het)	['smɔkələn]
contraband (smuggled goods)	smokkelwaar (de)	['smɔkəl·wār]

109. Finances

stock (share)	aandeel (het)	['āndēl]
bond (certificate)	obligatie (de)	[ɔbli'xatsi]
promissory note	wissel (de)	['wisəl]
stock exchange	beurs (de)	['børs]
stock price	aandelenkoers (de)	['āndələn·kurs]
to go down (become cheaper)	dalen	['dalən]
to go up (become more expensive)	stijgen	['stɛjxən]
share	deel (het)	[dēl]
controlling interest	meerderheids- belang (het)	['mērdərhɛjts bə'laŋ]
investment	investeringen	[invɛ'steriŋən]
to invest (vt)	investeren	[invɛ'sterən]
percent	procent (het)	[prɔ'sɛnt]
interest (on investment)	rente (de)	['rentə]
profit	winst (de)	[winst]
profitable (adj)	winstgevend	[winst'xevənt]
tax	belasting (de)	[bə'lastiŋ]
currency (foreign ~)	valuta (de)	[va'lʉta]
national (adj)	nationaal	[natsjo'nāl]
exchange (currency ~)	ruil (de)	[rœyl]
accountant	boekhouder (de)	[buk 'haudər]
accounting	boekhouding (de)	[buk 'haudiŋ]
bankruptcy	bankroet (het)	[bank'rut]
collapse, crash	ondergang (de)	['ɔndərxaŋ]
ruin	faillissement (het)	[fajis'mɛnt]
to be ruined (financially)	geruïneerd zijn	[xərui'nērt zɛjn]
inflation	inflatie (de)	[in'flatsi]
devaluation	devaluatie (de)	[devalj'vatsi]
capital	kapitaal (het)	[kapi'tāl]
income	inkomen (het)	['inkɔmən]
turnover	omzet (de)	['ɔmzɛt]

resources	**middelen**	['midələn]
monetary resources	**financiële middelen**	[finansi'elə 'midələn]
overhead	**operationele kosten**	[ɔpe'ratsjɔnələ 'kɔstən]
to reduce (expenses)	**reduceren**	[redʉ'serən]

110. Marketing

marketing	**marketing (de)**	['marketiŋ]
market	**markt (de)**	[markt]
market segment	**marktsegment (het)**	['markt·sɛx'mɛnt]
product	**product (het)**	[prɔ'dʉkt]
goods (merchandise)	**goederen**	['xudərən]
brand	**merk (het)**	[mɛrk]
trademark	**handelsmerk (het)**	['handəls·mɛrk]
logotype	**beeldmerk (het)**	['bēlt·mɛrk]
logo	**logo (het)**	['lɔxɔ]
demand	**vraag (de)**	[vrãx]
supply	**aanbod (het)**	['ãmbɔt]
need	**behoefte (de)**	[bə'huftə]
consumer	**consument (de)**	[kɔnsʉ'mɛnt]
analysis	**analyse (de)**	[ana'lizə]
to analyze (vt)	**analyseren**	[anali'zerən]
positioning	**positionering (de)**	[pɔzitsjɔ'neriŋ]
to position (vt)	**positioneren**	[pɔzitsjɔ'nerən]
price	**prijs (de)**	[prɛjs]
pricing policy	**prijspolitiek (de)**	['prɛjs·pɔli'tik]
price formation	**prijsvorming (de)**	['prɛjs·'vɔrmiŋ]

111. Advertising

advertising	**reclame (de)**	[re'klamə]
to advertise (vt)	**adverteren**	[advɛr'tɛrən]
budget	**budget (het)**	[bʉ'dʒɛt]
ad, advertisement	**advertentie, reclame (de)**	[advɛr'tɛntsi], [re'klamə]
TV advertising	**TV-reclame (de)**	[te've-re'klamə]
radio advertising	**radioreclame (de)**	['radio·re'klamə]
outdoor advertising	**buitenreclame (de)**	['bœytən·rək'lamə]
mass media	**massamedia (de)**	['masa·'media]
periodical (n)	**periodiek (de)**	[periɔ'dik]
image (public appearance)	**imago (het)**	[i'maxɔ]
slogan	**slagzin (de)**	['slax·sin]
motto (maxim)	**motto (het)**	['mɔtɔ]

campaign	campagne (de)	[kam'panjə]
advertising campaign	reclamecampagne (de)	[re'klamə·kam'panjə]
target group	doelpubliek (het)	[dul·pʉ'blik]

business card	visitekaartje (het)	[vi'zitə·'kārtʃə]
leaflet (promotional ~)	flyer (de)	['flajər]
brochure	brochure (de)	[brɔ'ʃʉrə]
(e.g., 12 pages ~)		
pamphlet	folder (de)	['fɔldər]
newsletter	nieuwsbrief (de)	['niusbrif]

signboard (store sign, etc.)	gevelreclame (de)	['xevəl·re'klamə]
poster	poster (de)	['pɔstər]
billboard	aanplakbord (het)	['ānplak·'bɔrt]

112. Banking

| bank | bank (de) | [bank] |
| branch (of bank, etc.) | bankfiliaal (het) | [bank·fili'āl] |

| bank clerk, consultant | bankbediende (de) | [bank·bə'dində] |
| manager (director) | manager (de) | ['mɛnədʒər] |

bank account	bankrekening (de)	[bank·'rekəniŋ]
account number	rekeningnummer (het)	['rekəniŋ·'nʉmər]
checking account	lopende rekening (de)	['lopəndə 'rekəniŋ]
savings account	spaarrekening (de)	['spār·'rekəniŋ]

to open an account	een rekening openen	[en 'rekəniŋ 'ɔpənən]
to close the account	de rekening sluiten	[də 'rekəniŋ slœytən]
to deposit into the account	op rekening storten	[ɔp 'rekəniŋ 'stɔrtən]
to withdraw (vt)	opnemen	['ɔpnemən]

deposit	storting (de)	['stɔrtiŋ]
to make a deposit	een storting maken	[en 'stɔrtiŋ 'makən]
wire transfer	overschrijving (de)	[ɔvər'sxrɛjviŋ]
to wire, to transfer	een overschrijving maken	[en ɔvər'sxrɛjviŋ 'makən]

| sum | som (de) | [sɔm] |
| How much? | Hoeveel? | [hu'vēl] |

| signature | handtekening (de) | ['hand·'tekəniŋ] |
| to sign (vt) | ondertekenen | ['ɔndər'tekənən] |

credit card	kredietkaart (de)	[kre'dit·kārt]
code (PIN code)	code (de)	['kɔdə]
credit card number	kredietkaart-nummer (het)	[kre'dit·kārt 'nʉmər]
ATM	geldautomaat (de)	[xɛlt·autɔ'māt]

check	cheque (de)	[ʃɛk]
to write a check	een cheque uitschrijven	[en ʃɛk œyt'sxrɛjvən]
checkbook	chequeboekje (het)	[ʃɛk·'bukjə]

loan (bank ~)	lening, krediet (de)	['leniŋ], [kre'dit]
to apply for a loan	een lening aanvragen	[en 'leniŋ 'ānvraxən]
to get a loan	een lening nemen	[en 'leniŋ 'nemən]
to give a loan	een lening verlenen	[en 'leniŋ vər'lenən]
guarantee	garantie (de)	[xa'rantsi]

113. Telephone. Phone conversation

telephone	telefoon (de)	[telə'fōn]
cell phone	mobieltje (het)	[mɔ'biltʃe]
answering machine	antwoordapparaat (het)	['antwōrt·apa'rāt]

| to call (by phone) | bellen | ['belən] |
| phone call | belletje (het) | ['beletʃe] |

to dial a number	een nummer draaien	[en 'nɵmər 'drājən]
Hello!	Hallo!	[ha'lɔ]
to ask (vt)	vragen	['vraxən]
to answer (vi, vt)	antwoorden	['antwōrdən]

to hear (vt)	horen	['hɔrən]
well (adv)	goed	[xut]
not well (adv)	slecht	[slɛxt]
noises (interference)	storingen	['stɔriŋən]
receiver	hoorn (de)	[hōrn]
to pick up (~ the phone)	opnemen	['ɔpnemən]
to hang up (~ the phone)	ophangen	['ɔphaŋən]

busy (engaged)	bezet	[bə'zɛt]
to ring (ab. phone)	overgaan	['ɔvərxān]
telephone book	telefoonboek (het)	[telə'fōn·buk]

local (adj)	lokaal	[lɔ'kāl]
local call	lokaal gesprek (het)	[lɔ'kāl xesp'rɛk]
long distance (~ call)	interlokaal	[intərlɔ'kāl]
long-distance call	interlokaal gesprek (het)	[intərlɔ'kāl xe'sprɛk]
international (adj)	buitenlands	['bœytənlants]
international call	buitenlands gesprek (het)	['bœytənlants xe'ʃprɛk]

114. Cell phone

| cell phone | mobieltje (het) | [mɔ'biltʃe] |
| display | scherm (het) | [sxɛrm] |

button	**toets, knop (de)**	[tuts], [knɔp]
SIM card	**simkaart (de)**	['sim·kãrt]
battery	**batterij (de)**	[batə'rɛj]
to be dead (battery)	**leeg zijn**	[lēx zɛjn]
charger	**acculader (de)**	[akʉ'ladər]
menu	**menu (het)**	[me'nʉ]
settings	**instellingen**	['instɛliŋən]
tune (melody)	**melodie (de)**	[melɔ'di]
to select (vt)	**selecteren**	[selɛk'terən]
calculator	**rekenmachine (de)**	['rekən·ma'ʃinə]
voice mail	**voicemail (de)**	['vɔjs·mɛjl]
alarm clock	**wekker (de)**	['wɛkər]
contacts	**contacten**	[kɔn'taktən]
SMS (text message)	**SMS-bericht (het)**	[ɛsɛ'mɛs-bə'rixt]
subscriber	**abonnee (de)**	[abɔ'nē]

115. Stationery

ballpoint pen	**balpen (de)**	['bal·pən]
fountain pen	**vulpen (de)**	['vʉl·pən]
pencil	**potlood (het)**	['pɔtlõt]
highlighter	**marker (de)**	['markər]
felt-tip pen	**viltstift (de)**	['vilt·stift]
notepad	**notitieboekje (het)**	[nɔ'titsi·'bukjə]
agenda (diary)	**agenda (de)**	[a'xɛnda]
ruler	**liniaal (de/het)**	[lini'ãl]
calculator	**rekenmachine (de)**	['rekən·ma'ʃinə]
eraser	**gom (de)**	[xɔm]
thumbtack	**punaise (de)**	[pʉ'nɛzə]
paper clip	**paperclip (de)**	['pɛjpər·klip]
glue	**lijm (de)**	[lɛjm]
stapler	**nietmachine (de)**	['nit·ma'ʃinə]
hole punch	**perforator (de)**	[perfɔ'ratɔr]
pencil sharpener	**potloodslijper (de)**	['pɔtlõt·'slɛjpər]

116. Various kinds of documents

account (report)	**verslag (het)**	[vər'slax]
agreement	**overeenkomst (de)**	[ɔvər'ēnkɔmst]
application form	**aanvraagformulier (het)**	['ãnvrãx·fɔrmu'lir]

authentic (adj)	origineel, authentiek	[ɔriʒi'nēl], [autən'tik]
badge (identity tag)	badge, kaart (de)	[bɛdʒ], [kārt]
business card	visitekaartje (het)	[vi'zitə·'kārtʃə]
certificate (~ of quality)	certificaat (het)	[sɛrtifi'kāt]
check (e.g., draw a ~)	cheque (de)	[ʃɛk]
check (in restaurant)	rekening (de)	['rekəniŋ]
constitution	grondwet (de)	['xrɔnt·wɛt]
contract (agreement)	contract (het)	[kɔn'trakt]
copy	kopie (de)	[kɔ'pi]
copy (of contract, etc.)	exemplaar (het)	[ɛksem'plār]
customs declaration	douaneaangifte (de)	[du'anə·'ānxiftə]
document	document (het)	[dɔkʉ'mɛnt]
driver's license	rijbewijs (het)	['rɛj·bɛwɛjs]
addendum	bijlage (de)	['bɛjlaxə]
form	formulier (het)	[fɔrmu'lir]
ID card (e.g., FBI ~)	identiteitskaart (de)	[idənti'tɛjts·kārt]
inquiry (request)	aanvraag (de)	['ānvrāx]
invitation card	uitnodigingskaart (de)	[œʏt'nɔdixiŋs·kārt]
invoice	factuur (de)	[fak'tūr]
law	wet (de)	[wɛt]
letter (mail)	brief (de)	[brif]
letterhead	briefhoofd (het)	['brifhōft]
list (of names, etc.)	lijst (de)	[lɛjst]
manuscript	manuscript (het)	[manʉsk'ript]
newsletter	nieuwsbrief (de)	['niusbrif]
note (short letter)	briefje (het)	['brifⁱə]
pass (for worker, visitor)	pasje (het)	['paɕə]
passport	paspoort (het)	['paspōrt]
permit	vergunning (de)	[vər'xʉniŋ]
résumé	CV, curriculum vitae (het)	[se've], [kʉ'rikʉlʉm 'vitə]
debt note, IOU	schuldbekentenis (de)	[sxjult·bə'kɛntənis]
receipt (for purchase)	kwitantie (de)	[kwi'tantsi]
sales slip, receipt	bon (de)	[bɔn]
report (mil.)	rapport (het)	[ra'pɔrt]
to show (ID, etc.)	tonen	['tɔnən]
to sign (vt)	ondertekenen	['ɔndər'tekənən]
signature	handtekening (de)	['hand·'tekəniŋ]
seal (stamp)	stempel (de)	['stɛmpəl]
text	tekst (de)	[tɛkst]
ticket (for entry)	biljet (het)	[bi'ljet]
to cross out	doorhalen	['dōrhalən]
to fill out (~ a form)	invullen	['invʉlən]
waybill (shipping invoice)	vrachtbrief (de)	['vraxt·brif]
will (testament)	testament (het)	[tɛsta'mɛnt]

117. Kinds of business

accounting services	boekhouddiensten	['bukhaut·'dinstən]
advertising	reclame (de)	[re'klamə]
advertising agency	reclamebureau (het)	[re'klamə·bʉ'ro]
air-conditioners	airconditioning (de)	[ɛr·kɔn'diʃəniŋ]
airline	luchtvaart- maatschappij (de)	['lʉxtvārt mātsxa'pɛj]
alcoholic beverages	alcoholische dranken	[alkɔ'hɔlisə 'drankən]
antiques (antique dealers)	antiek (het)	[an'tik]
art gallery (contemporary ~)	kunstgalerie (de)	['kʉnst·galə'ri]
audit services	audit diensten	['audit·'dinstən]
banking industry	banken	['bankən]
bar	bar (de)	[bar]
beauty parlor	schoonheids- salon (de/het)	['sxōnxɛjts sa'lɔn]
bookstore	boekhandel (de)	['bukən·'handəl]
brewery	bierbrouwerij (de)	[birb·rɔuwɛ'rɛj]
business center	zakencentrum (het)	['zakən·'sɛntrʉm]
business school	business school (de)	['biznes·sxōl]
casino	casino (het)	[ka'sinɔ]
construction	bouwbedrijven	['baubə'drɛjvən]
consulting	adviesbureau (het)	[at'vis·bʉ'ro]
dental clinic	tandheelkunde (de)	['tand·kli'nik]
design	design (het)	[di'zajn]
drugstore, pharmacy	apotheek (de)	[apɔ'tēk]
dry cleaners	stomerij (de)	[stɔmə'rɛj]
employment agency	uitzendbureau (het)	['œʏtzənt·by'ro]
financial services	financiële diensten	[finansi'elə 'dinstən]
food products	voedingswaren	['vudiŋs·warən]
funeral home	uitvaartcentrum (het)	['œʏtvārt·'sɛntrym]
furniture (e.g., house ~)	meubilair (het)	['møbi'lɛr]
clothing, garment	kleding (de)	['klediŋ]
hotel	hotel (het)	[hɔ'tɛl]
ice-cream	ijsje (het)	['ɛisjə], ['ɛiʃə]
industry (manufacturing)	industrie (de)	[indʉs'tri]
insurance	verzekering (de)	[vər'zekəriŋ]
Internet	Internet (het)	['intɛrnɛt]
investments (finance)	investeringen	[invɛ'steriŋən]
jeweler	juwelier (de)	[juwe'lir]
jewelry	juwelen	[ju'welən]
laundry (shop)	wasserette (de)	[wasə'rɛtə]

| legal advisor | juridische diensten | [ju'ridisə 'dinstən] |
| light industry | lichte industrie (de) | ['lixtə indɵs'tri] |

magazine	tijdschrift (het)	['tɛjtsxrift]
mail-order selling	postorderbedrijven	['post·ordər·bə'drɛjvən]
medicine	medicijnen	['mɛdisɛjnən]
movie theater	bioscoop (de)	[biɔ'skōp]
museum	museum (het)	[mɵ'zejum]

news agency	persbureau (het)	['pɛrs·bɵrɔ]
newspaper	krant (de)	[krant]
nightclub	nachtclub (de)	['naxt·klɵp]

oil (petroleum)	olie (de)	['ɔli]
courier services	koerierdienst (de)	[ku'rir·dinst]
pharmaceutics	farmacie (de)	[farma'si]
printing (industry)	drukkerij (de)	[drɵkə'rɛj]
publishing house	uitgeverij (de)	[œʏtxevə'rɛj]

radio (~ station)	radio (de)	['radiɔ]
real estate	vastgoed (het)	['vastxut]
restaurant	restaurant (het)	[rɛstɔ'rant]

security company	bewakingsfirma (de)	[bə'wakiŋs·'firma]
sports	sport (de)	[spɔrt]
stock exchange	handelsbeurs (de)	['handəls·bɵrs]
store	winkel (de)	['winkəl]
supermarket	supermarkt (de)	['sɵpərmarkt]
swimming pool (public ~)	zwembad (het)	['zwɛm·bat]

tailor shop	naaiatelier (het)	[nāj·atə'lje]
television	televisie (de)	[telə'vizi]
theater	theater (het)	[te'atər]
trade (commerce)	handel (de)	['handəl]
transportation	transport (het)	[trans'pɔrt]
travel	toerisme (het)	[tu'rismə]

veterinarian	dierenarts (de)	['dīrən·arts]
warehouse	magazijn (het)	[maxa'zɛjn]
waste collection	afvalinzameling (de)	['afval·'inzaməliŋ]

Job. Business. Part 2

118. Show. Exhibition

exhibition, show	beurs (de)	['børs]
trade show	vakbeurs,	['vak'børs],
	handelsbeurs (de)	['handəls·'børs]
participation	deelneming (de)	['dēlnemiŋ]
to participate (vi)	deelnemen	['dēlnemən]
participant (exhibitor)	deelnemer (de)	['dēlnemər]
director	directeur (de)	[dirɛk'tør]
organizers' office	organisatiecomité (het)	[ɔrxani'zatsi·kɔmi'tɛ]
organizer	organisator (de)	[ɔrxani'zatɔr]
to organize (vt)	organiseren	[ɔrxani'zerən]
participation form	deelnemingsaanvraag	['dēlnemiŋs 'ānvrãx]
to fill out (vt)	invullen	['invʉlən]
details	details	[de'tajs]
information	informatie (de)	[infɔr'matsi]
price (cost, rate)	prijs (de)	[prɛjs]
including	inclusief	[inklʉ'zif]
to include (vt)	inbegrepen	['inbəxrepən]
to pay (vi, vt)	betalen	[bə'talən]
registration fee	registratietarief (het)	[rexi'stratsi·ta'rif]
entrance	ingang (de)	['inxaŋ]
pavilion, hall	paviljoen (het), hal (de)	[pavi'ljun], [hal]
to register (vt)	registreren	[rexi'strerən]
badge (identity tag)	badge, kaart (de)	[bɛdʒ], [kārt]
booth, stand	beursstand (de)	['børs·stant]
to reserve, to book	reserveren	[rezɛr'verən]
display case	vitrine (de)	[vit'rinə]
spotlight	licht (het)	[lixt]
design	design (het)	[di'zajn]
to place (put, set)	plaatsen	['plātsən]
to be placed	geplaatst zijn	[xəp'lātst zɛjn]
distributor	distributeur (de)	[distribʉ'tør]
supplier	leverancier (de)	[levəran'sir]
to supply (vt)	leveren	['levərən]
country	land (het)	[lant]

| foreign (adj) | buitenlands | ['bœytənlants] |
| product | product (het) | [prɔ'dʉkt] |

association	associatie (de)	[asɔʃi'atsi]
conference hall	conferentiezaal (de)	[kɔnfə'rɛntsi·zāl]
congress	congres (het)	[kɔnx'res]
contest (competition)	wedstrijd (de)	['wɛtstrɛjt]

visitor (attendee)	bezoeker (de)	[bə'zukər]
to visit (attend)	bezoeken	[bə'zukən]
customer	afnemer (de)	['afnemər]

119. Mass Media

newspaper	krant (de)	[krant]
magazine	tijdschrift (het)	['tɛjtsxrift]
press (printed media)	pers (de)	[pɛrs]
radio	radio (de)	['radiɔ]
radio station	radiostation (het)	['radiɔ·sta'tsjɔn]
television	televisie (de)	[telə'vizi]

presenter, host	presentator (de)	[prezən'tatɔr]
newscaster	nieuwslezer (de)	['nius·lezər]
commentator	commentator (de)	[kɔmən'tatɔr]

journalist	journalist (de)	[ʒurna'list]
correspondent (reporter)	correspondent (de)	[kɔrɛspɔn'dɛnt]
press photographer	fotocorrespondent (de)	['fotɔ·kɔrɛspɔn'dɛnt]
reporter	reporter (de)	[re'pɔrtər]

| editor | redacteur (de) | [redak'tør] |
| editor-in-chief | chef-redacteur (de) | [ʃɛf-redak'tør] |

to subscribe (to …)	zich abonneren op	[zix abɔ'nerən ɔp]
subscription	abonnement (het)	[abɔne'mɛnt]
subscriber	abonnee (de)	[abɔ'nē]
to read (vi, vt)	lezen	['lezən]
reader	lezer (de)	['lezər]

circulation (of newspaper)	oplage (de)	['ɔplaxə]
monthly (adj)	maand-, maandelijks	[mānt], ['māndələks]
weekly (adj)	wekelijks	['wekələks]
issue (edition)	nummer (het)	['nʉmər]
new (~ issue)	vers	[vɛrs]

headline	kop (de)	[kɔp]
short article	korte artikel (het)	['kɔrtə ar'tikəl]
column (regular article)	rubriek (de)	[rʉ'brik]
article	artikel (het)	[ar'tikəl]
page	pagina (de)	['paxina]

reportage, report	**reportage (de)**	[repɔr'taʒə]
event (happening)	**gebeurtenis (de)**	[xə'bɔrtənis]
sensation (news)	**sensatie (de)**	[sɛn'satsi]
scandal	**schandaal (het)**	[sxan'dāl]
scandalous (adj)	**schandalig**	[sxan'daləx]
great (~ scandal)	**groot**	[xrōt]
show (e.g., cooking ~)	**programma (het)**	[prɔ'xrama]
interview	**interview (het)**	['intɛrvjʉ]
live broadcast	**live uitzending (de)**	[liv 'œʏtsɛndiŋ]
channel	**kanaal (het)**	[ka'nāl]

120. Agriculture

agriculture	**landbouw (de)**	['lantbau]
peasant (masc.)	**boer (de)**	[bur]
peasant (fem.)	**boerin (de)**	[bu'rin]
farmer	**landbouwer (de)**	['lantbauər]
tractor (farm ~)	**tractor (de)**	['traktɔr]
combine, harvester	**maaidorser (de)**	['mājdɔrsər]
plow	**ploeg (de)**	[plux]
to plow (vi, vt)	**ploegen**	['pluxən]
plowland	**akkerland (het)**	['akər·lant]
furrow (in field)	**voor (de)**	[vōr]
to sow (vi, vt)	**zaaien**	['zājən]
seeder	**zaaimachine (de)**	['zāi·ma'ʃinə]
sowing (process)	**zaaien (het)**	['zājən]
scythe	**zeis (de)**	[zɛjs]
to mow, to scythe	**maaien**	['mājən]
spade (tool)	**schop (de)**	[sxɔp]
to till (vt)	**spitten**	['spitən]
hoe	**schoffel (de)**	['sxɔfəl]
to hoe, to weed	**wieden**	['widən]
weed (plant)	**onkruid (het)**	['ɔnkrœʏt]
watering can	**gieter (de)**	['xitər]
to water (plants)	**begieten**	[bə'xitən]
watering (act)	**bewatering (de)**	[bə'watəriŋ]
pitchfork	**riek, hooivork (de)**	[rik], ['hōj·vɔrk]
rake	**hark (de)**	[hark]
fertilizer	**kunstmest (de)**	['kʉnstmɛst]
to fertilize (vt)	**bemesten**	[bə'mɛstən]

manure (fertilizer)	**mest (de)**	[mɛst]
field	**veld (het)**	[vɛlt]
meadow	**wei (de)**	[wɛj]
vegetable garden	**moestuin (de)**	['mus·tœyn]
orchard (e.g., apple ~)	**boomgaard (de)**	['bōm·xārt]
to graze (vi)	**weiden**	['wɛjdən]
herder (herdsman)	**herder (de)**	['hɛrdər]
pasture	**weiland (de)**	['wɛj·lant]
cattle breeding	**veehouderij (de)**	['vē·haudərɛj]
sheep farming	**schapenteelt (de)**	['sxapən·tēlt]
plantation	**plantage (de)**	[plan'taʒə]
row (garden bed ~s)	**rijtje (het)**	['rɛjtʃə]
hothouse	**broeikas (de)**	['brujkas]
drought (lack of rain)	**droogte (de)**	['drōxtə]
dry (~ summer)	**droog**	[drōx]
grain	**graan (het)**	[xrān]
cereal crops	**graangewassen**	['xrān·xɛ'wasən]
to harvest, to gather	**oogsten**	['ōxstən]
miller (person)	**molenaar (de)**	['molənār]
mill (e.g., gristmill)	**molen (de)**	['molən]
to grind (grain)	**malen**	['malən]
flour	**bloem (de)**	[blum]
straw	**stro (het)**	[strɔ]

121. Building. Building process

construction site	**bouwplaats (de)**	['bau·plāts]
to build (vt)	**bouwen**	['bauwən]
construction worker	**bouwvakker (de)**	['bau·'vakər]
project	**project (het)**	[pro'jekt]
architect	**architect (de)**	[arʃi'tɛkt]
worker	**arbeider (de)**	['arbɛjdər]
foundation (of a building)	**fundering (de)**	[fʉn'deriŋ]
roof	**dak (het)**	[dak]
foundation pile	**heipaal (de)**	['hɛjpāl]
wall	**muur (de)**	[mūr]
reinforcing bars	**betonstaal (het)**	[bə'ton·stāl]
scaffolding	**steigers**	['stɛjxərs]
concrete	**beton (het)**	[bə'ton]
granite	**graniet (het)**	[xra'nit]

stone	steen (de)	[stēn]
brick	baksteen (de)	['bakstēn]

sand	zand (het)	[zant]
cement	cement (de/het)	[sə'mɛnt]
plaster (for walls)	pleister (het)	['plɛjstər]
to plaster (vt)	pleisteren	['plɛjstərən]

paint	verf (de)	[vɛrf]
to paint (~ a wall)	verven	['vɛrvən]
barrel	ton (de)	[tɔn]

crane	kraan (de)	[krān]
to lift, to hoist (vt)	heffen, hijsen	['hefən], ['hɛjsən]
to lower (vt)	neerlaten	['nērlatən]

bulldozer	bulldozer (de)	[bʉl'dɔzər]
excavator	graafmachine (de)	[xrāf·ma'ʃinə]
scoop, bucket	graafbak (de)	[xrāf·bak]
to dig (excavate)	graven	['xravən]
hard hat	helm (de)	[hɛlm]

122. Science. Research. Scientists

science	wetenschap (de)	['wetənsxap]
scientific (adj)	wetenschappelijk	[wetən'sxapələk]
scientist	wetenschapper (de)	['wetənsxapər]
theory	theorie (de)	[teɔ'ri]

axiom	axioma (het)	[aksi'ɔma]
analysis	analyse (de)	[ana'lizə]
to analyze (vt)	analyseren	[anali'zerən]
argument (strong ~)	argument (het)	[arxju'mɛnt]
substance (matter)	substantie (de)	[sʉp'stansi]

hypothesis	hypothese (de)	[hipɔ'tezə]
dilemma	dilemma (het)	[di'lema]
dissertation	dissertatie (de)	[disɛr'tatsi]
dogma	dogma (het)	['dɔxma]

doctrine	doctrine (de)	[dɔk'trinə]
research	onderzoek (het)	['ɔndərzuk]
to research (vt)	onderzoeken	['ɔndər'zukən]
tests (laboratory ~)	toetsing (de)	['tutsiŋ]
laboratory	laboratorium (het)	[labɔra'tɔrijum]

method	methode (de)	[me'tɔdə]
molecule	molecule (de/het)	[mɔle'kʉlə]
monitoring	monitoring (de)	['mɔnitɔriŋ]
discovery (act, event)	ontdekking (de)	[ɔn'dɛkiŋ]

postulate	**postulaat (het)**	[pɔstʉ'lɑ̄t]
principle	**principe (het)**	[prin'sipə]
forecast	**voorspelling (de)**	[võr'spɛliŋ]
to forecast (vt)	**een prognose maken**	[ən prɔx'nɔzə 'makən]
synthesis	**synthese (de)**	[sin'tɛzə]
trend (tendency)	**tendentie (de)**	[ten'dɛnsi]
theorem	**theorema (het)**	[teɔ'rɛma]
teachings	**leerstellingen**	['lɛ̄rstɛliŋən]
fact	**feit (het)**	[fɛjt]
expedition	**expeditie (de)**	[ɛkspe'ditsi]
experiment	**experiment (het)**	[ɛksperi'mɛnt]
academician	**academicus (de)**	[aka'demikʉs]
bachelor (e.g., ~ of Arts)	**bachelor (de)**	['bɛtʃəlɔr]
doctor (PhD)	**doctor (de)**	['dɔktɔr]
Associate Professor	**universitair docent (de)**	['junivɛrsitər dɔ'sɛnt]
Master (e.g., ~ of Arts)	**master, magister (de)**	['mastər], [ma'xistər]
professor	**professor (de)**	[prɔ'fɛsɔr]

Professions and occupations

123. Job search. Dismissal

job	baan (de)	[bān]
staff (work force)	werknemers	['wɛrknemərs]
personnel	personeel (het)	[pɛrsɔ'nēl]
career	carrière (de)	[ka'rjerə]
prospects (chances)	vooruitzichten	[vōrœyt·'sixtən]
skills (mastery)	meesterschap (het)	['mēstər'sxap]
selection (screening)	keuze (de)	['køzə]
employment agency	uitzendbureau (het)	['œytzənt·by'rɔ]
résumé	CV, curriculum vitae (het)	[se've], [kʉ'rikʉlʉm 'vitə]
job interview	sollicitatiegesprek (het)	[sɔlisi'tatsi·xəsp'rɛk]
vacancy, opening	vacature (de)	[vaka'tʉrə]
salary, pay	salaris (het)	[sa'laris]
fixed salary	vaste salaris (het)	['vastə sa'laris]
pay, compensation	loon (het)	[lōn]
position (job)	betrekking (de)	[bə'trɛkiŋ]
duty (of employee)	taak, plicht (de)	[tāk], [plixt]
range of duties	takenpakket (het)	['takən·pa'ket]
busy (I'm ~)	bezig	['bezəx]
to fire (dismiss)	ontslagen	[ɔnt'slaxən]
dismissal	ontslag (het)	[ɔnt'slax]
unemployment	werkloosheid (de)	[wɛrk'lɔshɛjt]
unemployed (n)	werkloze (de)	[wɛrk'lozə]
retirement	pensioen (het)	[pɛn'ʃun]
to retire (from job)	met pensioen gaan	[mɛt pɛn'ʃun xān]

124. Business people

director	directeur (de)	[dirɛk'tør]
manager (director)	beheerder (de)	[bə'hērdər]
boss	hoofd (het)	[hōft]
superior	baas (de)	[bās]
superiors	superieuren	[sʉpə'rørən]

president	**president (de)**	[prezi'dɛnt]
chairman	**voorzitter (de)**	['vōrzitər]
deputy (substitute)	**adjunct (de)**	[ad'junkt]
assistant	**assistent (de)**	[asi'stɛnt]
secretary	**secretaris (de)**	[sekre'taris]
personal assistant	**persoonlijke assistent (de)**	[pɛr'sōnləkə asi'stɛnt]
businessman	**zakenman (de)**	['zakənman]
entrepreneur	**ondernemer (de)**	['ɔndər'nemər]
founder	**oprichter (de)**	['ɔprixtər]
to found (vt)	**oprichten**	['ɔprixtən]
incorporator	**stichter (de)**	['stixtər]
partner	**partner (de)**	['partnər]
stockholder	**aandeelhouder (de)**	['āndēl·haudər]
millionaire	**miljonair (de)**	[milju'nɛːr]
billionaire	**miljardair (de)**	[miljar'dɛːr]
owner, proprietor	**eigenaar (de)**	['ɛjxənār]
landowner	**landeigenaar (de)**	['lant·'ɛjxənār]
client	**klant (de)**	[klant]
regular client	**vaste klant (de)**	['vastə klant]
buyer (customer)	**koper (de)**	['kɔpər]
visitor	**bezoeker (de)**	[bə'zukər]
professional (n)	**professioneel (de)**	[prɔfesiɔ'nēl]
expert	**expert (de)**	[ɛk'spɛːr]
specialist	**specialist (de)**	[speʃia'list]
banker	**bankier (de)**	[baŋ'kir]
broker	**makelaar (de)**	['makəlār]
cashier, teller	**kassier (de)**	[ka'sir]
accountant	**boekhouder (de)**	[buk 'haudər]
security guard	**bewaker (de)**	[bə'wakər]
investor	**investeerder (de)**	[invɛ'stērdər]
debtor	**schuldenaar (de)**	['sxʉldənār]
creditor	**crediteur (de)**	[krədi'tør]
borrower	**lener (de)**	['lenər]
importer	**importeur (de)**	[impɔr'tør]
exporter	**exporteur (de)**	[ɛkspɔr'tør]
manufacturer	**producent (de)**	[prɔdʉ'sɛnt]
distributor	**distributeur (de)**	[distribʉ'tør]
middleman	**bemiddelaar (de)**	[bə'midəlār]
consultant	**adviseur, consulent (de)**	[atvi'zør], [kɔnsʉ'lent]

sales representative	vertegenwoordiger (de)	[vər'texən·'wōrdixər]
agent	agent (de)	[a'xɛnt]
insurance agent	verzekeringsagent (de)	[vər'zekəriŋs·a'xɛnt]

125. Service professions

cook	kok (de)	[kɔk]
chef (kitchen chef)	chef-kok (de)	[ʃɛf-'kɔk]
baker	bakker (de)	['bakər]

bartender	barman (de)	['barman]
waiter	kelner, ober (de)	['kɛlnər], ['ɔbər]
waitress	serveerster (de)	[sɛr'vērstər]

lawyer, attorney	advocaat (de)	[atvɔ'kāt]
lawyer (legal expert)	jurist (de)	[ju'rist]
notary	notaris (de)	[nɔ'taris]

electrician	elektricien (de)	[ɛlɛktri'sjen]
plumber	loodgieter (de)	['lōtxitər]
carpenter	timmerman (de)	['timərman]

masseur	masseur (de)	[mas'sør]
masseuse	masseuse (de)	[mas'søzə]
doctor	dokter, arts (de)	['dɔktər], [arts]

taxi driver	taxichauffeur (de)	['taksi·ʃɔ'før]
driver	chauffeur (de)	[ʃɔ'før]
delivery man	koerier (de)	[ku'rir]

chambermaid	kamermeisje (het)	['kamər·'mɛjɕə]
security guard	bewaker (de)	[bə'wakər]
flight attendant (fem.)	stewardess (de)	[stʉwər'dɛs]

schoolteacher	meester (de)	['mēstər]
librarian	bibliothecaris (de)	['bibliɔtə'kāris]
translator	vertaler (de)	[vər'talər]

| interpreter | tolk (de) | [tɔlk] |
| guide | gids (de) | [xits] |

hairdresser	kapper (de)	['kapər]
mailman	postbode (de)	['pɔst·bɔdə]
salesman (store staff)	verkoper (de)	[vər'kɔpər]

| gardener | tuinman (de) | ['tœyn·man] |
| domestic servant | huisbediende (de) | ['hœys·bə'dində] |

| maid (female servant) | dienstmeisje (het) | [dinst 'mɛjɕə] |
| cleaner (cleaning lady) | schoonmaakster (de) | ['sxōn·mākstər] |

126. Military professions and ranks

private	soldaat (de)	[sɔl'dāt]
sergeant	sergeant (de)	[sɛr'ʒant]
lieutenant	luitenant (de)	[lœytə'nant]
captain	kapitein (de)	[kapi'tɛjn]

major	majoor (de)	[ma'jōr]
colonel	kolonel (de)	[kɔlɔ'nɛl]
general	generaal (de)	[xenə'rāl]
marshal	maarschalk (de)	['mārsxalk]
admiral	admiraal (de)	[atmi'rāl]

military (n)	militair (de)	[mili'tɛːr]
soldier	soldaat (de)	[sɔl'dāt]
officer	officier (de)	[ɔfi'sir]
commander	commandant (de)	[kɔman'dant]

border guard	grenswachter (de)	[xrɛns·'wahtər]
radio operator	marconist (de)	[markɔ'nist]
scout (searcher)	verkenner (de)	[vər'kenər]
pioneer (sapper)	sappeur (de)	[sa'pør]
marksman	schutter (de)	['sxʉtər]
navigator	stuurman (de)	['stūrman]

127. Officials. Priests

| king | koning (de) | ['kɔniŋ] |
| queen | koningin (de) | [kɔniŋ'in] |

| prince | prins (de) | [prins] |
| princess | prinses (de) | [prin'sɛs] |

| czar | tsaar (de) | [tsār] |
| czarina | tsarina (de) | [tsa'rina] |

president	president (de)	[prezi'dɛnt]
Secretary (minister)	minister (de)	[mi'nistər]
prime minister	eerste minister (de)	['ērstə mi'nistər]
senator	senator (de)	[se'natɔr]

diplomat	diplomaat (de)	[diplɔ'māt]
consul	consul (de)	['kɔnsʉl]
ambassador	ambassadeur (de)	[ambasa'dør]

| counsilor (diplomatic officer) | adviseur (de) | [atvi'zør] |
| official, functionary (civil servant) | ambtenaar (de) | ['amtənār] |

| prefect | prefect (de) | [pre'fɛkt] |
| mayor | burgemeester (de) | [bʉrxə·'mēstər] |

| judge | rechter (de) | ['rɛxtər] |
| prosecutor (e.g., district attorney) | aanklager (de) | ['ānklahər] |

missionary	missionaris (de)	[misiɔ'naris]
monk	monnik (de)	['mɔnək]
abbot	abt (de)	[apt]
rabbi	rabbi, rabbijn (de)	['rabi], [ra'bɛjn]

vizier	vizier (de)	[vi'zir]
shah	sjah (de)	[ɕa]
sheikh	sjeik (de)	[ɕɛjk]

128. Agricultural professions

beekeeper	imker (de)	['imkər]
herder, shepherd	herder (de)	['hɛrdər]
agronomist	landbouwkundige (de)	['landbau·'kundixə]
cattle breeder	veehouder (de)	['vē·haudər]
veterinarian	dierenarts (de)	['dīrən·arts]

farmer	landbouwer (de)	['lantbauər]
winemaker	wijnmaker (de)	['wɛjn·makər]
zoologist	zoöloog (de)	[zoo'lōx]
cowboy	cowboy (de)	['kaubɔj]

129. Art professions

| actor | acteur (de) | [ak'tør] |
| actress | actrice (de) | [akt'risə] |

| singer (masc.) | zanger (de) | ['zaŋər] |
| singer (fem.) | zangeres (de) | [zaŋe'rɛs] |

| dancer (masc.) | danser (de) | ['dansər] |
| dancer (fem.) | danseres (de) | [danse'rɛs] |

| performer (masc.) | artiest (de) | [ar'tist] |
| performer (fem.) | artiest (de) | [ar'tist] |

musician	muzikant (de)	[mʉzi'kant]
pianist	pianist (de)	[pia'nist]
guitar player	gitarist (de)	[xita'rist]
conductor (orchestra ~)	orkestdirigent (de)	[ɔr'kɛst·diri'xɛnt]
composer	componist (de)	[kɔmpɔ'nist]

impresario	impresario (de)	[impre'sariɔ]
film director	filmregisseur (de)	[film·rexi'sør]
producer	filmproducent (de)	[film·prɔdy'sɛnt]
scriptwriter	scenarioschrijver (de)	[sɛ'nariɔ·'sxrɛjvər]
critic	criticus (de)	['kritikʉs]

writer	schrijver (de)	['sxrɛjvər]
poet	dichter (de)	['dixtər]
sculptor	beeldhouwer (de)	['bēlt·hauwər]
artist (painter)	kunstenaar (de)	['kʉnstənār]

juggler	jongleur (de)	[joŋ'lør]
clown	clown (de)	['klaun]
acrobat	acrobaat (de)	[akrɔ'bāt]
magician	goochelaar (de)	['xōxəlār]

130. Various professions

doctor	dokter, arts (de)	['dɔktər], [arts]
nurse	ziekenzuster (de)	['zikən·zʉstər]
psychiatrist	psychiater (de)	[psixi'atər]
dentist	tandarts (de)	['tand·arts]
surgeon	chirurg (de)	[ʃi'rʉrx]

astronaut	astronaut (de)	[astrɔ'naut]
astronomer	astronoom (de)	[astrɔ'nōm]
pilot	piloot (de)	[pi'lōt]

driver (of taxi, etc.)	chauffeur (de)	[ʃɔ'før]
engineer (train driver)	machinist (de)	[maʃi'nist]
mechanic	mecanicien (de)	[mekani'sjen]

miner	mijnwerker (de)	['mɛjn·wɛrkər]
worker	arbeider (de)	['arbɛjdər]
locksmith	bankwerker (de)	[bank·'wɛrkər]
joiner (carpenter)	houtbewerker (de)	['haut·bə'wɛrkər]
turner (lathe machine operator)	draaier (de)	['drājər]
construction worker	bouwvakker (de)	['bau·'vakər]
welder	lasser (de)	['lasər]

professor (title)	professor (de)	[prɔ'fɛsɔr]
architect	architect (de)	[arʃi'tɛkt]
historian	historicus (de)	[hi'stɔrikʉs]
scientist	wetenschapper (de)	['wetənsxapər]
physicist	fysicus (de)	['fisikʉs]
chemist (scientist)	scheikundige (de)	['sxɛjkʉndəxə]

| archeologist | archeoloog (de) | [arheɔ'lōx] |
| geologist | geoloog (de) | [xeo'lōx] |

researcher (scientist)	**onderzoeker (de)**	['ɔndər'zukər]
babysitter	**babysitter (de)**	['bɛjbisitər]
teacher, educator	**leraar, pedagoog (de)**	['lerār], [peda'xōx]
editor	**redacteur (de)**	[redak'tør]
editor-in-chief	**chef-redacteur (de)**	[ʃɛf-redak'tør]
correspondent	**correspondent (de)**	[kɔrɛspɔn'dɛnt]
typist (fem.)	**typiste (de)**	[ti'pistə]
designer	**designer (de)**	[di'zajnər]
computer expert	**computerexpert (de)**	[kɔm'pjutər·'ɛkspər]
programmer	**programmeur (de)**	[prɔxra'mør]
engineer (designer)	**ingenieur (de)**	[inxe'njør]
sailor	**matroos (de)**	[ma'trōs]
seaman	**zeeman (de)**	['zēman]
rescuer	**redder (de)**	['rɛdər]
fireman	**brandweerman (de)**	['brantwēr·man]
police officer	**politieagent (de)**	[pɔ'litsi·a'xɛnt]
watchman	**nachtwaker (de)**	['naxt·wakər]
detective	**detective (de)**	[de'tɛktif]
customs officer	**douanier (de)**	[dua'njē]
bodyguard	**lijfwacht (de)**	['lɛjf·waxt]
prison guard	**gevangenisbewaker (de)**	[xə'vaŋənis·bə'wakər]
inspector	**inspecteur (de)**	[inspɛk'tør]
sportsman	**sportman (de)**	['spɔrtman]
trainer, coach	**trainer (de)**	['trɛnər]
butcher	**slager, beenhouwer (de)**	['slaxər], ['bēnhauər]
cobbler (shoe repairer)	**schoenlapper (de)**	['sxun·'lapər]
merchant	**handelaar (de)**	['handəlār]
loader (person)	**lader (de)**	['ladər]
fashion designer	**kledingstilist (de)**	['klediŋ·sti'list]
model (fem.)	**model (het)**	[mɔ'dɛl]

131. Occupations. Social status

schoolboy	**scholier (de)**	[sxɔ'lir]
student (college ~)	**student (de)**	[stʉ'dɛnt]
philosopher	**filosoof (de)**	[filo'zōf]
economist	**econoom (de)**	[ɛkɔ'nōm]
inventor	**uitvinder (de)**	['œʏtvindər]
unemployed (n)	**werkloze (de)**	[wɛrk'lɔzə]
retiree	**gepensioneerde (de)**	[xəpɛnʃə'nērdə]
spy, secret agent	**spion (de)**	[spi'jon]

prisoner	gedetineerde (de)	[xədeti'nērdə]
striker	staker (de)	['stakər]
bureaucrat	bureaucraat (de)	[bʉrɔ'krāt]
traveler (globetrotter)	reiziger (de)	['rɛjzixər]

gay, homosexual (n)	homoseksueel (de)	[hɔmɔsɛksʉ'ēl]
hacker	hacker (de)	['hakər]
hippie	hippie (de)	['hippi]

bandit	bandiet (de)	[ban'dit]
hit man, killer	huurmoordenaar (de)	['hūr·mōrdənār]
drug addict	drugsverslaafde (de)	['drʉks·vər'slāfdə]
drug dealer	drugshandelaar (de)	['drʉks·'handəlār]
prostitute (fem.)	prostituee (de)	[prɔstitʉ'ē]
pimp	pooier (de)	['pōjər]

sorcerer	tovenaar (de)	[tɔvə'nār]
sorceress (evil ~)	tovenares (de)	[tɔvəna'rɛs]
pirate	piraat (de)	[pi'rāt]
slave	slaaf (de)	[slāf]
samurai	samoerai (de)	[samu'raj]
savage (primitive)	wilde (de)	['wildə]

Sports

132. Kinds of sports. Sportspersons

sportsman	**sportman (de)**	['sportman]
kind of sports	**soort sport (de/het)**	[sõrt sport]
basketball	**basketbal (het)**	['bãskətbal]
basketball player	**basketbalspeler (de)**	['bãskətbal·'spelər]
baseball	**baseball (het)**	['bejzbɔl]
baseball player	**baseballspeler (de)**	['bejzbɔl·'spelər]
soccer	**voetbal (het)**	['vutbal]
soccer player	**voetballer (de)**	['vutbalər]
goalkeeper	**doelman (de)**	['dulman]
hockey	**hockey (het)**	['hɔki]
hockey player	**hockeyspeler (de)**	['hɔki·'spelər]
volleyball	**volleybal (het)**	['vɔlibal]
volleyball player	**volleybalspeler (de)**	['vɔlibal·'spelər]
boxing	**boksen (het)**	['bɔksən]
boxer	**bokser (de)**	['bɔksər]
wrestling	**worstelen (het)**	['wɔrstələn]
wrestler	**worstelaar (de)**	['wɔrstəlãr]
karate	**karate (de)**	[ka'ratə]
karate fighter	**karateka (de)**	[kara'tɛka]
judo	**judo (de)**	[ju'dɔ]
judo athlete	**judoka (de)**	[ju'dɔka]
tennis	**tennis (het)**	['tɛnis]
tennis player	**tennisspeler (de)**	['tɛnis·'spelər]
swimming	**zwemmen (het)**	['zwɛmən]
swimmer	**zwemmer (de)**	['zwɛmər]
fencing	**schermen (het)**	['sxɛrmən]
fencer	**schermer (de)**	['sxɛrmər]
chess	**schaak (het)**	[sxãk]
chess player	**schaker (de)**	['sxakər]

| alpinism | alpinisme (het) | [alpi'nismə] |
| alpinist | alpinist (de) | [alpi'nist] |

| running | hardlopen (het) | ['hardlopən] |
| runner | renner (de) | ['renər] |

| athletics | atletiek (de) | [atle'tik] |
| athlete | atleet (de) | [at'lēt] |

| horseback riding | paardensport (de) | ['pārdən·sport] |
| horse rider | ruiter (de) | ['rœytər] |

figure skating	kunstschaatsen (het)	['kʉnst·'sxātsən]
figure skater (masc.)	kunstschaatser (de)	['kʉnst·'sxātsər]
figure skater (fem.)	kunstschaatsster (de)	['kʉnst·'sxātstər]

powerlifting	gewichtheffen (het)	[xə'wixt·'hefən]
powerlifter	gewichtheffer (de)	[xə'wixt·'hefər]
car racing	autoraces	['autɔ·'resəs]
racing driver	coureur (de)	[ku'rør]

| cycling | wielersport (de) | ['wilər·sport] |
| cyclist | wielrenner (de) | ['wil·renər] |

broad jump	verspringen (het)	[vər·'spriŋən]
pole vault	polsstokspringen (het)	['polstɔk·'spriŋən]
jumper	verspringer (de)	[vər'spriŋər]

133. Kinds of sports. Miscellaneous

football	Amerikaans voetbal (het)	[ameri'kāns 'vudbal]
badminton	badminton (het)	['bɛtminton]
biathlon	biatlon (de)	[biat'lon]
billiards	biljart (het)	[bi'ljart]

bobsled	bobsleeën (het)	[bɔb'slēən]
bodybuilding	bodybuilding (de)	[bɔdi·'bildiŋ]
water polo	waterpolo (het)	['watər·polɔ]
handball	handbal (de)	['hantbal]
golf	golf (het)	[gɔlf]
rowing, crew	roeisport (de)	['ruj·sport]
scuba diving	duiken (het)	['dœɣkən]
cross-country skiing	langlaufen (het)	[laŋ'laufən]
table tennis (ping-pong)	tafeltennis (het)	['tafəl·'tɛnis]

sailing	zeilen (het)	['zɛjlən]
rally racing	rally (de)	['rali]
rugby	rugby (het)	['ragbi]
snowboarding	snowboarden (het)	['snɔw·bordən]
archery	boogschieten (het)	['bōx·'sxitən]

134. Gym

barbell	lange halter (de)	['laŋə 'haltɛr]
dumbbells	halters	['haltərs]
training machine	training machine (de)	['trɛjniŋ·ma'ʃinə]
exercise bicycle	hometrainer (de)	[hɔm·'trɛnər]
treadmill	loopband (de)	['lōp·bant]
horizontal bar	rekstok (de)	['rɛkstɔk]
parallel bars	brug (de) gelijke leggers	[brʉx xə'lɛjkə 'lexərs]
vault (vaulting horse)	paardsprong (de)	['pārt·sprɔŋ]
mat (exercise ~)	mat (de)	[mat]
jump rope	springtouw (het)	['spriŋ·tau]
aerobics	aerobics (de)	[ɛj'rɔbiks]
yoga	yoga (de)	['jɔxa]

135. Hockey

hockey	hockey (het)	['hɔki]
hockey player	hockeyspeler (de)	['hɔki·'spelər]
to play hockey	hockey spelen	['hɔki 'spelən]
ice	ijs (het)	[ɛjs]
puck	puck (de)	[pʉk]
hockey stick	hockeystick (de)	['hɔki·stik]
ice skates	schaatsen (mv.)	['sxātsən]
board (ice hockey rink ~)	boarding (de)	['bɔrdiŋ]
shot	schot (het)	[sxɔt]
goaltender	doelman (de)	['dulman]
goal (score)	goal (de)	[gōl]
to score a goal	een goal scoren	[en gōl 'skɔrən]
period	periode (de)	[peri'ɔdə]
second period	tweede periode (de)	['twēdə peri'ɔdə]
substitutes bench	reservebank (de)	[re'zɛrvə·bank]

136. Soccer

soccer	voetbal (het)	['vutbal]
soccer player	voetballer (de)	['vutbalər]
to play soccer	voetbal spelen	['vutbal 'spelən]
major league	eredivisie (de)	['ɛrədi'vizi]
soccer club	voetbalclub (de)	['vutbal·klʉp]

coach	trainer (de)	['trɛnər]
owner, proprietor	eigenaar (de)	['ɛjxənãr]
team	team (het)	[tĩm]
team captain	aanvoerder (de)	['ãnvurdər]
player	speler (de)	['spelər]
substitute	reservespeler (de)	[re'zɛrvə·'spelər]
forward	aanvaller (de)	['ãnvalər]
center forward	centrale aanvaller (de)	[sɛn'tralə 'ãnvalər]
scorer	doelpuntmaker (de)	['dulpʉnt·'makər]
defender, back	verdediger (de)	[vər'dedixər]
midfielder, halfback	middenvelder (de)	['midən·'vɛldər]
match	match, wedstrijd (de)	[matʃ], ['wɛtstrɛjt]
to meet (vi, vt)	elkaar ontmoeten	[ɛl'kãr 'ɔntmutən]
final	finale (de)	[fi'nalə]
semi-final	halve finale (de)	['halvə fi'nalə]
championship	kampioenschap (het)	[kam'pjunsxap]
period, half	helft (de)	[hɛlft]
first period	eerste helft (de)	['ērstə hɛlft]
half-time	pauze (de)	['pauzə]
goal	doel (het)	[dul]
goalkeeper	doelman (de)	['dulman]
goalpost	doelpaal (de)	['dulpãl]
crossbar	lat (de)	[lat]
net	doelnet (het)	['dulnɛt]
to concede a goal	een goal incasseren	[en gōl inka'sɛrən]
ball	bal (de)	[bal]
pass	pass (de)	[pas]
kick	schot (het), schop (de)	[sxɔt], [sxɔp]
to kick (~ the ball)	schieten	['sxitən]
free kick (direct ~)	vrije schop (de)	['vrɛjə sxɔp]
corner kick	hoekschop, corner (de)	['huksxɔp], ['kɔrnər]
attack	aanval (de)	['ãnval]
counterattack	tegenaanval (de)	['texən·'ãnval]
combination	combinatie (de)	[kɔmbi'natsi]
referee	scheidsrechter (de)	['sxɛjts·'rɛxtər]
to blow the whistle	fluiten	['flœytən]
whistle (sound)	fluitsignaal (het)	['flœyt·si'njãl]
foul, misconduct	overtreding (de)	[ɔvər'trediŋ]
to commit a foul	een overtreding maken	[en ɔvər'trediŋ 'makən]
to send off	uit het veld te sturen	['œyt ət vɛlt 'styrən]
yellow card	gele kaart (de)	['xelə kãrt]
red card	rode kaart (de)	['rodə kãrt]
disqualification	diskwalificatie (de)	[diskwalifi'katsi]
to disqualify (vt)	diskwalificeren	[diskwalifi'serən]

penalty kick	**strafschop, penalty (de)**	['straf·sxɔp], ['pɛnalti]
wall	**muur (de)**	[mūr]
to score (vi, vt)	**scoren**	['skɔrən]
goal (score)	**goal (de), doelpunt (het)**	[gōl], ['dulpʉnt]
to score a goal	**een goal scoren**	[en gōl 'skɔrən]
substitution	**vervanging (de)**	[vər'vaŋiŋ]
to replace (a player)	**vervangen**	[vər'vaŋən]
rules	**regels**	['rexəls]
tactics	**tactiek (de)**	[tak'tik]
stadium	**stadion (het)**	[stadi'ɔn]
stand (bleachers)	**tribune (de)**	[tri'bʉnə]
fan, supporter	**fan, supporter (de)**	[fan], [sʉ'pɔrtər]
to shout (vi)	**schreeuwen**	['sxrēwən]
scoreboard	**scorebord (het)**	['skɔrə·bɔrt]
score	**stand (de)**	[stant]
defeat	**nederlaag (de)**	['nedərlāx]
to lose (not win)	**verliezen**	[vər'lizən]
tie	**gelijkspel (het)**	[xə'lɛjk·spɛl]
to tie (vi)	**in gelijk spel eindigen**	[in xə'lɛjk spɛl 'ɛjndixən]
victory	**overwinning (de)**	[ɔvər'winiŋ]
to win (vi, vt)	**overwinnen**	[ɔvər'winən]
champion	**kampioen (de)**	[kam'pjun]
best (adj)	**best**	[bɛst]
to congratulate (vt)	**feliciteren**	[felisi'terən]
commentator	**commentator (de)**	[kɔmən'tatɔr]
to commentate (vt)	**becommentariëren**	[bəkɔmən tari'erən]
broadcast	**uitzending (de)**	['œytsɛndiŋ]

137. Alpine skiing

skis	**ski's**	[skis]
to ski (vi)	**skiën**	['skiən]
mountain-ski resort	**skigebied (het)**	[ski·xəbit]
ski lift	**skilift (de)**	['ski·lift]
ski poles	**skistokken**	['ski·'stɔkən]
slope	**helling (de)**	['heliŋ]
slalom	**slalom (de)**	['slalɔm]

138. Tennis. Golf

golf	**golf (het)**	[gɔlf]
golf club	**golfclub (de)**	['gɔlf·klʉp]
golfer	**golfer (de)**	['gɔlfər]

hole	hole (de)	['houl]
club	golfclub (de)	['golf·klʉp]
golf trolley	trolley (de)	['troli]

tennis	tennis (het)	['tɛnis]
tennis court	tennisveld (het)	['tɛnis·vɛlt]
serve	opslag (de)	['ɔpslax]
to serve (vt)	serveren, opslaan	[sɛr'verən], ['ɔpslān]
racket	racket (het)	['rɛkət]
net	net (het)	[nɛt]
ball	bal (de)	[bal]

139. Chess

chess	schaak (het)	[sxāk]
chessmen	schaakstukken	['sxāk·'stʉkən]
chess player	schaker (de)	['sxakər]
chessboard	schaakbord (het)	['sxāk·bort]
chessman	schaakstuk (het)	['sxāk·stʉk]

| White (white pieces) | witte stukken | [witə 'stʉkən] |
| Black (black pieces) | zwarte stukken | ['zwartə 'stʉkən] |

pawn	pion (de)	[pi'ɔn]
bishop	loper (de)	['lopər]
knight	paard (het)	[pārt]
rook	toren (de)	['torən]
queen	dame, koningin (de)	['damə], [koniŋ'in]
king	koning (de)	['koniŋ]

move	zet (de)	[zɛt]
to move (vi, vt)	zetten	['zɛtən]
to sacrifice (vt)	opofferen	['ɔpoferən]
castling	rokade (de)	[ro'kadə]

| check | schaak (het) | [sxāk] |
| checkmate | schaakmat (het) | ['sxāk·mat] |

chess tournament	schaakwedstrijd (de)	['sxāk·'wɛtstrɛjt]
Grand Master	grootmeester (de)	['xrōt·mēstər]
combination	combinatie (de)	[kombi'natsi]
game (in chess)	partij (de)	[par'tɛj]
checkers	dammen (de)	['damən]

140. Boxing

| boxing | boksen (het) | ['boksən] |
| fight (bout) | boksgevecht (het) | [boks·xe'vɛht] |

| boxing match | bokswedstrijd (de) | [bɔks·'wɛtstrɛjt] |
| round (in boxing) | ronde (de) | ['rɔndə] |

| ring | ring (de) | [rɪŋ] |
| gong | gong (de) | [xɔŋ] |

punch	stoot (de)	[stōt]
knockdown	knock-down (de)	[nɔk'daun]
knockout	knock-out (de)	[nɔ'kaut]
to knock out	knock-out slaan	[nɔ'kaut slān]

| boxing glove | bokshandschoen (de) | [bɔks·'handsxun] |
| referee | referee (de) | ['refɛrī] |

lightweight	lichtgewicht (het)	['liht·xə'wixt]
middleweight	middengewicht (het)	['midən·xə'wixt]
heavyweight	zwaargewicht (het)	['zwār·xə'wixt]

141. Sports. Miscellaneous

Olympic Games	Olympische Spelen	[ɔ'limpisə 'spelən]
winner	winnaar (de)	['winār]
to be winning	overwinnen	[ɔvər'winən]
to win (vi)	winnen	['winən]

| leader | leider (de) | ['lɛjdər] |
| to lead (vi) | leiden | ['lɛjdən] |

first place	eerste plaats (de)	['ērstə plāts]
second place	tweede plaats (de)	['twēdə plāts]
third place	derde plaats (de)	['dɛrdə plāts]

medal	medaille (de)	[me'dajə]
trophy	trofee (de)	[trɔ'fē]
prize cup (trophy)	beker (de)	['bekər]
prize (in game)	prijs (de)	[prɛjs]
main prize	hoofdprijs (de)	[hōft·prɛjs]

| record | record (het) | [re'kōr] |
| to set a record | een record breken | [en re'kɔr 'brekən] |

| final | finale (de) | [fi'nalə] |
| final (adj) | finale | [fi'nalə] |

| champion | kampioen (de) | [kam'pjun] |
| championship | kampioenschap (het) | [kam'pjunsxap] |

stadium	stadion (het)	[stadi'ɔn]
stand (bleachers)	tribune (de)	[tri'bʉnə]
fan, supporter	fan, supporter (de)	[fan], [sʉ'portər]

opponent, rival	tegenstander (de)	['texən·'standər]
start (start line)	start (de)	[start]
finish line	finish (de)	['finiʃ]

| defeat | nederlaag (de) | ['nedərlāx] |
| to lose (not win) | verliezen | [vər'lizən] |

referee	rechter (de)	['rɛxtər]
jury (judges)	jury (de)	['ʒʉri]
score	stand (de)	[stant]
tie	gelijkspel (het)	[xə'lɛjk·spɛl]
to tie (vi)	in gelijk spel eindigen	[in xə'lɛjk spɛl 'ɛjndixən]
point	punt (het)	[pʉnt]
result (final score)	uitslag (de)	['œʏtslax]

period	periode (de)	[peri'ɔdə]
half-time	pauze (de)	['pauzə]
doping	doping (de)	['dɔpiŋ]
to penalize (vt)	straffen	['strafən]
to disqualify (vt)	diskwalificeren	[diskwalifi'serən]

apparatus	toestel (het)	['tustɛl]
javelin	speer (de)	[spēr]
shot (metal ball)	kogel (de)	['kɔxəl]
ball (snooker, etc.)	bal (de)	[bal]

aim (target)	doel (het)	[dul]
target	schietkaart (de)	['sxit·kārt]
to shoot (vi)	schieten	['sxitən]
accurate (~ shot)	precies	[prə'sis]

trainer, coach	trainer, coach (de)	['trɛnər], [kɔʧ]
to train (sb)	trainen	['trɛjnən]
to train (vi)	zich trainen	[zix 'trɛjnən]
training	training (de)	['trɛjniŋ]

gym	gymnastiekzaal (de)	[ximnas'tik·zāl]
exercise (physical)	oefening (de)	['ufəniŋ]
warm-up (athlete ~)	opwarming (de)	['ɔpwarmiŋ]

Education

142. School

school	**school (de)**	[sxōl]
principal (headmaster)	**schooldirecteur (de)**	[sxōl·dirɛk'tør]
pupil (boy)	**leerling (de)**	['lērliŋ]
pupil (girl)	**leerlinge (de)**	['lērliŋə]
schoolboy	**scholier (de)**	[sxɔ'lir]
schoolgirl	**scholiere (de)**	[sxɔ'lirə]
to teach (sb)	**leren**	['lerən]
to learn (language, etc.)	**studeren**	[stʉ'derən]
to learn by heart	**van buiten leren**	[van 'bœytən 'lerən]
to learn (~ to count, etc.)	**leren**	['lerən]
to be in school	**in school zijn**	[in 'sxōl zɛjn]
to go to school	**naar school gaan**	[nār 'sxōl xān]
alphabet	**alfabet (het)**	['alfabət]
subject (at school)	**vak (het)**	[vak]
classroom	**klaslokaal (het)**	['klas·lɔkāl]
lesson	**les (de)**	[lɛs]
recess	**pauze (de)**	['pauzə]
school bell	**bel (de)**	[bel]
school desk	**schooltafel (de)**	[sxōl·'tafəl]
chalkboard	**schoolbord (het)**	[sxōl·bɔrt]
grade	**cijfer (het)**	['sɛjfər]
good grade	**goed cijfer (het)**	[xut 'sɛjfər]
bad grade	**slecht cijfer (het)**	[slɛxt 'sɛjfər]
to give a grade	**een cijfer geven**	[en 'sɛjfər 'xevən]
mistake, error	**fout (de)**	['faut]
to make mistakes	**fouten maken**	['fautən 'makən]
to correct (an error)	**corrigeren**	[kɔri'dʒɛrən]
cheat sheet	**spiekbriefje (het)**	['spik·brifjə]
homework	**huiswerk (het)**	['hœʏs·wɛrk]
exercise (in education)	**oefening (de)**	['ufəniŋ]
to be present	**aanwezig zijn**	['ānwezəx zɛjn]
to be absent	**absent zijn**	[ap'sɛnt zɛjn]
to miss school	**school verzuimen**	[sxōl verzœymən]

to punish (vt)	**bestraffen**	[bə'strafən]
punishment	**bestraffing (de)**	[bə'strafiŋ]
conduct (behavior)	**gedrag (het)**	[xə'drax]
report card	**cijferlijst (de)**	['sɛjfər·lɛjst]
pencil	**potlood (het)**	['potlōt]
eraser	**gom (de)**	[xɔm]
chalk	**krijt (het)**	[krɛjt]
pencil case	**pennendoos (de)**	['penən·dōs]
schoolbag	**boekentas (de)**	['bukən·tas]
pen	**pen (de)**	[pen]
school notebook	**schrift (de)**	[sxrift]
textbook	**leerboek (het)**	['lēr·buk]
compasses	**passer (de)**	['pasɛr]
to make technical drawings	**technisch tekenen**	['tɛxnis 'tekənən]
technical drawing	**technische tekening (de)**	['tɛxnisə 'tekəniŋ]
poem	**gedicht (het)**	[xə'diht]
by heart (adv)	**van buiten**	[van 'bœytən]
to learn by heart	**van buiten leren**	[van 'bœytən 'lerən]
school vacation	**vakantie (de)**	[va'kantsi]
to be on vacation	**met vakantie zijn**	[mɛt va'kantsi zɛjn]
to spend one's vacation	**vakantie doorbrengen**	[va'kantsi 'dōrbreŋən]
test (written math ~)	**toets (de)**	[tuts]
essay (composition)	**opstel (het)**	['ɔpstəl]
dictation	**dictee (het)**	[dik'tē]
exam (examination)	**examen (het)**	[ɛk'samən]
to take an exam	**examen afleggen**	[ɛk'samən 'aflexən]
experiment (e.g., chemistry ~)	**experiment (het)**	[ɛksperi'mɛnt]

143. College. University

academy	**academie (de)**	[aka'demi]
university	**universiteit (de)**	[junivɛrsi'tɛjt]
faculty (e.g., ~ of Medicine)	**faculteit (de)**	[fakʉl'tɛjt]
student (masc.)	**student (de)**	[stʉ'dɛnt]
student (fem.)	**studente (de)**	[stʉ'dɛntə]
lecturer (teacher)	**leraar (de)**	['lerār]
lecture hall, room	**collegezaal (de)**	[kɔ'leʒə·zāl]
graduate	**afgestudeerde (de)**	['afxɛstʉ'dērdə]
diploma	**diploma (het)**	[di'plɔma]

dissertation	dissertatie (de)	[dɪsɛr'tatsi]
study (report)	onderzoek (het)	['ɔndərzuk]
laboratory	laboratorium (het)	[labɔra'tɔrijum]

lecture	college (het)	[kɔ'leʒə]
coursemate	medestudent (de)	['medə·stʉ'dɛnt]
scholarship	studiebeurs (de)	['stʉdi'børs]
academic degree	academische graad (de)	[aka'demisə xrāt]

144. Sciences. Disciplines

mathematics	wiskunde (de)	['wɪskʉndə]
algebra	algebra (de)	['alxəbra]
geometry	meetkunde (de)	['mētkʉndə]

astronomy	astronomie (de)	[astrɔnɔ'mi]
biology	biologie (de)	[biɔlɔ'xi]
geography	geografie (de)	[xeoxra'fi]
geology	geologie (de)	[xeolɔ'xi]
history	geschiedenis (de)	[xə'sxidənis]

medicine	geneeskunde (de)	[xə'nēs·kʉndə]
pedagogy	pedagogiek (de)	[peda'xɔxik]
law	rechten	['rɛxtən]

physics	fysica, natuurkunde (de)	['fizika], [na'tūrkʉndə]
chemistry	scheikunde (de)	['sxɛjkʉndə]
philosophy	filosofie (de)	[filɔzɔ'fi]
psychology	psychologie (de)	[psihɔlɔ'xi]

145. Writing system. Orthography

grammar	grammatica (de)	[xra'matika]
vocabulary	vocabulaire (het)	[vɔkabʉ'lɛ:r]
phonetics	fonetiek (de)	[fɔnɛ'tik]

noun	zelfstandig naamwoord (het)	[zɛlf'standix 'nāmwōrt]
adjective	bijvoeglijk naamwoord (het)	[bɛj'fuxlək 'nāmwōrt]
verb	werkwoord (het)	['wɛrk·vɔrt]
adverb	bijwoord (het)	['bɛj·wōrt]

pronoun	voornaamwoord (het)	['vōrnām·wōrt]
interjection	tussenwerpsel (het)	['tʉsən·'wɛrpsəl]
preposition	voorzetsel (het)	['vōrzɛtsəl]
root	stam (de)	[stam]
ending	achtervoegsel (het)	['axtər·vuxsəl]

prefix	voorvoegsel (het)	['vōr·vuxsəl]
syllable	lettergreep (de)	['lɛtər·xrēp]
suffix	achtervoegsel (het)	['axtər·vuxsəl]

| stress mark | nadruk (de) | ['nadrʉk] |
| apostrophe | afkappingsteken (het) | ['afkapiŋs·'tekən] |

period, dot	punt (de)	[pʉnt]
comma	komma (de/het)	['kɔma]
semicolon	puntkomma (de)	[pʉnt·'kɔma]
colon	dubbelpunt (de)	['dʉbəl·pʉnt]
ellipsis	beletselteken (het)	[bə'lɛtsel·'tekən]

| question mark | vraagteken (het) | ['vrāx·tekən] |
| exclamation point | uitroepteken (het) | ['œʏtrup·tekən] |

quotation marks	aanhalingstekens	['ānhaliŋs·'tekəns]
in quotation marks	tussen aanhalingstekens	['tʉsən 'ānhaliŋ's·tekəns]
parenthesis	haakjes	['hākjəs]
in parenthesis	tussen haakjes	['tʉsən 'hākjəs]

hyphen	streepje (het)	['strēpjə]
dash	gedachtestreepje (het)	[xə'dahtə 'strēpjə]
space (between words)	spatie (de)	['spatsi]

| letter | letter (de) | ['lɛtər] |
| capital letter | hoofdletter (de) | [hōft·'lɛtər] |

| vowel (n) | klinker (de) | ['klinkər] |
| consonant (n) | medeklinker (de) | ['medə·'klinkər] |

sentence	zin (de)	[zin]
subject	onderwerp (het)	['ɔndərwɛrp]
predicate	gezegde (het)	[xə'zɛxdə]

line	regel (de)	['rexəl]
on a new line	op een nieuwe regel	[ɔp en 'niuə 'rexəl]
paragraph	alinea (de)	[a'linɛa]

word	woord (het)	[wōrt]
group of words	woordgroep (de)	['wōrt·xrup]
expression	uitdrukking (de)	['œʏdrykiŋ]
synonym	synoniem (het)	[sinɔ'nim]
antonym	antoniem (het)	[antɔ'nim]

rule	regel (de)	['rexəl]
exception	uitzondering (de)	['œʏtzondəriŋ]
correct (adj)	correct	[kɔ'rɛkt]
conjugation	vervoeging, conjugatie (de)	[vər'vuxin], [kɔnju'xatsi]
declension	verbuiging, declinatie (de)	[vərbœʏxiŋ], [dekli'natsi]

nominal case	naamval (de)	['nāmval]
question	vraag (de)	[vrāx]
to underline (vt)	onderstrepen	['ɔndər'strepən]
dotted line	stippellijn (de)	['stipəl·lɛjn]

146. Foreign languages

language	taal (de)	[tāl]
foreign (adj)	vreemd	[vrēmt]
foreign language	vreemde taal (de)	['vrēmdə tāl]
to study (vt)	leren	['lerən]
to learn (language, etc.)	studeren	[stʉ'derən]

to read (vi, vt)	lezen	['lezən]
to speak (vi, vt)	spreken	['sprekən]
to understand (vt)	begrijpen	[bə'xrɛjpən]
to write (vt)	schrijven	['sxrɛjvən]

fast (adv)	snel	[snɛl]
slowly (adv)	langzaam	['laŋzām]
fluently (adv)	vloeiend	['vlujənt]

rules	regels	['rexəls]
grammar	grammatica (de)	[xra'matika]
vocabulary	vocabulaire (het)	[vɔkabʉ'lɛːr]
phonetics	fonetiek (de)	[fɔnɛ'tik]

textbook	leerboek (het)	['lēr·buk]
dictionary	woordenboek (het)	['wōrdən·buk]
teach-yourself book	leerboek (het) voor zelfstudie	['lērbuk vōr 'zɛlfstʉdi]
phrasebook	taalgids (de)	['tāl·xits]

cassette, tape	cassette (de)	[ka'sɛtə]
videotape	videocassette (de)	['videɔ·ka'sɛtə]
CD, compact disc	CD (de)	[se'de]
DVD	DVD (de)	[deve'de]

alphabet	alfabet (het)	['alfabət]
to spell (vt)	spellen	['spɛlən]
pronunciation	uitspraak (de)	['œʏtsprāk]

accent	accent (het)	[ak'sɛnt]
with an accent	met een accent	[mɛt en ak'sɛnt]
without an accent	zonder accent	['zɔndər ak'sɛnt]

word	woord (het)	[wōrt]
meaning	betekenis (de)	[bə'tekənis]
course (e.g., a French ~)	cursus (de)	['kʉrzʉs]
to sign up	zich inschrijven	[zix 'insxrɛjvən]

teacher	leraar (de)	['lerãr]
translation (process)	vertaling (de)	[vər'taliŋ]
translation (text, etc.)	vertaling (de)	[vər'taliŋ]
translator	vertaler (de)	[vər'talər]
interpreter	tolk (de)	[tɔlk]
polyglot	polyglot (de)	[poli'xlɔt]
memory	geheugen (het)	[xə'høxən]

147. Fairy tale characters

Santa Claus	Sinterklaas (de)	[sintər·'klãs]
Cinderella	Assepoester (de)	[asə'pustər]
mermaid	zeemeermin (de)	['zē·mērmin]
Neptune	Neptunus (de)	[nep'tunʉs]
magician, wizard	magiër, tovenaar (de)	['maxjər], [tovə'nãr]
fairy	goede heks (de)	['xudə hɛks]
magic (adj)	magisch	['maxis]
magic wand	toverstokje (het)	['tovər·stɔkjə]
fairy tale	sprookje (het)	['sprõkjə]
miracle	wonder (het)	['wɔndər]
dwarf	dwerg (de)	[dwɛrx]
to turn into ...	veranderen in ...	[və'randərən in]
ghost	geest (de)	[xēst]
phantom	spook (het)	[spõk]
monster	monster (het)	['mɔnstər]
dragon	draak (de)	[drãk]
giant	reus (de)	['røs]

148. Zodiac Signs

Aries	Ram (de)	[ram]
Taurus	Stier (de)	[stir]
Gemini	Tweelingen	['twēliŋən]
Cancer	Kreeft (de)	[krēft]
Leo	Leeuw (de)	[lēw]
Virgo	Maagd (de)	[mãxt]
Libra	Weegschaal (de)	['wēxsxãl]
Scorpio	Schorpioen (de)	[sxɔrpi'un]
Sagittarius	Boogschutter (de)	['bõx·'sxʉtər]
Capricorn	Steenbok (de)	['stēnbok]
Aquarius	Waterman (de)	['watərman]
Pisces	Vissen	['visən]
character	karakter (het)	[ka'raktər]

character traits	**karaktertrekken**	[ka'raktər·'trɛkən]
behavior	**gedrag (het)**	[xə'drax]
to tell fortunes	**waarzeggen**	[wār'zexən]
fortune-teller	**waarzegster (de)**	[wār'zexstər]
horoscope	**horoscoop (de)**	[hɔrɔ'skōp]

Arts

149. Theater

theater	theater (het)	[te'atər]
opera	opera (de)	['ɔpəra]
operetta	operette (de)	[ɔpe'rɛtə]
ballet	ballet (het)	[ba'lɛt]
theater poster	affiche (de/het)	[a'fiʃə]
troupe (theatrical company)	theatergezelschap (het)	[te'atər·xəzɛlsxap]
tour	tournee (de)	[tur'nē]
to be on tour	op tournee zijn	[ɔp tur'nē zɛjn]
to rehearse (vi, vt)	repeteren	[repɛ'terən]
rehearsal	repetitie (de)	[repɛ'titsi]
repertoire	repertoire (het)	[repɛrtu'ar]
performance	voorstelling (de)	['vōrstɛliŋ]
theatrical show	spektakel (het)	[spɛk'takəl]
play	toneelstuk (het)	[tɔ'nēl·stʉk]
ticket	biljet (het)	[bi'ljet]
box office (ticket booth)	kassa (de)	['kasa]
lobby, foyer	foyer (de)	[fua'je]
coat check (cloakroom)	garderobe (de)	[xardə'rɔbə]
coat check tag	garderobe nummer (het)	[xardə'rɔbə 'nʉmɛr]
binoculars	verrekijker (de)	['vɛrəkɛjkər]
usher	plaatsaanwijzer (de)	[plāts·'ānwɛjzər]
orchestra seats	parterre (de)	[par'tɛ:rə]
balcony	balkon (het)	[bal'kɔn]
dress circle	gouden rang (de)	['xaudən raŋ]
box	loge (de)	['lɔʒə]
row	rij (de)	[rɛj]
seat	plaats (de)	[plāts]
audience	publiek (het)	[pʉ'blik]
spectator	kijker (de)	['kɛjkər]
to clap (vi, vt)	klappen	['klapən]
applause	applaus (het)	[a'plaus]
ovation	ovatie (de)	[ɔ'vatsi]
stage	toneel (het)	[tɔ'nēl]
curtain	gordijn, doek (het)	[xɔr'dɛjn], [duk]
scenery	toneeldecor (het)	[tɔ'nēl·de'kɔr]

backstage	backstage (de)	[bɛk·'stɛjdʒ]
scene (e.g., the last ~)	scène (de)	['sɛjnə]
act	bedrijf (het)	[bə'drɛjf]
intermission	pauze (de)	['pauzə]

150. Cinema

| actor | acteur (de) | [ak'tør] |
| actress | actrice (de) | [akt'risə] |

movies (industry)	bioscoop (de)	[biɔ'skōp]
movie	speelfilm (de)	['spēl·film]
episode	aflevering (de)	['afleverin]

detective movie	detectivefilm (de)	[de'tɛktif·film]
action movie	actiefilm (de)	['aktsi·film]
adventure movie	avonturenfilm (de)	[avɔn'tʉrən·film]
science fiction movie	sciencefictionfilm (de)	['sajəns·'fikʃən·film]
horror movie	griezelfilm (de)	['xrizəl·film]

comedy movie	komedie (de)	[kɔ'medi]
melodrama	melodrama (het)	[melɔ'drama]
drama	drama (het)	['drama]

fictional movie	speelfilm (de)	['spēl·film]
documentary	documentaire (de)	[dɔkʉmen'tɛ:r]
cartoon	tekenfilm (de)	['tekən·film]
silent movies	stomme film (de)	['stɔmə film]

role (part)	rol (de)	[rɔl]
leading role	hoofdrol (de)	['hōft·rɔl]
to play (vi, vt)	spelen	['spelən]

movie star	filmster (de)	['film·stɛr]
well-known (adj)	bekend	[bə'kɛnt]
famous (adj)	beroemd	[bə'rumt]
popular (adj)	populair	[pɔpʉ'lɛr]

script (screenplay)	scenario (het)	[sɛ'nariɔ]
scriptwriter	scenarioschrijver (de)	[sɛ'nariɔ·'sxrɛjvər]
movie director	regisseur (de)	[rexi'sør]
producer	filmproducent (de)	[film·prɔdʉ'sɛnt]
assistant	assistent (de)	[asi'stɛnt]
cameraman	cameraman (de)	['kaməraman]
stuntman	stuntman (de)	['stʉnt·man]
double (stuntman)	stuntdubbel (de)	['stʉnt·dʉbəl]

to shoot a movie	een film maken	[en film 'makən]
audition, screen test	auditie (de)	[au'ditsi]
shooting	opnamen	['ɔpnamən]

movie crew	filmploeg (de)	['film·plux]
movie set	filmset (de)	['film·sɛt]
camera	filmcamera (de)	[film·'kamǝra]

movie theater	bioscoop (de)	[biɔ'skōp]
screen (e.g., big ~)	scherm (het)	[sxɛrm]
to show a movie	een film vertonen	[en film vǝr'tɔnǝn]

soundtrack	geluidsspoor (de)	[xǝ'lœyts·spōr]
special effects	speciale effecten	[speʃi'alǝ ɛ'fɛktǝn]
subtitles	ondertiteling (de)	['ɔndǝr'titǝliŋ]
credits	voortiteling, aftiteling (de)	[vōr'titǝliŋ], [af'titǝliŋ]
translation	vertaling (de)	[vǝr'taliŋ]

151. Painting

art	kunst (de)	['kʉnst]
fine arts	schone kunsten	['sxɔnǝ 'kʉnstǝn]
art gallery	kunstgalerie (de)	['kʉnst·galǝ'ri]
art exhibition	kunsttentoonstelling (de)	['kʉnst·tɛn'tōnstɛliŋ]

painting (art)	schilderkunst (de)	['sxildǝr·kʉnst]
graphic art	grafiek (de)	[xra'fik]
abstract art	abstracte kunst (de)	[ap'straktǝ kʉnst]
impressionism	impressionisme (het)	[impresiɔ'nismǝ]

picture (painting)	schilderij (het)	[sxildǝ'rɛj]
drawing	tekening (de)	['tekǝniŋ]
poster	poster (de)	['pɔstǝr]

illustration (picture)	illustratie (de)	[ilʉ'stratsi]
miniature	miniatuur (de)	[minia'tūr]
copy (of painting, etc.)	kopie (de)	[kɔ'pi]
reproduction	reproductie (de)	[reprɔ'dʉksi]

| mosaic | mozaïek (het) | [mɔza'ik] |
| stained glass window | gebrandschilderd glas (het) | [xǝ'brant·sxildǝrt xlas] |

| fresco | fresco (het) | ['frɛskɔ] |
| engraving | gravure (de) | [xra'vʉrǝ] |

bust (sculpture)	buste (de)	['bʉstǝ]
sculpture	beeldhouwwerk (het)	['bēlt·hauwɛrk]
statue	beeld (het)	[bēlt]
plaster of Paris	gips (het)	[xips]
plaster (as adj)	gipsen	['xipsǝn]

| portrait | portret (het) | [pɔrt'rɛt] |
| self-portrait | zelfportret (het) | ['zɛlf·pɔr'trɛt] |

landscape painting	landschap (het)	['landsxap]
still life	stilleven (het)	[sti'levən]
caricature	karikatuur (de)	[karika'tūr]
sketch	schets (de)	[sxɛts]
paint	verf (de)	[vɛrf]
watercolor paint	aquarel (de)	[akva'rɛl]
oil (paint)	olieverf (de)	['ɔli·vɛrf]
pencil	potlood (het)	['potlōt]
India ink	Oostindische inkt (de)	[ōst 'indisə inkt]
charcoal	houtskool (de)	['haut·skōl]
to draw (vi, vt)	tekenen	['tekənən]
to paint (vi, vt)	schilderen	['sxilderən]
to pose (vi)	poseren	[pɔ'zerən]
artist's model (masc.)	naaktmodel (het)	[nākt·mɔ'dɛl]
artist's model (fem.)	naaktmodel (het)	[nākt·mɔ'dɛl]
artist (painter)	kunstenaar (de)	['kʉnstənār]
work of art	kunstwerk (het)	['kʉnst·wɛrk]
masterpiece	meesterwerk (het)	['mēstər·wɛrk]
studio (artist's workroom)	studio, werkruimte (de)	['stydiɔ], [wɛrk·rœymtə]
canvas (cloth)	schildersdoek (het)	['sxildər·duk]
easel	schildersezel (de)	['sxildərs·'ezəl]
palette	palet (het)	[pa'lɛt]
frame (picture ~, etc.)	lijst (de)	[lɛjst]
restoration	restauratie (de)	[rɛstɔ'ratsi]
to restore (vt)	restaureren	[rɛstɔ'rerən]

152. Literature & Poetry

literature	literatuur (de)	[litəra'tūr]
author (writer)	auteur (de)	[au'tør]
pseudonym	pseudoniem (het)	[psødɔ'nim]
book	boek (het)	[buk]
volume	boekdeel (het)	['bukdēl]
table of contents	inhoudsopgave (de)	['inhauts·'ɔpxavə]
page	pagina (de)	['paxina]
main character	hoofdpersoon (de)	[hōft·pɛr'sɔn]
autograph	handtekening (de)	['hand·'tekəniŋ]
short story	verhaal (het)	[vər'hāl]
story (novella)	novelle (de)	[nɔ'velə]
novel	roman (de)	[rɔ'man]
work (writing)	werk (het)	[wɛrk]
fable	fabel (de)	['fabəl]

detective novel	detectiveroman (de)	[de'tɛktif·rɔ'man]
poem (verse)	gedicht (het)	[xə'diht]
poetry	poëzie (de)	[pɔɛ'zi]
poem (epic, ballad)	epos (het)	['ɛpɔs]
poet	dichter (de)	['dixtər]

fiction	fictie (de)	['fiksi]
science fiction	sciencefiction (de)	['sajəns·'fikʃən]
adventures	avonturenroman (de)	[avɔn'tʉrən·rɔ'man]
educational literature	opvoedkundige literatuur (de)	['ɔpvud'kundəxə litəra'tʉr]
children's literature	kinderliteratuur (de)	['kindər·litəra'tʉr]

153. Circus

| circus | circus (de/het) | ['sirkʉs] |
| traveling circus | chapiteau circus (de/het) | [ʃʌpi'tɔ 'sirkʉs] |

| program | programma (het) | [prɔ'xrama] |
| performance | voorstelling (de) | ['vɔrstɛliŋ] |

| act (circus ~) | nummer (het) | ['nʉmər] |
| circus ring | arena (de) | [a'rena] |

| pantomime (act) | pantomime (de) | [pantɔ'mim] |
| clown | clown (de) | ['klaun] |

acrobat	acrobaat (de)	[akrɔ'bāt]
acrobatics	acrobatiek (de)	[akrɔba'tik]
gymnast	gymnast (de)	[xim'nast]

| gymnastics | gymnastiek (de) | [ximnas'tik] |
| somersault | salto (de) | ['saltɔ] |

| athlete (strongman) | sterke man (de) | ['stɛrkə man] |
| tamer (e.g., lion ~) | temmer (de) | ['tɛmər] |

| rider (circus horse ~) | ruiter (de) | ['rœytər] |
| assistant | assistent (de) | [asi'stɛnt] |

stunt	stunt (de)	[stʉnt]
magic trick	goocheltruc (de)	['xōxəl·trʉk]
conjurer, magician	goochelaar (de)	['xōxəlãr]

| juggler | jongleur (de) | [jɔŋ'lør] |
| to juggle (vi, vt) | jongleren | [jɔŋ'lerən] |

animal trainer	dierentrainer (de)	['dīrən·trɛjnər]
animal training	dressuur (de)	[drɛ'sūr]
to train (animals)	dresseren	[drɛ'serən]

154. Music. Pop music

music	muziek (de)	[mʉ'zik]
musician	muzikant (de)	[mʉzi'kant]
musical instrument	muziekinstrument (het)	[mʉ'zik·instrʉ'mɛnt]
to play ...	... spelen	['spelən]
guitar	gitaar (de)	[xi'tār]
violin	viool (de)	[vi'jõl]
cello	cello (de)	['ʧɛlo]
double bass	contrabas (de)	['kɔntrabas]
harp	harp (de)	[harp]
piano	piano (de)	[pi'ano]
grand piano	vleugel (de)	['vløxəl]
organ	orgel (het)	['ɔrxəl]
wind instruments	blaasinstrumenten	[blāz·instrʉ'mɛntən]
oboe	hobo (de)	[ho'bo]
saxophone	saxofoon (de)	[saksɔ'fõn]
clarinet	klarinet (de)	[klari'nɛt]
flute	fluit (de)	['flœyt]
trumpet	trompet (de)	[trɔm'pɛt]
accordion	accordeon (de/het)	[akɔrdɛ'ɔn]
drum	trommel (de)	['trɔməl]
duo	duet (het)	[dʉ'wɛt]
trio	trio (het)	['trio]
quartet	kwartet (het)	['kwar'tɛt]
choir	koor (het)	[kõr]
orchestra	orkest (het)	[ɔr'kɛst]
pop music	popmuziek (de)	[pɔp·mʉ'zik]
rock music	rockmuziek (de)	[rɔk·mʉ'zik]
rock group	rockgroep (de)	['rɔk·xrup]
jazz	jazz (de)	[dʒaz]
idol	idool (het)	[i'dõl]
admirer, fan	bewonderaar (de)	[bə'wɔndərār]
concert	concert (het)	[kɔn'sɛrt]
symphony	symfonie (de)	[simfo'ni]
composition	compositie (de)	[kɔmpo'zitsi]
to compose (write)	componeren	[kɔmpo'nerən]
singing (n)	zang (de)	[zaŋ]
song	lied (het)	[lit]
tune (melody)	melodie (de)	[melɔ'di]
rhythm	ritme (het)	['ritmə]
blues	blues (de)	[blʉs]

sheet music	**bladmuziek (de)**	['blat·mʉ'zik]
baton	**dirigeerstok (de)**	[diri'xēr·stɔk]
bow	**strijkstok (de)**	['strɛjk·stɔk]
string	**snaar (de)**	[snār]
case (e.g., guitar ~)	**koffer (de)**	['kɔfər]

Rest. Entertainment. Travel

155. Trip. Travel

tourism, travel	**toerisme (het)**	[tu'rismə]
tourist	**toerist (de)**	[tu'rist]
trip, voyage	**reis (de)**	[rɛjs]
adventure	**avontuur (het)**	[avɔn'tūr]
trip, journey	**tocht (de)**	[tɔxt]
vacation	**vakantie (de)**	[va'kantsi]
to be on vacation	**met vakantie zijn**	[mɛt va'kantsi zɛjn]
rest	**rust (de)**	[rʉst]
train	**trein (de)**	[trɛjn]
by train	**met de trein**	[mɛt də trɛjn]
airplane	**vliegtuig (het)**	['vlixtœʏx]
by airplane	**met het vliegtuig**	[mɛt ət 'vlixtœʏx]
by car	**met de auto**	[mɛt də 'autɔ]
by ship	**per schip**	[pər sxip]
luggage	**bagage (de)**	[ba'xaʒə]
suitcase	**valies (de)**	[va'lis]
luggage cart	**bagagekarretje (het)**	[ba'xaʒə·'karɛtʃə]
passport	**paspoort (het)**	['paspōrt]
visa	**visum (het)**	['vizʉm]
ticket	**kaartje (het)**	['kārtʃə]
air ticket	**vliegticket (het)**	['vlix·'tikət]
guidebook	**reisgids (de)**	['rɛjs·xids]
map (tourist ~)	**kaart (de)**	[kārt]
area (rural ~)	**gebied (het)**	[xə'bit]
place, site	**plaats (de)**	[plāts]
exotica (n)	**exotische bestemming (de)**	[ɛ'ksɔtise bɛ'stemiŋ]
exotic (adj)	**exotisch**	[ɛk'sɔtis]
amazing (adj)	**verwonderlijk**	[vər'wɔndərlək]
group	**groep (de)**	[xrup]
excursion, sightseeing tour	**rondleiding (de)**	['rɔntlɛjdiŋ]
guide (person)	**gids (de)**	[xits]

156. Hotel

hotel	**hotel (het)**	[ho'tɛl]
motel	**motel (het)**	[mɔ'tɛl]
three-star (~ hotel)	**3-sterren**	[dri-'stɛrən]
five-star	**5-sterren**	[vɛjf-'stɛrən]
to stay (in a hotel, etc.)	**overnachten**	[ɔvər'naxtən]
room	**kamer (de)**	['kamər]
single room	**eenpersoonskamer (de)**	[ēnpɛr'sōns·'kamər]
double room	**tweepersoonskamer (de)**	[twē·pɛr'sōns·'kamər]
to book a room	**een kamer reserveren**	[en 'kamər rezər'verən]
half board	**halfpension (het)**	[half·pɛn'ʃɔn]
full board	**volpension (het)**	['vɔl·pɛn'ʃɔn]
with bath	**met badkamer**	[mɛt 'batkamər]
with shower	**met douche**	[mɛt 'duʃ]
satellite television	**satelliet-tv (de)**	[satə'lit-te've]
air-conditioner	**airconditioner (de)**	[ɛr·kɔn'diʃənər]
towel	**handdoek (de)**	['handuk]
key	**sleutel (de)**	['sløtəl]
administrator	**administrateur (de)**	[atministra'tør]
chambermaid	**kamermeisje (het)**	['kamər·'mɛjɕə]
porter, bellboy	**piccolo (de)**	['pikɔlɔ]
doorman	**portier (de)**	[pɔ'rtīr]
restaurant	**restaurant (het)**	[rɛstɔ'rant]
pub, bar	**bar (de)**	[bar]
breakfast	**ontbijt (het)**	[ɔn'bɛjt]
dinner	**avondeten (het)**	['avɔntetən]
buffet	**buffet (het)**	[bʉ'fɛt]
lobby	**hal (de)**	[hal]
elevator	**lift (de)**	[lift]
DO NOT DISTURB	**NIET STOREN**	[nit 'stɔrən]
NO SMOKING	**VERBODEN TE ROKEN!**	[vər'bodən tə 'rokən]

157. Books. Reading

book	**boek (het)**	[buk]
author	**auteur (de)**	[au'tør]
writer	**schrijver (de)**	['sxrɛjvər]
to write (~ a book)	**schrijven**	['sxrɛjvən]
reader	**lezer (de)**	['lezər]
to read (vi, vt)	**lezen**	['lezən]

reading (activity)	**lezen (het)**	['lezən]
silently (to oneself)	**stil**	[stil]
aloud (adv)	**hardop**	['hartɔp]
to publish (vt)	**uitgeven**	['œʏtxevən]
publishing (process)	**uitgeven (het)**	['œʏtxevən]
publisher	**uitgever (de)**	['œʏtxevər]
publishing house	**uitgeverij (de)**	[œʏtxeve'rɛj]
to come out (be released)	**verschijnen**	[vər'sxɛjnən]
release (of a book)	**verschijnen (het)**	[vər'sxɛjnən]
print run	**oplage (de)**	['ɔplaxə]
bookstore	**boekhandel (de)**	['bukən·'handəl]
library	**bibliotheek (de)**	[bibliɔ'tēk]
story (novella)	**novelle (de)**	[nɔ'velə]
short story	**verhaal (het)**	[vər'hāl]
novel	**roman (de)**	[rɔ'man]
detective novel	**detectiveroman (de)**	[de'tɛktif·rɔ'man]
memoirs	**memoires**	[memu'arəs]
legend	**legende (de)**	[le'xɛndə]
myth	**mythe (de)**	['mitə]
poetry, poems	**gedichten**	[xə'dihtən]
autobiography	**autobiografie (de)**	['autɔ·bioxra'fi]
selected works	**bloemlezing (de)**	[blum'leziŋ]
science fiction	**sciencefiction (de)**	['sajəns·'fikʃən]
title	**naam (de)**	[nām]
introduction	**inleiding (de)**	[in'lɛjdiŋ]
title page	**voorblad (het)**	['vōr·blat]
chapter	**hoofdstuk (het)**	['hōftstʉk]
extract	**fragment (het)**	[frax'mɛnt]
episode	**episode (de)**	[ɛpi'zɔdə]
plot (storyline)	**intrige (de)**	[in'trīʒə]
contents	**inhoud (de)**	['inhaut]
table of contents	**inhoudsopgave (de)**	['inhauts·'ɔpxavə]
main character	**hoofdpersonage (het)**	[hōft·pɛrsɔ'naʒə]
volume	**boekdeel (het)**	['bukdēl]
cover	**omslag (de/het)**	['ɔmslax]
binding	**boekband (de)**	['buk·bant]
bookmark	**bladwijzer (de)**	[blat·'wɛjzər]
page	**pagina (de)**	['paxina]
to page through	**bladeren**	['bladerən]
margins	**marges**	['marʒəs]
annotation (marginal note, etc.)	**annotatie (de)**	[anɔ'tatsi]

footnote	opmerking (de)	['ɔpmɛrkiŋ]
text	tekst (de)	[tɛkst]
type, font	lettertype (het)	['lɛtər·tipə]
misprint, typo	drukfout (de)	['druk·faut]

translation	vertaling (de)	[vər'taliŋ]
to translate (vt)	vertalen	[vər'talən]
original (n)	origineel (het)	[ɔriʒi'nēl]

famous (adj)	beroemd	[bə'rumt]
unknown (not famous)	onbekend	[ɔmbə'kɛnt]
interesting (adj)	interessant	[intərə'sant]
bestseller	bestseller (de)	[bɛst'sɛlər]

dictionary	woordenboek (het)	['wōrdən·buk]
textbook	leerboek (het)	['lēr·buk]
encyclopedia	encyclopedie (de)	[ɛnsiklɔpə'di]

158. Hunting. Fishing

hunting	jacht (de)	[jaxt]
to hunt (vi, vt)	jagen	['jaxən]
hunter	jager (de)	['jaxər]

to shoot (vi)	schieten	['sxitən]
rifle	geweer (het)	[xə'wēr]
bullet (shell)	patroon (de)	[pa'trōn]
shot (lead balls)	hagel (de)	['haxəl]

steel trap	val (de)	[val]
snare (for birds, etc.)	valstrik (de)	['valstrək]
to fall into the steel trap	in de val trappen	[in də val t'rapən]
to lay a steel trap	een val zetten	[ən val 'zetən]

poacher	stroper (de)	['strɔpər]
game (in hunting)	wild (het)	[wilt]
hound dog	jachthond (de)	['jaxt·hɔnt]
safari	safari (de)	[sa'fari]
mounted animal	opgezet dier (het)	['ɔpxezət dīr]

fisherman, angler	visser (de)	['visər]
fishing (angling)	visvangst (de)	['visvaŋst]
to fish (vi)	vissen	['visən]

fishing rod	hengel (de)	['hɛŋəl]
fishing line	vislijn (de)	['vis·lɛjn]
hook	haak (de)	[hāk]
float, bobber	dobber (de)	['dɔbər]
bait	aas (het)	[ās]
to cast a line	de hengel uitwerpen	[də 'hɛŋɛl œyt'wɛrpən]

to bite (ab. fish)	bijten	['bɛjtən]
catch (of fish)	vangst (de)	['vaŋst]
ice-hole	wak (het)	[wak]

fishing net	net (het)	[nɛt]
boat	boot (de)	[bõt]
to net (to fish with a net)	vissen met netten	['visən mɛt 'nɛtən]
to cast[throw] the net	het net uitwerpen	[ət nɛt œyt'wɛrpən]
to haul the net in	het net binnenhalen	[də nɛt 'binənhalən]
to fall into the net	in het net vallen	[in ət nɛt 'valən]

whaler (person)	walvisvangst (de)	['walvis·vaŋst]
whaleboat	walvisvaarder (de)	['walvis·vãrdər]
harpoon	harpoen (de)	[har'pun]

159. Games. Billiards

billiards	biljart (het)	[bi'ljart]
billiard room, hall	biljartzaal (de)	[bi'ljart·zãl]
ball (snooker, etc.)	biljartbal (de)	[bi'ljart·bal]

to pocket a ball	een bal in het gat jagen	[en 'bal in het xat 'jaxən]
cue	keu (de)	['kø]
pocket	gat (het)	[xat]

160. Games. Playing cards

diamonds	ruiten	['rœytən]
spades	schoppen	['sxɔpən]
hearts	klaveren	['klavərən]
clubs	harten	['hartən]

ace	aas (de)	[ãs]
king	koning (de)	['kɔniŋ]
queen	dame (de)	['damə]
jack, knave	boer (de)	[bur]

| playing card | speelkaart (de) | ['spēl·kãrt] |
| cards | kaarten | ['kãrtən] |

| trump | troef (de) | ['truf] |
| deck of cards | pak (het) kaarten | [pak 'kãrtən] |

point	punt (het)	[pʉnt]
to deal (vi, vt)	uitdelen	['œytdelən]
to shuffle (cards)	schudden	['sxʉdən]
lead, turn (n)	beurt (de)	['børt]
cardsharp	valsspeler (de)	['vals·spelər]

161. Casino. Roulette

casino	**casino (het)**	[ka'sinɔ]
roulette (game)	**roulette (de)**	[ru'letə]
bet	**inzet (de)**	['inzɛt]
to place bets	**een bod doen**	[en 'bɔt dun]
red	**rood (de)**	[rõt]
black	**zwart (de)**	[zwart]
to bet on red	**inzetten op rood**	['inzɛtən ɔp rõt]
to bet on black	**inzetten op zwart**	['inzɛtən ɔp 'zwart]
croupier (dealer)	**croupier (de)**	[kru'pje]
to spin the wheel	**de cilinder draaien**	[dɛ si'lindər 'drãin]
rules (of game)	**spelregels**	['spɛl·'rexəls]
chip	**fiche (de)**	['fiʃə]
to win (vi, vt)	**winnen**	['winən]
win (winnings)	**winst (de)**	[winst]
to lose (~ 100 dollars)	**verliezen**	[vər'lizən]
loss (losses)	**verlies (het)**	[vər'lis]
player	**speler (de)**	['spelər]
blackjack (card game)	**blackjack (het)**	[blɛk'dʒɛk]
craps (dice game)	**dobbelspel (het)**	['dɔbəl·spɛl]
dice (a pair of ~)	**dobbelstenen**	['dɔbəl·'stɛnən]
slot machine	**speelautomaat (de)**	['spēl·autɔ'māt]

162. Rest. Games. Miscellaneous

to stroll (vi, vt)	**wandelen**	['wandələn]
stroll (leisurely walk)	**wandeling (de)**	['wandəliŋ]
car ride	**trip (de)**	[trip]
adventure	**avontuur (het)**	[avɔn'tūr]
picnic	**picknick (de)**	['piknik]
game (chess, etc.)	**spel (het)**	[spɛl]
player	**speler (de)**	['spelər]
game (one ~ of chess)	**partij (de)**	[par'tɛj]
collector (e.g., philatelist)	**collectioneur (de)**	[kɔlektsjɔ'nør]
to collect (stamps, etc.)	**collectioneren**	[kɔlektsjɔ'nerən]
collection	**collectie (de)**	[kɔ'lɛksi]
crossword puzzle	**kruiswoordraadsel (het)**	['krœyswõrt·'rādsəl]
racetrack (horse racing venue)	**hippodroom (de)**	[hipɔ'drõm]
disco (discotheque)	**discotheek (de)**	[diskɔ'tēk]

| sauna | sauna (de) | ['sauna] |
| lottery | loterij (de) | [lotə'rɛj] |

camping trip	trektocht (de)	['trɛk·tɔxt]
camp	kamp (het)	[kamp]
tent (for camping)	tent (de)	[tɛnt]
compass	kompas (het)	[kɔm'pas]
camper	rugzaktoerist (de)	['rʉxzak·tu'rist]

to watch (movie, etc.)	bekijken	[bə'kɛjkən]
viewer	kijker (de)	['kɛjkər]
TV show (TV program)	televisie-uitzending (de)	[telə'vizi-'œʏtsɛndiŋ]

163. Photography

| camera (photo) | fotocamera (de) | ['fɔtɔ·'kaməra] |
| photo, picture | foto (de) | ['fɔtɔ] |

photographer	fotograaf (de)	[fotɔx'rāf]
photo studio	fotostudio (de)	[fɔtɔ·'stʉdiɔ]
photo album	fotoalbum (het)	[fɔtɔ·'albʉm]

camera lens	lens (de), objectief (het)	[lɛns], [ɔbjek'tif]
telephoto lens	telelens (de)	[telə·'lɛns]
filter	filter (de/het)	['filtər]
lens	lens (de)	[lɛns]

optics (high-quality ~)	optiek (de)	[ɔp'tik]
diaphragm (aperture)	diafragma (het)	[dia'fraxma]
exposure time (shutter speed)	belichtingstijd (de)	[bə'lixtiŋs·tɛjt]
viewfinder	zoeker (de)	['zukər]

digital camera	digitale camera (de)	[dixi'talə 'kaməra]
tripod	statief (het)	[sta'tif]
flash	flits (de)	[flits]

to photograph (vt)	fotograferen	[fɔtɔxra'ferən]
to take pictures	foto's maken	['fɔtɔs 'makən]
to have one's picture taken	zich laten fotograferen	[zih 'latən fɔtɔxra'ferən]

focus	focus (de)	['fɔkəs]
to focus	scherpstellen	['sxɛrpstɛlən]
sharp, in focus (adj)	scherp	[sxɛrp]
sharpness	scherpte (de)	['sxɛrptə]

contrast	contrast (het)	[kɔn'trast]
contrast (as adj)	contrastrijk	[kɔn'trastrɛjk]
picture (photo)	kiekje (het)	['kikjə]
negative (n)	negatief (het)	[nexa'tif]

film (a roll of ~)	**filmpje (het)**	['filmpjə]
frame (still)	**beeld (het)**	[bēlt]
to print (photos)	**afdrukken**	['afdrʉkən]

164. Beach. Swimming

beach	**strand (het)**	[strant]
sand	**zand (het)**	[zant]
deserted (beach)	**leeg**	[lēx]

suntan	**bruine kleur (de)**	['brœynə 'klør]
to get a tan	**zonnebaden**	['zɔnə·badən]
tan (adj)	**gebruind**	[xə'brœynt]
sunscreen	**zonnecrème (de)**	['zɔnə·krɛ:m]

bikini	**bikini (de)**	[bi'kini]
bathing suit	**badpak (het)**	['bad·pak]
swim trunks	**zwembroek (de)**	['zwɛm·brʉk]

swimming pool	**zwembad (het)**	['zwɛm·bat]
to swim (vi)	**zwemmen**	['zwɛmən]
shower	**douche (de)**	[duʃ]
to change (one's clothes)	**zich omkleden**	[zix 'ɔmkledən]
towel	**handdoek (de)**	['handuk]

| boat | **boot (de)** | [bōt] |
| motorboat | **motorboot (de)** | ['mɔtɔr·bōt] |

water ski	**waterski's**	['watər·skis]
paddle boat	**waterfiets (de)**	['watər·fits]
surfing	**surfen (het)**	['sʉrfən]
surfer	**surfer (de)**	['sʉrfər]

scuba set	**scuba, aqualong (de)**	['skʉba], [akwa'lɔŋ]
flippers (swim fins)	**zwemvliezen**	['zwɛm·vlizən]
mask (diving ~)	**duikmasker (het)**	['dœyk·'maskər]
diver	**duiker (de)**	['dœykər]
to dive (vi)	**duiken**	['dœykən]
underwater (adv)	**onder water**	['ɔndər 'watər]

beach umbrella	**parasol (de)**	[para'sɔl]
sunbed (lounger)	**ligstoel (de)**	['lix·stul]
sunglasses	**zonnebril (de)**	[zɔnə·bril]
air mattress	**luchtmatras (de/het)**	['lʉxt·ma'tras]

| to play (amuse oneself) | **spelen** | ['spelən] |
| to go for a swim | **gaan zwemmen** | [xān 'zwɛmən] |

| beach ball | **bal (de)** | [bal] |
| to inflate (vt) | **opblazen** | ['ɔpblazən] |

inflatable, air (adj)	**lucht-, opblaasbare**	[lʉxt], [ɔpblās'barə]
wave	**golf (de)**	[xɔlf]
buoy (line of ~s)	**boei (de)**	[buj]
to drown (ab. person)	**verdrinken**	[vər'drinkən]
to save, to rescue	**redden**	['rɛdən]
life vest	**reddingsvest (de)**	['rɛdiŋs·vɛst]
to observe, to watch	**waarnemen**	['wārnemən]
lifeguard	**redder (de)**	['rɛdər]

TECHNICAL EQUIPMENT. TRANSPORTATION

Technical equipment

165. Computer

computer	**computer (de)**	[kɔm'pjutər]
notebook, laptop	**laptop (de)**	['laptɔp]
to turn on	**aanzetten**	['ānzɛtən]
to turn off	**uitzetten**	['œʏtzɛtən]
keyboard	**toetsenbord (het)**	['tutsən·bɔrt]
key	**toets (de)**	[tuts]
mouse	**muis (de)**	[mœʏs]
mouse pad	**muismat (de)**	['mœʏs·mat]
button	**knopje (het)**	['knɔpjə]
cursor	**cursor (de)**	['kʉrzɔr]
monitor	**monitor (de)**	['mɔnitɔr]
screen	**scherm (het)**	[sxɛrm]
hard disk	**harde schijf (de)**	['hardə sxɛjf]
hard disk capacity	**volume (het)** **van de harde schijf**	[vɔ'lʉmə van də 'hardə sxɛjf]
memory	**geheugen (het)**	[xə'høxən]
random access memory	**RAM-geheugen (het)**	[rɛm-xə'høxən]
file	**bestand (het)**	[bə'stant]
folder	**folder (de)**	['fɔldər]
to open (vt)	**openen**	['ɔpənən]
to close (vt)	**sluiten**	['slœʏtən]
to save (vt)	**opslaan**	['ɔpslān]
to delete (vt)	**verwijderen**	[vər'wɛjdərən]
to copy (vt)	**kopiëren**	[kɔpi'erən]
to sort (vt)	**sorteren**	[sɔr'terən]
to transfer (copy)	**overplaatsen**	[ɔvər'platsən]
program	**programma (het)**	[prɔ'xrama]
software	**software (de)**	[sɔft'wɛr]
programmer	**programmeur (de)**	[prɔxra'mør]
to program (vt)	**programmeren**	[prɔxra'merən]
hacker	**hacker (de)**	['hakər]

password	wachtwoord (het)	['waxt·wōrt]
virus	virus (het)	['virʉs]
to find, to detect	ontdekken	[ɔn'dɛkən]
byte	byte (de)	[bajt]
megabyte	megabyte (de)	['mexabajt]
data	data (de)	['data]
database	databank (de)	['data·bank]
cable (USB, etc.)	kabel (de)	['kabəl]
to disconnect (vt)	afsluiten	['afslœytən]
to connect (sth to sth)	aansluiten op	['ānslœytən ɔp]

166. Internet. E-mail

Internet	internet (het)	['intɛrnɛt]
browser	browser (de)	['brausər]
search engine	zoekmachine (de)	['zuk·ma'ʃinə]
provider	internetprovider (de)	['intɛrnɛt·prɔ'vajdər]
webmaster	webmaster (de)	[wɛb·'mastər]
website	website (de)	[wɛbsajt]
webpage	webpagina (de)	[wɛb·'paxina]
address (e-mail ~)	adres (het)	[ad'rɛs]
address book	adresboek (het)	[ad'rɛs·buk]
mailbox	postvak (het)	['pɔst·vak]
mail	post (de)	[pɔst]
full (adj)	vol	[vɔl]
message	bericht (het)	[bə'rixt]
incoming messages	binnenkomende berichten	['binənkɔmɛndə bə'rixtən]
outgoing messages	uitgaande berichten	['œytxāndə bə'rihtən]
sender	verzender (de)	[vər'zɛndər]
to send (vt)	verzenden	[vər'zɛndən]
sending (of mail)	verzending (de)	[vər'zɛndiŋ]
receiver	ontvanger (de)	[ɔnt'faŋər]
to receive (vt)	ontvangen	[ɔnt'faŋən]
correspondence	correspondentie (de)	[kɔrɛspɔn'dɛntsi]
to correspond (vi)	corresponderen	[kɔrɛspɔn'derən]
file	bestand (het)	[bə'stant]
to download (vt)	downloaden	[daun'lɔudən]
to create (vt)	creëren	[kre'jerən]
to delete (vt)	verwijderen	[vər'wɛjdərən]

deleted (adj)	verwijderd	[vər'wɛjdərt]
connection (ADSL, etc.)	verbinding (de)	[vər'bindiŋ]
speed	snelheid (de)	['snɛlhɛjt]
modem	modem (de)	['mɔdɛm]
access	toegang (de)	['tuxaŋ]
port (e.g., input ~)	poort (de)	['põrt]
connection (make a ~)	aansluiting (de)	['ānslœytiŋ]
to connect to ... (vi)	zich aansluiten	[zix 'ānslœytən]
to select (vt)	selecteren	[selɛk'terən]
to search (for ...)	zoeken	['zukən]

167. Electricity

electricity	elektriciteit (de)	[ɛlɛktrisi'tɛjt]
electric, electrical (adj)	elektrisch	[ɛ'lɛktris]
electric power plant	elektriciteits-centrale (de)	[ɛlɛktrisi'tɛjt sən'tralə]
energy	energie (de)	[ɛnɛr'ʒi]
electric power	elektrisch vermogen (het)	[ɛ'lɛktris vər'mɔxən]
light bulb	lamp (de)	[lamp]
flashlight	zaklamp (de)	['zak·lamp]
street light	straatlantaarn (de)	['strāt·lan'tārn]
light	licht (het)	[lixt]
to turn on	aandoen	['āndun]
to turn off	uitdoen	['œytdun]
to turn off the light	het licht uitdoen	[ət 'lixt 'œytdun]
to burn out (vi)	doorbranden	['dõrbrandən]
short circuit	kortsluiting (de)	['kɔrt·slœytiŋ]
broken wire	onderbreking (de)	['ɔndər'brekiŋ]
contact (electrical ~)	contact (het)	[kɔn'takt]
light switch	schakelaar (de)	['sxakəlār]
wall socket	stopcontact (het)	['stɔp·kɔn'takt]
plug	stekker (de)	['stɛkər]
extension cord	verlengsnoer (de)	[vər'lɛŋ·snur]
fuse	zekering (de)	['zekəriŋ]
cable, wire	kabel (de)	['kabəl]
wiring	bedrading (de)	[bə'dradiŋ]
ampere	ampère (de)	[am'pɛrə]
amperage	stroomsterkte (de)	[strõm·'stɛrktə]
volt	volt (de)	[vɔlt]
voltage	spanning (de)	['spaniŋ]

| electrical device | elektrisch toestel (het) | [ɛ'lɛktris 'tustəl] |
| indicator | indicator (de) | [indi'katɔr] |

electrician	elektricien (de)	[ɛlɛktri'sjen]
to solder (vt)	solderen	[sɔl'derən]
soldering iron	soldeerbout (de)	[sɔl'dēr·baut]
electric current	stroom (de)	[strōm]

168. Tools

tool, instrument	werktuig (het)	['wɛrktœɣx]
tools	gereedschap (het)	[xə'rētsxap]
equipment (factory ~)	uitrusting (de)	['œɣtrystiŋ]

hammer	hamer (de)	['hamər]
screwdriver	schroevendraaier (de)	['sxruvən·'drājər]
ax	bijl (de)	[bɛjl]

saw	zaag (de)	[zãx]
to saw (vt)	zagen	['zaxən]
plane (tool)	schaaf (de)	[sxãf]
to plane (vt)	schaven	['sxavən]
soldering iron	soldeerbout (de)	[sɔl'dēr·baut]
to solder (vt)	solderen	[sɔl'derən]

file (tool)	vijl (de)	[vɛjl]
carpenter pincers	nijptang (de)	['nɛjp·taŋ]
lineman's pliers	combinatietang (de)	[kɔmbi'natsi·taŋ]
chisel	beitel (de)	['bɛjtəl]

drill bit	boorkop (de)	['bōrkɔp]
electric drill	boormachine (de)	[bōr·ma'ʃinə]
to drill (vi, vt)	boren	['bɔrən]

| knife | mes (het) | [mɛs] |
| blade | lemmet (het) | ['lemət] |

sharp (blade, etc.)	scherp	[sxɛrp]
dull, blunt (adj)	bot	[bɔt]
to get blunt (dull)	bot raken	[bɔt 'rakən]
to sharpen (vt)	slijpen	['slɛjpən]

bolt	bout (de)	['baut]
nut	moer (de)	[mur]
thread (of a screw)	schroefdraad (de)	['sxruf·drãt]
wood screw	houtschroef (de)	['haut·sxruf]

nail	spijker (de)	['spɛjkər]
nailhead	kop (de)	[kɔp]
ruler (for measuring)	liniaal (de/het)	[lini'ãl]

tape measure	rolmeter (de)	['rɔl·metər]
spirit level	waterpas (de/het)	['watərpas]
magnifying glass	loep (de)	[lup]

measuring instrument	meetinstrument (het)	['mēt·instrʉ'mɛnt]
to measure (vt)	opmeten	['ɔpmetən]
scale	schaal (de)	[sxāl]
(of thermometer, etc.)		
readings	gegevens	[xə'xevəns]

| compressor | compressor (de) | [kɔm'presɔr] |
| microscope | microscoop (de) | [mikrɔ'skōp] |

pump (e.g., water ~)	pomp (de)	[pɔmp]
robot	robot (de)	['robɔt]
laser	laser (de)	['lezər]

wrench	moersleutel (de)	['mur·'sløtəl]
adhesive tape	plakband (de)	['plak·bant]
glue	lijm (de)	[lɛjm]

sandpaper	schuurpapier (het)	[sxūr·pa'pir]
spring	veer (de)	[vēr]
magnet	magneet (de)	[max'nēt]
gloves	handschoenen	['xand 'sxunən]

rope	touw (het)	['tau]
cord	snoer (het)	[snur]
wire (e.g., telephone ~)	draad (de)	[drāt]
cable	kabel (de)	['kabəl]

sledgehammer	moker (de)	['mɔkər]
prybar	breekijzer (het)	['brē'kɛjzər]
ladder	ladder (de)	['ladər]
stepladder	trapje (het)	['trapje]

to screw (tighten)	aanschroeven	['ānsxruvən]
to unscrew (lid, filter, etc.)	losschroeven	[lɔs'sxruvən]
to tighten	dichtpersen	['dixtpɛrsən]
(e.g., with a clamp)		
to glue, to stick	vastlijmen	[vast'lɛjmən]
to cut (vt)	snijden	['snɛjdən]

malfunction (fault)	defect (het)	[de'fɛkt]
repair (mending)	reparatie (de)	[repa'ratsi]
to repair, to fix (vt)	repareren	[repa'rerən]
to adjust (machine, etc.)	regelen	['rexələn]

to check (to examine)	checken	['ʧɛkən]
checking	controle (de)	[kɔn'trɔlə]
readings	gegevens	[xə'xevəns]
reliable, solid (machine)	degelijk	['dexələk]

complex (adj)	**ingewikkeld**	[inxe'wikəlt]
to rust (get rusted)	**roesten**	['rustən]
rusty, rusted (adj)	**roestig**	['rustəx]
rust	**roest (de/het)**	[rust]

Transportation

169. Airplane

airplane	**vliegtuig (het)**	['vlixtœɣx]
air ticket	**vliegticket (het)**	['vlix·'tikət]
airline	**luchtvaart-maatschappij (de)**	['lʉxtvārt mātsxa'pɛj]
airport	**luchthaven (de)**	['lʉxthavən]
supersonic (adj)	**supersonisch**	[sʉpər'sɔnis]
captain	**gezagvoerder (de)**	[xəzax·'vurdər]
crew	**bemanning (de)**	[bə'maniŋ]
pilot	**piloot (de)**	[pi'lōt]
flight attendant (fem.)	**stewardess (de)**	[stʉwər'dɛs]
navigator	**stuurman (de)**	['stūrman]
wings	**vleugels**	['vløxəls]
tail	**staart (de)**	[stārt]
cockpit	**cabine (de)**	[ka'binə]
engine	**motor (de)**	['mɔtɔr]
undercarriage (landing gear)	**landingsgestel (het)**	['landiŋs·xə'stɛl]
turbine	**turbine (de)**	[tʉr'binə]
propeller	**propeller (de)**	[prɔ'pelər]
black box	**zwarte doos (de)**	['zwartə dōs]
yoke (control column)	**stuur (het)**	[stūr]
fuel	**brandstof (de)**	['brandstɔf]
safety card	**veiligheidskaart (de)**	['vɛjləxhɛjts·kārt]
oxygen mask	**zuurstofmasker (het)**	['zūrstɔf·'maskər]
uniform	**uniform (het)**	['juniform]
life vest	**reddingsvest (de)**	['rɛdiŋs·vɛst]
parachute	**parachute (de)**	[para'ʃʉtə]
takeoff	**opstijgen (het)**	['ɔpstɛjxən]
to take off (vi)	**opstijgen**	['ɔpstɛjxən]
runway	**startbaan (de)**	['start·bān]
visibility	**zicht (het)**	[zixt]
flight (act of flying)	**vlucht (de)**	[vlʉxt]
altitude	**hoogte (de)**	['hōxtə]
air pocket	**luchtzak (de)**	['lʉxt·zak]
seat	**plaats (de)**	[plāts]
headphones	**koptelefoon (de)**	['kɔp·telə'fōn]

folding tray (tray table)	**tafeltje (het)**	['tafɛltʃə]
airplane window	**venster (het)**	['vɛnstər]
aisle	**gangpad (het)**	['haŋpat]

170. Train

train	**trein (de)**	[trɛjn]
commuter train	**elektrische trein (de)**	[ɛ'lɛktrisə trɛjn]
express train	**sneltrein (de)**	['snɛl·trɛjn]
diesel locomotive	**diesellocomotief (de)**	['dizəl·lɔkɔmɔ'tif]
steam locomotive	**stoomlocomotief (de)**	[stōm·lɔkɔmɔ'tif]
passenger car	**rijtuig (het)**	['rɛjtœɣx]
dining car	**restauratierijtuig (het)**	[rɛstɔ'ratsi·'rɛjtœɣx]
rails	**rails**	['rɛjls]
railroad	**spoorweg (de)**	['spōr·wɛx]
railway tie	**dwarsligger (de)**	['dwars·lixə]
platform (railway ~)	**perron (het)**	[pɛ'rɔn]
track (~ 1, 2, etc.)	**spoor (het)**	[spōr]
semaphore	**semafoor (de)**	[səma'fōr]
station	**halte (de)**	['haltə]
engineer (train driver)	**machinist (de)**	[maʃi'nist]
porter (of luggage)	**kruier (de)**	['krœyər]
car attendant	**conducteur (de)**	[kɔndʉk'tør]
passenger	**passagier (de)**	[pasa'xir]
conductor	**controleur (de)**	[kɔntrɔ'lør]
(ticket inspector)		
corridor (in train)	**gang (de)**	[xaŋ]
emergency brake	**noodrem (de)**	['nōd·rɛm]
compartment	**coupé (de)**	[ku'pɛ]
berth	**bed (het)**	[bɛt]
upper berth	**bovenste bed (het)**	['bovənstə bɛt]
lower berth	**onderste bed (het)**	['ɔndərstə bɛt]
bed linen, bedding	**beddengoed (het)**	['bɛdən·xut]
ticket	**kaartje (het)**	['kārtʃə]
schedule	**dienstregeling (de)**	[dinst·'rexəliŋ]
information display	**informatiebord (het)**	[infor'matsi·bɔrt]
to leave, to depart	**vertrekken**	[vər'trɛkən]
departure (of train)	**vertrek (het)**	[vər'trɛk]
to arrive (ab. train)	**aankomen**	['ānkɔmən]
arrival	**aankomst (de)**	['ānkɔmst]
to arrive by train	**aankomen per trein**	['ānkɔmən pɛr trɛjn]
to get on the train	**in de trein stappen**	[in də 'trɛjn 'stapən]

to get off the train	uit de trein stappen	['œyt də 'trɛjn 'stapən]
train wreck	treinwrak (het)	['trɛjn·wrak]
to derail (vi)	ontspoord zijn	[ɔnt'spɔrt zɛjn]
steam locomotive	stoomlocomotief (de)	[stõm·lɔkɔmɔ'tif]
stoker, fireman	stoker (de)	['stɔkər]
firebox	stookplaats (de)	['stõk·plāts]
coal	steenkool (de)	['stēn·kõl]

171. Ship

ship	schip (het)	[sxip]
vessel	vaartuig (het)	['vārtœyx]
steamship	stoomboot (de)	['stõm·bõt]
riverboat	motorschip (het)	['mɔtɔr·sxip]
cruise ship	lijnschip (het)	['lɛjn·sxip]
cruiser	kruiser (de)	['krœysər]
yacht	jacht (het)	[jaxt]
tugboat	sleepboot (de)	['slēp·bõt]
barge	duwbak (de)	['dʉwbak]
ferry	ferryboot (de)	['fɛri·bõt]
sailing ship	zeilboot (de)	['zɛjl·bõt]
brigantine	brigantijn (de)	[brixan'tɛjn]
ice breaker	ijsbreker (de)	['ɛjs·brekər]
submarine	duikboot (de)	['dœyk·bõt]
boat (flat-bottomed ~)	boot (de)	[bõt]
dinghy	sloep (de)	[slup]
lifeboat	reddingssloep (de)	['rɛdiŋs·slup]
motorboat	motorboot (de)	['mɔtɔr·bõt]
captain	kapitein (de)	[kapi'tɛjn]
seaman	zeeman (de)	['zēman]
sailor	matroos (de)	[ma'trõs]
crew	bemanning (de)	[bə'maniŋ]
boatswain	bootsman (de)	['bõtsman]
ship's boy	scheepsjongen (de)	['sxēps·'joŋən]
cook	kok (de)	[kɔk]
ship's doctor	scheepsarts (de)	['sxēps·arts]
deck	dek (het)	[dɛk]
mast	mast (de)	[mast]
sail	zeil (het)	[zɛjl]
hold	ruim (het)	[rœym]
bow (prow)	voorsteven (de)	['võrstevən]

stern	achtersteven (de)	['axtər·stevən]
oar	roeispaan (de)	['rujs·pān]
screw propeller	schroef (de)	[sxruf]

cabin	kajuit (de)	[kajœyt]
wardroom	officierskamer (de)	[ɔfi'sir·'kamər]
engine room	machinekamer (de)	[ma'ʃinə·'kamər]
bridge	brug (de)	[brʉx]
radio room	radiokamer (de)	['radiɔ·'kamər]

| wave (radio) | radiogolf (de) | ['radiɔ·xɔlf] |
| logbook | logboek (het) | ['lɔxbuk] |

spyglass	verrekijker (de)	['vɛrəkɛjkər]
bell	klok (de)	[klɔk]
flag	vlag (de)	[vlax]

| hawser (mooring ~) | kabel (de) | ['kabəl] |
| knot (bowline, etc.) | knoop (de) | [knōp] |

| deckrails | leuning (de) | ['løniŋ] |
| gangway | trap (de) | [trap] |

| anchor | anker (het) | ['ankər] |
| to weigh anchor | het anker lichten | [ət 'ankər 'lixtən] |

| to drop anchor | het anker neerlaten | [ət 'ankər 'nērlatən] |
| anchor chain | ankerketting (de) | ['ankər·'ketiŋ] |

| port (harbor) | haven (de) | ['havən] |
| quay, wharf | kaai (de) | [kāj] |

| to berth (moor) | aanleggen | ['ānlexən] |
| to cast off | wegvaren | ['wɛxvarən] |

| trip, voyage | reis (de) | [rɛjs] |
| cruise (sea trip) | cruise (de) | [krus] |

| course (route) | koers (de) | [kurs] |
| route (itinerary) | route (de) | ['rutə] |

fairway (safe water channel)	vaarwater (het)	['vār·watər]
shallows	zandbank (de)	['zant·bank]
to run aground	stranden	['strandən]

storm	storm (de)	[stɔrm]
signal	signaal (het)	[si'njāl]
to sink (vi)	zinken	['zinkən]
Man overboard!	Man overboord!	[man ɔvər'bōrt]
SOS (distress signal)	SOS	[ɛs ɔ ɛs]
ring buoy	reddingsboei (de)	['rɛdiŋs·bui]

172. Airport

airport	luchthaven (de)	['lʉxthavən]
airplane	vliegtuig (het)	['vlixtœyx]
airline	luchtvaart-maatschappij (de)	['lʉxtvārt mātsxa'pɛj]
air traffic controller	luchtverkeersleider (de)	['lʉxt·verkērs·'lɛjdər]
departure	vertrek (het)	[vər'trɛk]
arrival	aankomst (de)	['ānkɔmst]
to arrive (by plane)	aankomen	['ānkɔmən]
departure time	vertrektijd (de)	[vər'trɛk·tɛjt]
arrival time	aankomstuur (het)	['ānkɔmst·'ūr]
to be delayed	vertraagd zijn	[vər'trāxt zɛjn]
flight delay	vluchtvertraging (de)	['vlʉxt·vərt'raxiŋ]
information board	informatiebord (het)	[infɔr'matsi·bɔrt]
information	informatie (de)	[infɔr'matsi]
to announce (vt)	aankondigen	['ānkɔndəxən]
flight (e.g., next ~)	vlucht (de)	[vlʉxt]
customs	douane (de)	[du'anə]
customs officer	douanier (de)	[dua'njē]
customs declaration	douaneaangifte (de)	[du'anə·'ānxiftə]
to fill out (vt)	invullen	['invʉlən]
to fill out the declaration	een douaneaangifte invullen	[en du'anə·'ānxiftə 'invʉlən]
passport control	paspoortcontrole (de)	['paspōrt·kɔn'trɔlə]
luggage	bagage (de)	[ba'xaʒə]
hand luggage	handbagage (de)	[hant·ba'xaʒə]
luggage cart	bagagekarretje (het)	[ba'xaʒə·'karɛtʃə]
landing	landing (de)	['landiŋ]
landing strip	landingsbaan (de)	['landiŋs·bān]
to land (vi)	landen	['landən]
airstairs	vliegtuigtrap (de)	['vlixtœyx·trap]
check-in	inchecken (het)	['intʃɛkən]
check-in counter	incheckbalie (de)	['intʃɛk·'bali]
to check-in (vi)	inchecken	['intʃɛkən]
boarding pass	instapkaart (de)	['instap·kārt]
departure gate	gate (de)	[gejt]
transit	transit (de)	['transit]
to wait (vt)	wachten	['waxtən]
departure lounge	wachtzaal (de)	['waxt·zāl]
to see off	begeleiden	[bəxe'lɛjdən]
to say goodbye	afscheid nemen	['afsxɛjt 'nemən]

173. Bicycle. Motorcycle

bicycle	**fiets (de)**	[fits]
scooter	**bromfiets (de)**	['brɔmfits]
motorcycle, bike	**motorfiets (de)**	['motɔrfits]
to go by bicycle	**met de fiets rijden**	[mɛt də fits 'rɛjdən]
handlebars	**stuur (het)**	[stūr]
pedal	**pedaal (de/het)**	[pe'dāl]
brakes	**remmen**	['rɛmən]
bicycle seat (saddle)	**fietszadel (de/het)**	['fits·zadəl]
pump	**pomp (de)**	[pɔmp]
luggage rack	**bagagedrager (de)**	[ba'xaʒə·'draxər]
front lamp	**fietslicht (het)**	['fits·lixt]
helmet	**helm (de)**	[hɛlm]
wheel	**wiel (het)**	[wil]
fender	**spatbord (het)**	['spat·bɔrt]
rim	**velg (de)**	[vɛlx]
spoke	**spaak (de)**	[spāk]

Cars

174. Types of cars

automobile, car	auto (de)	['autɔ]
sports car	sportauto (de)	[spɔrt·'autɔ]
limousine	limousine (de)	[limu'zinə]
off-road vehicle	terreinwagen (de)	[te'rɛjn·'waxən]
convertible (n)	cabriolet (de)	[kabriɔ'let]
minibus	minibus (de)	['minibʉs]
ambulance	ambulance (de)	[ambʉ'lansə]
snowplow	sneeuwruimer (de)	['snēw·'rœymər]
truck	vrachtwagen (de)	['vraht·'waxən]
tanker truck	tankwagen (de)	['tank·'waxən]
van (small truck)	bestelwagen (de)	[bə'stɛl·'waxən]
road tractor (trailer truck)	trekker (de)	['trɛkər]
trailer	aanhangwagen (de)	['ānhaŋ·'wahən]
comfortable (adj)	comfortabel	[kɔmfɔr'tabəl]
used (adj)	tweedehands	[twēdə'hants]

175. Cars. Bodywork

hood	motorkap (de)	['motɔr·kap]
fender	spatbord (het)	['spat·bɔrt]
roof	dak (het)	[dak]
windshield	voorruit (de)	['vōr·rœyt]
rear-view mirror	achterruit (de)	['axtər·rœyt]
windshield washer	ruitensproeier (de)	['rœytən·'sprujər]
windshield wipers	wisserbladen	['wisər·bladən]
side window	zijruit (de)	['zɛj·rœyt]
window lift (power window)	raamlift (de)	['rām·lift]
antenna	antenne (de)	[an'tɛnə]
sunroof	zonnedak (het)	['zɔnə·dak]
bumper	bumper (de)	['bʉmpər]
trunk	koffer (de)	['kɔfər]
roof luggage rack	imperiaal (de/het)	[imperi'jāl]
door	portier (het)	[pɔ'rtīr]

| door handle | handvat (het) | ['hand·fat] |
| door lock | slot (het) | [slɔt] |

license plate	nummerplaat (de)	['nʉmər·plāt]
muffler	knalpot (de)	['knal·pɔt]
gas tank	benzinetank (de)	[bɛn'zinə·tank]
tailpipe	uitlaatpijp (de)	['œytlāt·pɛjp]

gas, accelerator	gas (het)	[xas]
pedal	pedaal (de/het)	[pe'dāl]
gas pedal	gaspedaal (de/het)	[xas·pe'dāl]

brake	rem (de)	[rɛm]
brake pedal	rempedaal (de/het)	[rɛm·pə'dāl]
to brake (use the brake)	remmen	['rɛmən]
parking brake	handrem (de)	['hand·rɛm]

clutch	koppeling (de)	['kɔpəliŋ]
clutch pedal	koppelings-pedaal (de/het)	['kɔpəliŋs pə'dāl]
clutch disc	koppelingsschijf (de)	['kɔpəliŋs·sxɛjf]
shock absorber	schokdemper (de)	['sxɔk·dɛmpər]

wheel	wiel (het)	[wil]
spare tire	reservewiel (het)	[re'zɛrvə·wil]
tire	band (de)	[bant]
hubcap	wieldop (de)	['wil·dɔp]

driving wheels	aandrijfwielen	['āndrɛjf·'wilən]
front-wheel drive (as adj)	met voorwielaandrijving	[mɛt 'vōr·wilān·'drɛjviŋ]
rear-wheel drive (as adj)	met achterwielaandrijving	[mɛt 'axtər·wilān·'drɛjviŋ]
all-wheel drive (as adj)	met vierwielaandrijving	[mɛt 'vir·wilān·'drɛjviŋ]

| gearbox | versnellingsbak (de) | [vər'sneliŋs·bak] |
| automatic (adj) | automatisch | [autɔ'matis] |

| mechanical (adj) | mechanisch | [me'xanis] |
| gear shift | versnellingspook (de) | [vər'sneliŋs·pōk] |

| headlight | voorlicht (het) | ['vōrlixt] |
| headlights | voorlichten | ['vōrlixtən] |

low beam	dimlicht (het)	['dim·lixt]
high beam	grootlicht (het)	[xrōt·'liht]
brake light	stoplicht (het)	['stɔp·lixt]

parking lights	standlichten	['stant·'lixtən]
hazard lights	noodverlichting (de)	['nōtvər·'lixtiŋ]
fog lights	mistlichten	['mist·'lixtən]
turn signal	pinker (de)	['pinkər]
back-up light	achteruitrijdlicht (het)	['axtərœyt·rɛjt·'lixt]

176. Cars. Passenger compartment

car inside (interior)	interieur (het)	[intə'rør]
leather (as adj)	leren	['lerən]
velour (as adj)	fluwelen	[flʉ'welən]
upholstery	bekleding (de)	[bə'klediŋ]
instrument (gage)	toestel (het)	['tustɛl]
dashboard	instrumentenbord (het)	[instrʉ'mɛntən·bɔrt]
speedometer	snelheidsmeter (de)	['snɛlhɛjts·'metər]
needle (pointer)	pijltje (het)	['pɛjltjə]
odometer	kilometerteller (de)	[kilometər·'tɛlər]
indicator (sensor)	sensor (de)	['sɛnsɔr]
level	niveau (het)	[ni'vɔ]
warning light	controlelampje (het)	[kɔn'trolə·'lampjə]
steering wheel	stuur (het)	[stūr]
horn	toeter (de)	['tutər]
button	knopje (het)	['knɔpjə]
switch	schakelaar (de)	['sxakəlãr]
seat	stoel (de)	[stul]
backrest	rugleuning (de)	['rʉx·'løniŋ]
headrest	hoofdsteun (de)	['hõft'støn]
seat belt	veiligheidsgordel (de)	['vɛjləxhɛjts·'xɔrdəl]
to fasten the belt	de gordel aandoen	[də 'xɔrdəl 'āndun]
adjustment (of seats)	regeling (de)	['rexəliŋ]
airbag	airbag (de)	['ɛjrbax]
air-conditioner	airconditioner (de)	[ɛr·kɔn'diʃənər]
radio	radio (de)	['radiɔ]
CD player	CD-speler (de)	[se'de-'spelər]
to turn on	aanzetten	['ānzɛtən]
antenna	antenne (de)	[an'tɛnə]
glove box	handschoenen-kastje (het)	['xand·'sxunən 'kaɕə]
ashtray	asbak (de)	['asbak]

177. Cars. Engine

engine, motor	motor (de)	['mɔtɔr]
diesel (as adj)	diesel-	['dizəl]
gasoline (as adj)	benzine-	[bɛn'zinə]
engine volume	motorinhoud (de)	['mɔtɔr·'inhaut]
power	vermogen (het)	[vər'mɔxən]
horsepower	paardenkracht (de)	['pārdən·kraxt]

piston	zuiger (de)	['zœyxər]
cylinder	cilinder (de)	[si'lindər]
valve	klep (de)	[klɛp]

injector	injectie (de)	[inj'eksi]
generator (alternator)	generator (de)	[xenə'ratɔr]
carburetor	carburator (de)	[karbʉ'ratɔr]
motor oil	motorolie (de)	['mɔtɔr·ɔli]

radiator	radiator (de)	[radi'atɔr]
coolant	koelvloeistof (de)	['kul·vlujstɔf]
cooling fan	ventilator (de)	[vənti'latɔr]

battery (accumulator)	accu (de)	['akʉ]
starter	starter (de)	['startər]
ignition	contact (het)	[kɔn'takt]
spark plug	bougie (de)	[bu'ʒi]

terminal (of battery)	pool (de)	[pōl]
positive terminal	positieve pool (de)	[pozi'tivə pōl]
negative terminal	negatieve pool (de)	[nexa'tivə pōl]
fuse	zekering (de)	['zekəriŋ]

air filter	luchtfilter (de)	['lʉxt·'filtər]
oil filter	oliefilter (de)	['ɔli·'filtər]
fuel filter	benzinefilter (de)	[bɛn'zinə·'filtər]

178. Cars. Crash. Repair

car crash	auto-ongeval (het)	['autɔ-'ɔŋɛval]
traffic accident	verkeersongeluk (het)	[vər'kērs·'ɔŋəlʉk]
to crash (into the wall, etc.)	aanrijden	['ānrɛjdən]
to get smashed up	verongelukken	[və'rɔnxəlʉkən]
damage	beschadiging (de)	[bə'sxadəxiŋ]
intact (unscathed)	heelhuids	['hēlhœyts]

breakdown	pech (de)	[pɛx]
to break down (vi)	kapot gaan	[ka'pɔt xān]
towrope	sleeptouw (het)	['slēp·tau]

puncture	lek (het)	[lɛk]
to be flat	lekke krijgen	['lɛkə 'krɛjxən]
to pump up	oppompen	['ɔpɔmpən]
pressure	druk (de)	[drʉk]
to check (to examine)	checken	['ʧɛkən]

repair	reparatie (de)	[repa'ratsi]
auto repair shop	garage (de)	[xa'raʒə]
spare part	wisselstuk (het)	['wisəl·stʉk]

part	onderdeel (het)	['ɔndərdēl]
bolt (with nut)	bout (de)	['baut]
screw (fastener)	schroef (de)	[sxruf]
nut	moer (de)	[mur]
washer	sluitring (de)	['slœytriŋ]
bearing	kogellager (de/het)	['kɔxəllahər]

tube	pijp (de)	[pɛjp]
gasket (head ~)	pakking (de)	['pakiŋ]
cable, wire	kabel (de)	['kabəl]

jack	dommekracht (de)	['dɔməkraxt]
wrench	moersleutel (de)	['mur·'sløtəl]
hammer	hamer (de)	['hamər]
pump	pomp (de)	[pɔmp]
screwdriver	schroevendraaier (de)	['sxruvən·'drājər]

| fire extinguisher | brandblusser (de) | ['brant·blʉsər] |
| warning triangle | gevarendriehoek (de) | [xə'varən·'drihuk] |

to stall (vi)	afslaan	['afslān]
stall (n)	uitvallen (het)	['œytvalən]
to be broken	zijn gebroken	[zɛjn xə'brɔkən]

to overheat (vi)	oververhitten	[ɔvərvər'hitən]
to be clogged up	verstopt raken	[vər'stɔpt 'rakən]
to freeze up (pipes, etc.)	bevriezen	[bə'vrizən]
to burst (vi, ab. tube)	barsten	['barstən]

pressure	druk (de)	[drʉk]
level	niveau (het)	[ni'vɔ]
slack (~ belt)	slap	[slap]

dent	deuk (de)	['døk]
knocking noise (engine)	geklop (het)	[xə'klɔp]
crack	barst (de)	[barst]
scratch	kras (de)	[kras]

179. Cars. Road

road	weg (de)	[wɛx]
highway	snelweg (de)	['snɛlwɛx]
freeway	autoweg (de)	['autowɛx]
direction (way)	richting (de)	['rixtiŋ]
distance	afstand (de)	['afstant]

bridge	brug (de)	[brʉx]
parking lot	parking (de)	['parkiŋ]
square	plein (het)	[plɛjn]
interchange	verkeersknooppunt (het)	[vər'kērs·'knōp·pʉnt]

tunnel	tunnel (de)	['tʉnəl]
gas station	benzinestation (het)	[bɛn'zinə·sta'tsjɔn]
parking lot	parking (de)	['parkiŋ]
gas pump (fuel dispenser)	benzinepomp (de)	[bɛn'zinə·pɔmp]
auto repair shop	garage (de)	[xa'raʒə]
to get gas (to fill up)	tanken	['tankən]
fuel	brandstof (de)	['brandstɔf]
jerrycan	jerrycan (de)	['dʒɛrikən]
asphalt	asfalt (het)	['asfalt]
road markings	markering (de)	[mar'keriŋ]
curb	trottoirband (de)	[trɔtu'ar·bant]
guardrail	geleiderail (de)	[xəlɛjdə'rel]
ditch	greppel (de)	['xrepəl]
roadside (shoulder)	vluchtstrook (de)	['vlʉxt·strɔk]
lamppost	lichtmast (de)	['lixt·mast]
to drive (a car)	besturen	[bə'stʉrən]
to turn (e.g., ~ left)	afslaan	['afslān]
to make a U-turn	U-bocht maken	[ju-bɔxt 'makən]
reverse (~ gear)	achteruit (de)	['axtərœʏt]
to honk (vi)	toeteren	['tutərən]
honk (sound)	toeter (de)	['tutər]
to get stuck (in the mud, etc.)	vastzitten	['vastzitən]
to spin the wheels	spinnen	['spinən]
to cut, to turn off (vt)	uitzetten	['œʏtzɛtən]
speed	snelheid (de)	['snɛlhɛjt]
to exceed the speed limit	een snelheids-overtreding maken	[en 'snɛlhɛjts ɔvər'trediŋ 'makən]
to give a ticket	bekeuren	[bə'køren]
traffic lights	verkeerslicht (het)	[vər'kĕrs·lixt]
driver's license	rijbewijs (het)	['rɛj·bɛwɛjs]
grade crossing	overgang (de)	['ɔvərxaŋ]
intersection	kruispunt (het)	['krœʏs·pynt]
crosswalk	zebrapad (het)	['zɛbra·pat]
bend, curve	bocht (de)	[bɔxt]
pedestrian zone	voetgangerszone (de)	['vutxaŋərs·'zɔnə]

180. Traffic signs

rules of the road	verkeersregels	[vər'kĕrs·'rexəls]
road sign (traffic sign)	verkeersbord (het)	[vər'kĕrs·bort]
passing (overtaking)	inhalen (het)	['inhalən]
curve	bocht (de)	[bɔxt]
U-turn	U-bocht, kering (de)	[ju-bɔxt], ['kɛriŋ]

traffic circle	**Rotonde (de)**	[rɔ'tɔndə]
No entry	**Verboden richting**	[vər'bodən 'rixtiŋ]
No vehicles allowed	**Verboden toegang**	[vər'bodən 'tuxaŋ]
No passing	**Inhalen verboden**	['inhalən vər'bodən]
No parking	**Parkeerverbod**	['parkēr·vər'bɔt]
No stopping	**Verbod stil te staan**	[vər'bɔt 'stil tə stān]

dangerous bend	**Gevaarlijke bocht**	[xe'vārləkə bɔht]
steep descent	**Gevaarlijke daling**	[xe'vārləkə 'daliŋ]
one-way traffic	**Eenrichtingsweg**	[ēn'rixtiŋs·wɛx]
crosswalk	**Voetgangers**	['vutxaŋərs]
slippery road	**Slipgevaar**	['slipxəvār]
YIELD	**Voorrang verlenen**	['vōrraŋ vər'lenən]

PEOPLE. LIFE EVENTS

Life events

181. Holidays. Event

celebration, holiday	feest (het)	[fēst]
national day	nationale feestdag (de)	[natsjo'nalə 'fēstdax]
public holiday	feestdag (de)	['fēst·dax]
to commemorate (vt)	herdenken	['hɛrdɛŋkən]
event (happening)	gebeurtenis (de)	[xə'børtənis]
event (organized activity)	evenement (het)	[ɛvənə'mɛnt]
banquet (party)	banket (het)	[ban'ket]
reception (formal party)	receptie (de)	[re'sɛpsi]
feast	feestmaal (het)	['fēst·māl]
anniversary	verjaardag (de)	[vər'jār·dax]
jubilee	jubileum (het)	[jubi'lejum]
to celebrate (vt)	vieren	['virən]
New Year	Nieuwjaar (het)	[niu'jār]
Happy New Year!	Gelukkig Nieuwjaar!	[xə'lʉkəx niu'jār]
Santa Claus	Sinterklaas (de)	[sintər·'klās]
Christmas	Kerstfeest (het)	['kɛrstfēst]
Merry Christmas!	Vrolijk kerstfeest!	['vrɔlək 'kɛrstfēst]
Christmas tree	kerstboom (de)	['kɛrst·bōm]
fireworks (fireworks show)	vuurwerk (het)	['vūr·wɛrk]
wedding	bruiloft (de)	['brœyloft]
groom	bruidegom (de)	['brœydəxɔm]
bride	bruid (de)	['brœyd]
to invite (vt)	uitnodigen	['œytnodixən]
invitation card	uitnodigingskaart (de)	[œyt'nodixiŋs·kārt]
guest	gast (de)	[xast]
to visit	op bezoek gaan	[ɔp bə'zuk xān]
(~ your parents, etc.)		
to meet the guests	gasten verwelkomen	['xastən vər'wɛlkomən]
gift, present	geschenk, cadeau (het)	[xə'sxɛnk]
to give (sth as present)	geven	['xevən]
to receive gifts	geschenken ontvangen	[xə'sxɛnkən ɔnt'vaŋən]

bouquet (of flowers)	**boeket (het)**	[bu'kɛt]
congratulations	**felicitaties**	[felisi'tatsis]
to congratulate (vt)	**feliciteren**	[felisi'terən]
greeting card	**wenskaart (de)**	['wɛns·kārt]
to send a postcard	**een kaartje versturen**	[en 'kārtʃe vər'sturən]
to get a postcard	**een kaartje ontvangen**	[en 'kārtʃe ɔnt'vaŋen]
toast	**toast (de)**	[tɔst]
to offer (a drink, etc.)	**aanbieden**	[ām'bidən]
champagne	**champagne (de)**	[ʃʌm'panjə]
to enjoy oneself	**plezier hebben**	[plɛ'zir 'hɛbən]
merriment (gaiety)	**plezier (het)**	[plɛ'zir]
joy (emotion)	**vreugde (de)**	['vrøhdə]
dance	**dans (de)**	[dans]
to dance (vi, vt)	**dansen**	['dansən]
waltz	**wals (de)**	[wals]
tango	**tango (de)**	['tangɔ]

182. Funerals. Burial

cemetery	**kerkhof (het)**	['kɛrkhɔf]
grave, tomb	**graf (het)**	[xraf]
cross	**kruis (het)**	['krœɤs]
gravestone	**grafsteen (de)**	['xraf·stēn]
fence	**omheining (de)**	[ɔm'hɛjniŋ]
chapel	**kapel (de)**	[ka'pɛl]
death	**dood (de)**	[dōt]
to die (vi)	**sterven**	['stɛrvən]
the deceased	**overledene (de)**	[ɔvər'ledenə]
mourning	**rouw (de)**	['rau]
to bury (vt)	**begraven**	[bə'xravən]
funeral home	**begrafenis-onderneming (de)**	[bə'xrafenis ɔndər'nemiŋ]
funeral	**begrafenis (de)**	[bə'xrafənis]
wreath	**krans (de)**	[krans]
casket, coffin	**doodskist (de)**	['dōd·skist]
hearse	**lijkwagen (de)**	['lɛjk·waxən]
shroud	**lijkkleed (het)**	['lɛjk·klēt]
funeral procession	**begrafenisstoet (de)**	[bə'xrafenis·stut]
funerary urn	**urn (de)**	[jurn]
crematory	**crematorium (het)**	[krema'tɔrijum]
obituary	**overlijdensbericht (het)**	[ɔvər'lɛjdəns·bə'rixt]

| to cry (weep) | huilen | ['hœylən] |
| to sob (vi) | snikken | ['snikən] |

183. War. Soldiers

platoon	peloton (het)	[pelɔ'tɔn]
company	compagnie (de)	[kɔmpa'njɪ]
regiment	regiment (het)	[rexi'mɛnt]
army	leger (het)	['lexər]
division	divisie (de)	[di'vizi]

| section, squad | sectie (de) | ['sɛksi] |
| host (army) | troep (de) | [trup] |

| soldier | soldaat (de) | [sɔl'dāt] |
| officer | officier (de) | [ɔfi'sir] |

private	soldaat (de)	[sɔl'dāt]
sergeant	sergeant (de)	[sɛr'ʒant]
lieutenant	luitenant (de)	[lœytə'nant]
captain	kapitein (de)	[kapi'tɛjn]
major	majoor (de)	[ma'jōr]
colonel	kolonel (de)	[kɔlɔ'nɛl]
general	generaal (de)	[xenə'rāl]

sailor	matroos (de)	[ma'trōs]
captain	kapitein (de)	[kapi'tɛjn]
boatswain	bootsman (de)	['bōtsman]

artilleryman	artillerist (de)	[artile'rist]
paratrooper	valschermjager (de)	['valsxɛrm·'jaxər]
pilot	piloot (de)	[pi'lōt]
navigator	stuurman (de)	['stūrman]
mechanic	mecanicien (de)	[mekani'sjen]

pioneer (sapper)	sappeur (de)	[sa'pør]
parachutist	parachutist (de)	[paraʃu'tist]
reconnaissance scout	verkenner (de)	[vər'kenər]
sniper	scherpschutter (de)	['sxɛrp·sxʉtər]

patrol (group)	patrouille (de)	[pa'trujə]
to patrol (vt)	patrouilleren	[patru'jerən]
sentry, guard	wacht (de)	[waxt]

warrior	krijger (de)	['krɛjxə]
patriot	patriot (de)	[patri'ɔt]
hero	held (de)	[hɛlt]
heroine	heldin (de)	[hɛl'din]
traitor	verrader (de)	[və'radər]
to betray (vt)	verraden	[və'radən]

| deserter | deserteur (de) | [dezɛr'tør] |
| to desert (vi) | deserteren | [dezɛr'terən] |

mercenary	huurling (de)	['hʉrliŋ]
recruit	rekruut (de)	[rek'rʉt]
volunteer	vrijwilliger (de)	[vrɛj'wiləxər]

dead (n)	gedode (de)	[xə'dɔdə]
wounded (n)	gewonde (de)	[xə'wɔndə]
prisoner of war	krijgsgevangene (de)	['krɛjxs·xə'vaŋənə]

184. War. Military actions. Part 1

war	oorlog (de)	['ôrlɔx]
to be at war	oorlog voeren	['ôrlɔx 'vurən]
civil war	burgeroorlog (de)	['bʉrxər·'ôrlɔx]

treacherously (adv)	achterbaks	['axtərbaks]
declaration of war	oorlogsverklaring (de)	['ôrlɔxs·vər'klariŋ]
to declare (~ war)	verklaren	[vər'klarən]
aggression	agressie (de)	[ax'rɛsi]
to attack (invade)	aanvallen	['ânvalən]

to invade (vt)	binnenvallen	['binənvalən]
invader	invaller (de)	['invalə]
conqueror	veroveraar (de)	[və'rɔvərãr]

defense	verdediging (de)	[vər'dedəxiŋ]
to defend (a country, etc.)	verdedigen	[vər'dedixən]
to defend (against …)	zich verdedigen	[zih vər'dedixən]

enemy	vijand (de)	['vɛjant]
foe, adversary	tegenstander (de)	['texən·'standər]
enemy (as adj)	vijandelijk	[vɛ'jandələk]

| strategy | strategie (de) | [stratə'xi] |
| tactics | tactiek (de) | [tak'tik] |

order	order (de)	['ɔrdər]
command (order)	bevel (het)	[bə'vɛl]
to order (vt)	bevelen	[bə'velən]
mission	opdracht (de)	['ɔpdraxt]
secret (adj)	geheim	[xə'hɛjm]

battle	slag (de)	[slax]
battle	veldslag (de)	['vɛlt·slax]
combat	strijd (de)	[strɛjt]

| attack | aanval (de) | ['ânval] |
| charge (assault) | bestorming (de) | [bə'stɔrmiŋ] |

| to storm (vt) | bestormen | [bə'stɔrmən] |
| siege (to be under ~) | bezetting (de) | [bə'zɛtiŋ] |

| offensive (n) | aanval (de) | ['ānval] |
| to go on the offensive | in het offensief te gaan | [in ət ɔfɛn'sif te xān] |

| retreat | terugtrekking (de) | [te'rʉx·trɛkiŋ] |
| to retreat (vi) | zich terugtrekken | [zih tə'rʉxtrɛkən] |

| encirclement | omsingeling (de) | [ɔm'siŋəliŋ] |
| to encircle (vt) | omsingelen | [ɔm'siŋələn] |

bombing (by aircraft)	bombardement (het)	[bɔmbardə'mɛnt]
to drop a bomb	een bom gooien	[en bɔm 'xōjən]
to bomb (vt)	bombarderen	[bɔmbar'derən]
explosion	ontploffing (de)	[ɔnt'plɔfiŋ]

shot	schot (het)	[sxɔt]
to fire (~ a shot)	een schot lossen	[en sxɔt 'lɔsən]
firing (burst of ~)	schieten (het)	['sxitən]

to aim (to point a weapon)	mikken op	['mikən ɔp]
to point (a gun)	aanleggen	['ānlexən]
to hit (the target)	treffen	['trefən]

to sink (~ a ship)	zinken	['zinkən]
hole (in a ship)	kogelgat (het)	['kɔxəlxat]
to founder, to sink (vi)	zinken	['zinkən]

front (war ~)	front (het)	[frɔnt]
evacuation	evacuatie (de)	[ɛvakʉ'atsi]
to evacuate (vt)	evacueren	[ɛvakʉ'erən]
trench	loopgraaf (de)	['lōpxrāf]
barbwire	prikkeldraad (de)	['prikəl·drāt]
barrier (anti tank ~)	verdedigings-obstakel (het)	[vər'dedəhiŋ ɔp'stakəl]
watchtower	wachttoren (de)	['waxt·tɔrən]

military hospital	hospitaal (het)	['hɔspitāl]
to wound (vt)	verwonden	[vər'wɔndən]
wound	wond (de)	[wɔnt]
wounded (n)	gewonde (de)	[xə'wɔndə]
to be wounded	gewond raken	[xə'wɔnt 'rakən]
serious (wound)	ernstig	['ɛrnstəx]

185. War. Military actions. Part 2

| captivity | krijgs-gevangenschap (de) | ['krɛjxs xə'vaŋənsxap] |
| to take captive | krijgsgevangen nemen | ['krɛjxs·xə'vaŋən 'nemən] |

to be held captive	**krijgsgevangene zijn**	['krɛjxs·xə'vaŋənə zɛjn]
to be taken captive	**krijgsgevangen genomen worden**	['krɛjxs·xə'vaŋən xə'nɔmən 'wɔrdən]
concentration camp	**concentratiekamp (het)**	[kɔnsən'tratsi·kamp]
prisoner of war	**krijgsgevangene (de)**	['krɛjxs·xə'vaŋənə]
to escape (vi)	**vluchten**	['vlʉxtən]
to betray (vt)	**verraden**	[və'radən]
betrayer	**verrader (de)**	[və'radər]
betrayal	**verraad (het)**	[və'rāt]
to execute (by firing squad)	**fusilleren**	[fʉzi'jerən]
execution (by firing squad)	**executie (de)**	[ɛkse'kʉtsi]
equipment (military gear)	**uitrusting (de)**	['œytrystiŋ]
shoulder board	**schouderstuk (het)**	['sxaudər·'stʉk]
gas mask	**gasmasker (het)**	[xas·'maskər]
field radio	**portofoon (de)**	[pɔrtɔ'fōn]
cipher, code	**geheime code (de)**	[xə'hɛjmə 'kɔdə]
secrecy	**samenzwering (de)**	['samənzweriŋ]
password	**wachtwoord (het)**	['waxt·wōrt]
land mine	**mijn (de)**	[mɛjn]
to mine (road, etc.)	**ondermijnen**	['ɔndər'mɛjnən]
minefield	**mijnenveld (het)**	['mɛjnən·vɛlt]
air-raid warning	**luchtalarm (het)**	['lʉxt·a'larm]
alarm (alert signal)	**alarm (het)**	[a'larm]
signal	**signaal (het)**	[si'njāl]
signal flare	**vuurpijl (de)**	['vūr·pɛjl]
headquarters	**staf (de)**	['staf]
reconnaissance	**verkenning (de)**	[vər'keniŋ]
situation	**toestand (de)**	['tustant]
report	**rapport (het)**	[ra'pɔrt]
ambush	**hinderlaag (de)**	['hindər·lāx]
reinforcement (of army)	**versterking (de)**	[vər'stɛrkiŋ]
target	**doel (het)**	[dul]
proving ground	**proefterrein (het)**	['pruf·te'rɛjn]
military exercise	**manoeuvres**	[ma'nøvrɛs]
panic	**paniek (de)**	[pa'nik]
devastation	**verwoesting (de)**	[vər'wustiŋ]
destruction, ruins	**verwoestingen**	[vər'wustiŋən]
to destroy (vt)	**verwoesten**	[vər'wustən]
to survive (vi, vt)	**overleven**	[ɔvər'levən]
to disarm (vt)	**ontwapenen**	[ɔnt'wapənən]

to handle (~ a gun)	**behandelen**	[bə'handələn]
Attention!	**Geeft acht!**	[xĕft 'aht]
At ease!	**Op de plaats rust!**	[ɔp də plãts 'rʉst]
act of courage	**heldendaad (de)**	['hɛldən·dãt]
oath (vow)	**eed (de)**	[ĕd]
to swear (an oath)	**zweren**	['zwerən]
decoration (medal, etc.)	**decoratie (de)**	[dekɔ'ratsi]
to award (give medal to)	**onderscheiden**	['ɔndər'sxɛjdən]
medal	**medaille (de)**	[me'dajə]
order (e.g., ~ of Merit)	**orde (de)**	['ɔrdə]
victory	**overwinning (de)**	[ɔvər'winiŋ]
defeat	**verlies (het)**	[vər'lis]
armistice	**wapenstilstand (de)**	['wapən·'stilstant]
standard (battle flag)	**wimpel (de)**	['wimpəl]
glory (honor, fame)	**roem (de)**	[rum]
parade	**parade (de)**	[pa'radə]
to march (on parade)	**marcheren**	[mar'ʃerən]

186. Weapons

weapons	**wapens**	['wapəns]
firearms	**vuurwapens**	[vūr·'wapəns]
cold weapons (knives, etc.)	**koude wapens**	['kaudə 'wapəns]
chemical weapons	**chemische wapens**	['hemisə 'wapəns]
nuclear (adj)	**kern-, nucleair**	[kɛrn], [nʉkle'ɛr]
nuclear weapons	**kernwapens**	[kɛrn·'wapəns]
bomb	**bom (de)**	[bɔm]
atomic bomb	**atoombom (de)**	[a'tõm·bɔm]
pistol (gun)	**pistool (het)**	[pi'stõl]
rifle	**geweer (het)**	[xə'wĕr]
submachine gun	**machinepistool (het)**	[ma'ʃinə·pis'tõl]
machine gun	**machinegeweer (het)**	[ma'ʃinə·xə'wĕr]
muzzle	**loop (de)**	[lõp]
barrel	**loop (de)**	[lõp]
caliber	**kaliber (het)**	[ka'libər]
trigger	**trekker (de)**	['trɛkər]
sight (aiming device)	**korrel (de)**	['kɔrəl]
magazine	**magazijn (het)**	[maxa'zɛjn]
butt (shoulder stock)	**geweerkolf (de)**	[xə'wĕr·kɔlf]
hand grenade	**granaat (de)**	[xra'nãt]

explosive	explosieven	[ɛksplɔ'zivən]
bullet	kogel (de)	['koxəl]
cartridge	patroon (de)	[pa'trõn]
charge	lading (de)	['ladiŋ]
ammunition	ammunitie (de)	[amʉ'nitsi]

bomber (aircraft)	bommenwerper (de)	['bɔmən·'wɛrpər]
fighter	straaljager (de)	['strāl·'jaxər]
helicopter	helikopter (de)	[heli'kɔptər]

anti-aircraft gun	afweergeschut (het)	['afwēr·xəsxʉt]
tank	tank (de)	[tank]
tank gun	kanon (het)	[ka'nɔn]

artillery	artillerie (de)	[artile'ri]
gun (cannon, howitzer)	kanon (het)	[ka'nɔn]
to lay (a gun)	aanleggen	['ānlexən]

shell (projectile)	projectiel (het)	[prɔjek'til]
mortar bomb	mortiergranaat (de)	[mɔr'tir·xra'nāt]
mortar	mortier (de)	[mɔr'tir]
splinter (shell fragment)	granaatscherf (de)	[xra'nāt·'sxerf]

submarine	duikboot (de)	['dœʏk·bōt]
torpedo	torpedo (de)	[tɔr'pedɔ]
missile	raket (de)	[ra'kɛt]

to load (gun)	laden	['ladən]
to shoot (vi)	schieten	['sxitən]
to point at (the cannon)	richten op	['rixtən ɔp]
bayonet	bajonet (de)	[bajo'nɛt]

rapier	degen (de)	['dexən]
saber (e.g., cavalry ~)	sabel (de)	['sabəl]
spear (weapon)	speer (de)	[spēr]
bow	boog (de)	[bōx]
arrow	pijl (de)	[pɛjl]
musket	musket (de)	[mʉs'kɛt]
crossbow	kruisboog (de)	['krœʏs·bōx]

187. Ancient people

primitive (prehistoric)	primitief	[primi'tif]
prehistoric (adj)	voorhistorisch	['vōrhis'tɔris]
ancient (~ civilization)	eeuwenoude	[ēwə'naudə]

Stone Age	Steentijd (de)	['stēn·tɛjt]
Bronze Age	Bronstijd (de)	['brɔns·tɛjt]
Ice Age	IJstijd (de)	['ɛjs·tɛjt]
tribe	stam (de)	[stam]

cannibal	menseneter (de)	['mɛnsən·'ɛtər]
hunter	jager (de)	['jaxər]
to hunt (vi, vt)	jagen	['jaxən]
mammoth	mammoet (de)	[ma'mut]

cave	grot (de)	[xrɔt]
fire	vuur (het)	[vūr]
campfire	kampvuur (het)	['kampvūr]
cave painting	rotstekening (de)	['rɔts·tekəniŋ]

tool (e.g., stone ax)	werkinstrument (het)	['wɛrk·instru'mɛnt]
spear	speer (de)	[spēr]
stone ax	stenen bijl (de)	['stenən bɛjl]
to be at war	oorlog voeren	['ōrlɔx 'vurən]
to domesticate (vt)	temmen	['tɛmən]

idol	idool (het)	[i'dōl]
to worship (vt)	aanbidden	[ām'bidən]
superstition	bijgeloof (het)	['bɛjxəlōf]
rite	ritueel (het)	[ritu'ēl]

evolution	evolutie (de)	[ɛvo'lutsi]
development	ontwikkeling (de)	[ɔnt'wikəliŋ]
disappearance (extinction)	verdwijning (de)	[vərd'wɛjniŋ]
to adapt oneself	zich aanpassen	[zix 'ānpasən]

archeology	archeologie (de)	[arheɔlɔ'xi]
archeologist	archeoloog (de)	[arheɔ'lōx]
archeological (adj)	archeologisch	[arheɔ'lɔxis]

excavation site	opgravingsplaats (de)	['ɔpxraviŋs·plāts]
excavations	opgravingen	['ɔpxraviŋən]
find (object)	vondst (de)	[vɔntst]
fragment	fragment (het)	[frax'mɛnt]

188. Middle Ages

people (ethnic group)	volk (het)	[vɔlk]
peoples	volkeren	['vɔlkərən]
tribe	stam (de)	[stam]
tribes	stammen	['stamən]

barbarians	barbaren	[bar'barən]
Gauls	Galliërs	['xaliers]
Goths	Goten	['xɔtən]
Slavs	Slaven	['slavən]
Vikings	Vikings	['vikiŋs]

| Romans | Romeinen | [rɔ'mɛjnən] |
| Roman (adj) | Romeins | [rɔ'mɛjns] |

Byzantines	**Byzantijnen**	[bizan'tɛjnən]
Byzantium	**Byzantium (het)**	[bi'zantijum]
Byzantine (adj)	**Byzantijns**	[bizan'tɛjns]
emperor	**keizer (de)**	['kɛjzər]
leader, chief (tribal ~)	**opperhoofd (het)**	['ɔpərhõft]
powerful (~ king)	**machtig**	['mahtəx]
king	**koning (de)**	['kɔniŋ]
ruler (sovereign)	**heerser (de)**	['hẽrsər]
knight	**ridder (de)**	['ridər]
feudal lord	**feodaal (de)**	[feɔ'dãl]
feudal (adj)	**feodaal**	[feɔ'dãl]
vassal	**vazal (de)**	[va'zal]
duke	**hertog (de)**	['hɛrtɔx]
earl	**graaf (de)**	[xrãf]
baron	**baron (de)**	[ba'rɔn]
bishop	**bisschop (de)**	['bisxɔp]
armor	**harnas (het)**	['harnas]
shield	**schild (het)**	[sxilt]
sword	**zwaard (het)**	[zwãrt]
visor	**vizier (het)**	[vi'zir]
chainmail	**maliënkolder (de)**	['malien·'kɔldər]
Crusade	**kruistocht (de)**	['krœys·tɔxt]
crusader	**kruisvaarder (de)**	['krœys·'vãrdər]
territory	**gebied (het)**	[xə'bit]
to attack (invade)	**aanvallen**	['ãnvalən]
to conquer (vt)	**veroveren**	[və'rɔvərən]
to occupy (invade)	**innemen**	['innemən]
siege (to be under ~)	**bezetting (de)**	[bə'zɛtiŋ]
besieged (adj)	**belegerd**	[bə'lexert]
to besiege (vt)	**belegeren**	[bə'lexərən]
inquisition	**inquisitie (de)**	[inkvi'zitsi]
inquisitor	**inquisiteur (de)**	[inkvizi'tør]
torture	**foltering (de)**	['foltəriŋ]
cruel (adj)	**wreed**	[wrẽt]
heretic	**ketter (de)**	['kɛtər]
heresy	**ketterij (de)**	[kɛtə'rɛj]
seafaring	**zeevaart (de)**	['zẽ·vãrt]
pirate	**piraat (de)**	[pi'rãt]
piracy	**piraterij (de)**	[piratə'rɛj]
boarding (attack)	**enteren (het)**	['ɛntərən]
loot, booty	**buit (de)**	['bœyt]
treasures	**schatten**	['sxatən]
discovery	**ontdekking (de)**	[ɔn'dɛkiŋ]

| to discover (new land, etc.) | ontdekken | [ɔn'dɛkən] |
| expedition | expeditie (de) | [ɛkspe'ditsi] |

musketeer	musketier (de)	[mʉskə'tir]
cardinal	kardinaal (de)	[kardi'nāl]
heraldry	heraldiek (de)	[hɛral'dik]
heraldic (adj)	heraldisch	[hɛ'raldis]

189. Leader. Chief. Authorities

king	koning (de)	['kɔniŋ]
queen	koningin (de)	[kɔniŋ'in]
royal (adj)	koninklijk	['kɔninklək]
kingdom	koninkrijk (het)	['kɔninkrɛjk]

| prince | prins (de) | [prins] |
| princess | prinses (de) | [prin'sɛs] |

president	president (de)	[prezi'dɛnt]
vice-president	vicepresident (de)	['visə·prezi'dɛnt]
senator	senator (de)	[se'natɔr]

monarch	monarch (de)	[mɔ'narx]
ruler (sovereign)	heerser (de)	['hērsər]
dictator	dictator (de)	[dik'tatɔr]
tyrant	tiran (de)	[ti'ran]
magnate	magnaat (de)	[max'nāt]

director	directeur (de)	[dirɛk'tør]
chief	chef (de)	[ʃɛf]
manager (director)	beheerder (de)	[bə'hērdər]
boss	baas (de)	[bās]
owner	eigenaar (de)	['ɛjxənār]

leader	leider (de)	['lɛjdər]
head (~ of delegation)	hoofd (het)	[hōft]
authorities	autoriteiten	[autɔri'tɛjtən]
superiors	superieuren	[sʉpə'rørən]

governor	gouverneur (de)	[xuvɛr'nør]
consul	consul (de)	['kɔnsʉl]
diplomat	diplomaat (de)	[diplɔ'māt]

| mayor | burgemeester (de) | [bʉrxə·'mēstər] |
| sheriff | sheriff (de) | ['ʃerif] |

emperor	keizer (de)	['kɛjzər]
tsar, czar	tsaar (de)	[tsār]
pharaoh	farao (de)	['faraɔ]
khan	kan (de)	[kan]

190. Road. Way. Directions

road	weg (de)	[wɛx]
way (direction)	route (de)	['rutə]
freeway	autoweg (de)	['autɔwɛx]
highway	snelweg (de)	['snɛlwɛx]
interstate	rijksweg (de)	['rɛjks·wɛx]
main road	hoofdweg (de)	['hōft·wɛx]
dirt road	landweg (de)	['land·wɛx]
pathway	pad (het)	[pat]
footpath (troddenpath)	paadje (het)	['pādjə]
Where?	Waar?	[wār]
Where (to)?	Waarheen?	[wār'hēn]
From where?	Waarvandaan?	[ʋār·van'dān]
direction (way)	richting (de)	['rixtiŋ]
to point (~ the way)	aanwijzen	['ānwɛjzən]
to the left	naar links	[nār 'links]
to the right	naar rechts	[nār 'rɛxts]
straight ahead (adv)	rechtdoor	[rɛx'dōr]
back (e.g., to turn ~)	terug	[te'rʉx]
bend, curve	bocht (de)	[bɔxt]
to turn (e.g., ~ left)	afslaan	['afslān]
to make a U-turn	U-bocht maken	[ju-bɔxt 'makən]
to be visible (mountains, castle, etc.)	zichtbaar worden	['zixtbār 'wordən]
to appear (come into view)	verschijnen	[vər'sxɛjnən]
stop, halt (e.g., during a trip)	stop (de)	[stɔp]
to rest, to pause (vi)	zich verpozen	[zix vər'pozən]
rest (pause)	rust (de)	[rʉst]
to lose one's way	verdwalen (de weg kwijt zijn)	[vərd'walən]
to lead to ... (ab. road)	leiden naar ...	['lɛjdən nār]
to come out (e.g., on the highway)	bereiken	[bə'rɛjkən]
stretch (of road)	deel (het)	[dēl]
asphalt	asfalt (het)	['asfalt]
curb	trottoirband (de)	[trɔtu'ar·bant]
ditch	greppel (de)	['xrepəl]
manhole	putdeksel (het)	[pʉt'dɛksəl]

| roadside (shoulder) | vluchtstrook (de) | ['vlʉxt·strɔk] |
| pit, pothole | kuil (de) | ['kœyl] |

| to go (on foot) | gaan | [xān] |
| to pass (overtake) | inhalen | ['inhalən] |

| step (footstep) | stap (de) | [stap] |
| on foot (adv) | te voet | [tə 'vut] |

to block (road)	blokkeren (de weg ~)	[blɔ'kerən]
boom gate	slagboom (de)	['slaxbōm]
dead end	doodlopende straat (de)	[dōd'lɔpəndə strāt]

191. Breaking the law. Criminals. Part 1

bandit	bandiet (de)	[ban'dit]
crime	misdaad (de)	['misdāt]
criminal (person)	misdadiger (de)	[mis'dadixər]

thief	dief (de)	[dif]
to steal (vi, vt)	stelen	['stelən]
stealing (larceny)	stelen (de)	['stelən]
theft	diefstal (de)	['difstal]

to kidnap (vt)	kidnappen	[kid'nɛpən]
kidnapping	kidnapping (de)	[kid'nɛpiŋ]
kidnapper	kidnapper (de)	[kid'nɛpər]

| ransom | losgeld (het) | ['lɔshəlt] |
| to demand ransom | eisen losgeld | ['ɛjsən 'lɔshəlt] |

to rob (vt)	overvallen	[ɔvər'valən]
robbery	overval (de)	[ɔvər'val]
robber	overvaller (de)	[ɔvər'valər]

to extort (vt)	afpersen	['afpɛrsən]
extortionist	afperser (de)	['afpɛrsər]
extortion	afpersing (de)	['afpɛrsiŋ]

to murder, to kill	vermoorden	[vər'mōrdən]
murder	moord (de)	[mōrt]
murderer	moordenaar (de)	['mōrdənār]

gunshot	schot (het)	[sxɔt]
to fire (~ a shot)	een schot lossen	[en sxɔt 'lɔsən]
to shoot to death	neerschieten	[nēr'sxitən]
to shoot (vi)	schieten	['sxitən]
shooting	schieten (het)	['sxitən]
incident (fight, etc.)	ongeluk (het)	['ɔnxəlʉk]
fight, brawl	gevecht (het)	[xə'vɛxt]

Help!	Help!	[hɛlp]
victim	slachtoffer (het)	['slaxtɔfər]
to damage (vt)	beschadigen	[bə'sxadəxən]
damage	schade (de)	['sxadə]
dead body, corpse	lijk (het)	[lɛjk]
grave (~ crime)	zwaar	[zwãr]
to attack (vt)	aanvallen	['ãnvalən]
to beat (to hit)	slaan	[slãn]
to beat up	in elkaar slaan	[in ɛl'kãr slãn]
to take (rob of sth)	ontnemen	[ɔnt'nemən]
to stab to death	steken	['stekən]
to maim (vt)	verminken	[vər'minkən]
to wound (vt)	verwonden	[vər'wɔndən]
blackmail	chantage (de)	[ʃʌn'taʒə]
to blackmail (vt)	chanteren	[ʃʌn'terən]
blackmailer	chanteur (de)	[ʃʌn'tør]
protection racket	afpersing (de)	['afpɛrsiŋ]
racketeer	afperser (de)	['afpɛrsər]
gangster	gangster (de)	['xɛŋstər]
mafia, Mob	maffia (de)	['mafia]
pickpocket	kruimeldief (de)	['krœymɛldif]
burglar	inbreker (de)	['inbrekər]
smuggling	smokkelen (het)	['smɔkələn]
smuggler	smokkelaar (de)	['smɔkəlãr]
forgery	namaak (de)	['namãk]
to forge (counterfeit)	namaken	['namakən]
fake (forged)	vals, namaak-	[vals], ['namãk]

192. Breaking the law. Criminals. Part 2

rape	verkrachting (de)	[vər'kraxtiŋ]
to rape (vt)	verkrachten	[vər'kraxtən]
rapist	verkrachter (de)	[vər'kraxtər]
maniac	maniak (de)	[mani'ak]
prostitute (fem.)	prostituee (de)	[prɔstitʉ'ē]
prostitution	prostitutie (de)	[prɔsti'tʉtsi]
pimp	pooier (de)	['põjər]
drug addict	drugsverslaafde (de)	['drʉks·vər'slãfdə]
drug dealer	drugshandelaar (de)	['drʉks·'handəlãr]
to blow up (bomb)	opblazen	['ɔpblazən]
explosion	explosie (de)	[ɛks'plɔzi]

to set fire	**in brand steken**	[in brant 'stekən]
arsonist	**brandstichter (de)**	['brant·stixtər]
terrorism	**terrorisme (het)**	[tɛrɔ'rismə]
terrorist	**terrorist (de)**	[tɛrɔ'rist]
hostage	**gijzelaar (de)**	['xɛjzəlãr]
to swindle (deceive)	**bedriegen**	[bə'drixən]
swindle, deception	**bedrog (het)**	[bə'drɔx]
swindler	**oplichter (de)**	['ɔplixtər]
to bribe (vt)	**omkopen**	[ɔmkɔpən]
bribery	**omkoperij (de)**	[ɔmkɔpərɛj]
bribe	**smeergeld (het)**	['smẽr·xɛlt]
poison	**vergif (het)**	[vər'xif]
to poison (vt)	**vergiftigen**	[vər'xiftixən]
to poison oneself	**vergif innemen**	[vər'xif 'innemən]
suicide (act)	**zelfmoord (de)**	['zɛlf·mõrt]
suicide (person)	**zelfmoordenaar (de)**	['zɛlf·mõrdə'nãr]
to threaten (vt)	**bedreigen**	[bə'drɛjxən]
threat	**bedreiging (de)**	[bə'drɛjxiŋ]
to make an attempt	**een aanslag plegen**	[en 'ãnslax 'plexən]
attempt (attack)	**aanslag (de)**	['ãnslax]
to steal (a car)	**stelen**	['stelən]
to hijack (a plane)	**kapen**	['kapən]
revenge	**wraak (de)**	[wrãk]
to avenge (get revenge)	**wreken**	['wrekən]
to torture (vt)	**martelen**	['martələn]
torture	**foltering (de)**	['foltəriŋ]
to torment (vt)	**folteren**	['foltərən]
pirate	**piraat (de)**	[pi'rãt]
hooligan	**straatschender (de)**	['strãt·sxəndə]
armed (adj)	**gewapend**	[xə'wapənt]
violence	**geweld (het)**	[xə'wɛlt]
illegal (unlawful)	**onwettig**	[ɔn'wɛtəx]
spying (espionage)	**spionage (de)**	[spijo'naʒə]
to spy (vi)	**spioneren**	[spijo'nerən]

193. Police. Law. Part 1

justice	**justitie (de)**	[jus'titsi]
court (see you in ~)	**gerechtshof (het)**	[xe'rɛhtshof]

judge	rechter (de)	['rɛxtər]
jurors	jury (de)	['ʒʉri]
jury trial	juryrechtspraak (de)	['ʒʉri·'rɛxtsprāk]
to judge (vt)	berechten	[bə'rɛxtən]

lawyer, attorney	advocaat (de)	[atvɔ'kāt]
defendant	beklaagde (de)	[bə'klāxdə]
dock	beklaagdenbank (de)	[bə'klāxdən·bank]

| charge | beschuldiging (de) | [bə'sxʉldəxiŋ] |
| accused | beschuldigde (de) | [bə'sxʉldəxdə] |

| sentence | vonnis (het) | ['vɔnis] |
| to sentence (vt) | veroordelen | [və'rōrdələn] |

guilty (culprit)	schuldige (de)	['sxʉldixə]
to punish (vt)	straffen	['strafən]
punishment	bestraffing (de)	[bə'strafiŋ]

fine (penalty)	boete (de)	['butə]
life imprisonment	levenslange opsluiting (de)	['levənslaŋə 'ɔpslœytiŋ]
death penalty	doodstraf (de)	['dōd·straf]
electric chair	elektrische stoel (de)	[ɛ'lɛktrisə stul]
gallows	schavot (het)	[sxa'vɔt]

| to execute (vt) | executeren | [ɛksekʉ'terən] |
| execution | executie (de) | [ɛkse'kʉtsi] |

| prison, jail | gevangenis (de) | [xə'vaŋənis] |
| cell | cel (de) | [sɛl] |

escort	konvooi (het)	[kɔn'vōj]
prison guard	gevangenisbewaker (de)	[xə'vaŋənis·bə'wakər]
prisoner	gedetineerde (de)	[xədeti'nērdə]

| handcuffs | handboeien | ['hant·bujən] |
| to handcuff (vt) | handboeien omdoen | ['hantbujən 'ɔmdun] |

prison break	ontsnapping (de)	[ɔnt'snapiŋ]
to break out (vi)	ontsnappen	[ɔnt'snapən]
to disappear (vi)	verdwijnen	[vərd'wɛjnən]
to release (from prison)	vrijlaten	['vrɛjlatən]
amnesty	amnestie (de)	[amnɛs'ti]

police	politie (de)	[pɔ'litsi]
police officer	politieagent (de)	[pɔ'litsi·a'xɛnt]
police station	politiebureau (het)	[pɔ'litsi·bʉ'rɔ]
billy club	knuppel (de)	['knʉpəl]
bullhorn	megafoon (de)	[mexa'fōn]
patrol car	patrouilleerwagen (de)	[patru'jēr·'waxən]
siren	sirene (de)	[si'renə]

to turn on the siren	de sirene aansteken	[də si'renə 'ānstekən]
siren call	geloei (het)	[xə'lui
	van de sirene	van də si'renə]

crime scene	plaats delict (de)	[plāts dɛ'likt]
witness	getuige (de)	[xə'tœyxə]
freedom	vrijheid (de)	['vrɛjhɛjt]
accomplice	handlanger (de)	['hantlaŋər]
to flee (vi)	ontvluchten	[ɔn'flʉxtən]
trace (to leave a ~)	spoor (het)	[spōr]

194. Police. Law. Part 2

search (investigation)	opsporing (de)	['ɔpspɔriŋ]
to look for ...	opsporen	['ɔpspɔrən]
suspicion	verdenking (de)	[vər'dɛnkiŋ]
suspicious (e.g., ~ vehicle)	verdacht	[vər'daxt]
to stop (cause to halt)	aanhouden	['ānhaudən]
to detain (keep in custody)	tegenhouden	['texən·'haudən]

case (lawsuit)	strafzaak (de)	['straf·zāk]
investigation	onderzoek (het)	['ɔndərzuk]
detective	detective (de)	[de'tɛktif]
investigator	onderzoeksrechter (de)	['ɔndərzuks 'rɛxtər]
hypothesis	versie (de)	['vɛrsi]

motive	motief (het)	[mɔ'tif]
interrogation	verhoor (het)	[vər'hōr]
to interrogate (vt)	ondervragen	['ɔndər'vraxən]
to question	ondervragen	['ɔndər'vraxən]
(~ neighbors, etc.)		
check (identity ~)	controle (de)	[kɔn'trɔlə]

round-up	razzia (de)	['razia]
search (~ warrant)	huiszoeking (de)	['hœys·'zukiŋ]
chase (pursuit)	achtervolging (de)	['axtərvɔlxiŋ]
to pursue, to chase	achtervolgen	['axtərvɔlxən]
to track (a criminal)	opsporen	['ɔpspɔrən]

arrest	arrest (het)	[a'rɛst]
to arrest (sb)	arresteren	[arɛ'sterən]
to catch (thief, etc.)	vangen, aanhouden	['vaŋən], [ān'haudən]
capture	aanhouding (de)	['ānhaudiŋ]

document	document (het)	[dɔkʉ'mɛnt]
proof (evidence)	bewijs (het)	[bə'wɛjs]
to prove (vt)	bewijzen	[bə'wɛjzən]
footprint	voetspoor (het)	['vutspōr]
fingerprints	vingerafdrukken	['viŋər·'afdrʉkən]
piece of evidence	bewijs (het)	[bə'wɛjs]

alibi	**alibi (het)**	['alibi]
innocent (not guilty)	**onschuldig**	[ɔn'sxʉldəx]
injustice	**onrecht (het)**	['ɔnrɛxt]
unjust, unfair (adj)	**onrechtvaardig**	['ɔnrɛxt 'vārdəx]

criminal (adj)	**crimineel**	[krimi'nēl]
to confiscate (vt)	**confisqueren**	[kɔnfi'skerən]
drug (illegal substance)	**drug (de)**	[drʉx]
weapon, gun	**wapen (het)**	['wapən]
to disarm (vt)	**ontwapenen**	[ɔnt'wapənən]
to order (command)	**bevelen**	[bə'velən]
to disappear (vi)	**verdwijnen**	[vərd'wɛjnən]

law	**wet (de)**	[wɛt]
legal, lawful (adj)	**wettelijk**	['wɛtələk]
illegal, illicit (adj)	**onwettelijk**	[ɔn'wɛtələk]

| responsibility (blame) | **verantwoordelijk-heid (de)** | [vərant·'wōrdələk 'hɛjt] |
| responsible (adj) | **verantwoordelijk** | [vərant·'wōrdələk] |

NATURE

The Earth. Part 1

195. Outer space

space	kosmos (de)	['kɔsmɔs]
space (as adj)	kosmisch	['kɔsmis]
outer space	kosmische ruimte (de)	['kɔsmisə 'rœʏmtə]
world	wereld (de)	['werəlt]
universe	heelal (het)	[hē'lal]
galaxy	sterrenstelsel (het)	['stɛrən·'stɛlsəl]
star	ster (de)	[stɛr]
constellation	sterrenbeeld (het)	['stɛrən·bēlt]
planet	planeet (de)	[pla'nēt]
satellite	satelliet (de)	[satə'lit]
meteorite	meteoriet (de)	[meteɔ'rit]
comet	komeet (de)	[kɔ'mēt]
asteroid	asteroïde (de)	[aste'rɔidə]
orbit	baan (de)	[bān]
to revolve	draaien	['drājən]
(~ around the Earth)		
atmosphere	atmosfeer (de)	[atmɔ'sfēr]
the Sun	Zon (de)	[zɔn]
solar system	zonnestelsel (het)	['zɔnə·stɛlsəl]
solar eclipse	zonsverduistering (de)	['zɔns·vər'dœʏsteriŋ]
the Earth	Aarde (de)	['ārdə]
the Moon	Maan (de)	[mān]
Mars	Mars (de)	[mars]
Venus	Venus (de)	['venʉs]
Jupiter	Jupiter (de)	[jupi'tɛr]
Saturn	Saturnus (de)	[sa'tʉrnʉs]
Mercury	Mercurius (de)	[mər'kʉrijus]
Uranus	Uranus (de)	[u'ranʉs]
Neptune	Neptunus (de)	[nep'tʉnʉs]
Pluto	Pluto (de)	['plʉtɔ]
Milky Way	Melkweg (de)	['mɛlk·wɛx]

| Great Bear (Ursa Major) | **Grote Beer (de)** | ['xrɔtə bĕr] |
| North Star | **Poolster (de)** | ['pōlstər] |

Martian	**marsmannetje (het)**	['mars·'manɛtʃə]
extraterrestrial (n)	**buitenaards wezen (het)**	['bœytən·ārts 'wezən]
alien	**bovenaards (het)**	['bɔvən·ārts]
flying saucer	**vliegende schotel (de)**	['vlixəndə 'sxɔtəl]

spaceship	**ruimtevaartuig (het)**	['rœymtə·'vārtœyx]
space station	**ruimtestation (het)**	['rœymtə·sta'tsjɔn]
blast-off	**start (de)**	[start]

engine	**motor (de)**	['mɔtɔr]
nozzle	**straalpijp (de)**	['strāl·pɛjp]
fuel	**brandstof (de)**	['brandstɔf]

cockpit, flight deck	**cabine (de)**	[ka'binə]
antenna	**antenne (de)**	[an'tɛnə]
porthole	**patrijspoort (de)**	[pa'trɛjs·pōrt]
solar panel	**zonnebatterij (de)**	['zɔnə·batə'rɛj]
spacesuit	**ruimtepak (het)**	['rœymtə·pak]

| weightlessness | **gewichtloosheid (de)** | [xə'wixtlō'shɛjt] |
| oxygen | **zuurstof (de)** | ['zūrstɔf] |

| docking (in space) | **koppeling (de)** | ['kɔpəliŋ] |
| to dock (vi, vt) | **koppeling maken** | ['kɔpəliŋ 'makən] |

observatory	**observatorium (het)**	[ɔbsərva'tɔrijum]
telescope	**telescoop (de)**	[telə'skōp]
to observe (vt)	**waarnemen**	['wārnemən]
to explore (vt)	**exploreren**	[ɛksplɔ'rerən]

196. The Earth

the Earth	**Aarde (de)**	['ārdə]
the globe (the Earth)	**aardbol (de)**	['ārd·bɔl]
planet	**planeet (de)**	[pla'nēt]

atmosphere	**atmosfeer (de)**	[atmɔ'sfēr]
geography	**aardrijkskunde (de)**	['ārdrɛjkskʉndə]
nature	**natuur (de)**	[na'tūr]

globe (table ~)	**wereldbol (de)**	['werəld·bɔl]
map	**kaart (de)**	[kārt]
atlas	**atlas (de)**	['atlas]

Europe	**Europa (het)**	[ø'rɔpa]
Asia	**Azië (het)**	['āzijə]
Africa	**Afrika (het)**	['afrika]

Australia	Australië (het)	[ɔu'straliə]
America	Amerika (het)	[a'merika]
North America	Noord-Amerika (het)	[nõrd-a'merika]
South America	Zuid-Amerika (het)	['zœyd-a'merika]
Antarctica	Antarctica (het)	[an'tarktika]
the Arctic	Arctis (de)	['arktis]

197. Cardinal directions

north	noorden (het)	['nõrdən]
to the north	naar het noorden	[nãr ət 'nõrdən]
in the north	in het noorden	[in ət 'nõrdən]
northern (adj)	noordelijk	['nõrdələk]
south	zuiden (het)	['zœydən]
to the south	naar het zuiden	[nãr ət zœydən]
in the south	in het zuiden	[in ət 'zœydən]
southern (adj)	zuidelijk	['zœydələk]
west	westen (het)	['wɛstən]
to the west	naar het westen	[nãr ət 'wɛstən]
in the west	in het westen	[in ət 'wɛstən]
western (adj)	westelijk	['wɛstələk]
east	oosten (het)	['õstən]
to the east	naar het oosten	[nãr ət 'õstən]
in the east	in het oosten	[in ət 'õstən]
eastern (adj)	oostelijk	['õstələk]

198. Sea. Ocean

sea	zee (de)	[zẽ]
ocean	oceaan (de)	[ɔse'ãn]
gulf (bay)	golf (de)	[xɔlf]
straits	straat (de)	[strãt]
land (solid ground)	grond (de)	['xrɔnt]
continent (mainland)	continent (het)	[kɔnti'nɛnt]
island	eiland (het)	['ɛjlant]
peninsula	schiereiland (het)	['sxir·ɛjlant]
archipelago	archipel (de)	[arxipɛl]
bay, cove	baai, bocht (de)	[bãj], [bɔxt]
harbor	haven (de)	['havən]
lagoon	lagune (de)	[la'xʉnə]
cape	kaap (de)	[kãp]
atoll	atol (de)	[a'tɔl]

reef	rif (het)	[rif]
coral	koraal (het)	[kɔ'rāl]
coral reef	koraalrif (het)	[kɔ'rāl·rif]

deep (adj)	diep	[dip]
depth (deep water)	diepte (de)	['diptə]
abyss	diepzee (de)	[dip·zē]
trench (e.g., Mariana ~)	trog (de)	[trɔx]

current (Ocean ~)	stroming (de)	['strɔmiŋ]
to surround (bathe)	omspoelen	['ɔmspulən]

shore	oever (de)	['uvər]
coast	kust (de)	[kʉst]

flow (flood tide)	vloed (de)	['vlut]
ebb (ebb tide)	eb (de)	[ɛb]
shoal	ondiepte (de)	[ɔn'diptə]
bottom (~ of the sea)	bodem (de)	['bɔdəm]
wave	golf (de)	[xɔlf]
crest (~ of a wave)	golfkam (de)	['xɔlfkam]
spume (sea foam)	schuim (het)	['sxœʏm]

storm (sea storm)	storm (de)	[stɔrm]
hurricane	orkaan (de)	[ɔr'kān]
tsunami	tsunami (de)	[tsʉ'nami]
calm (dead ~)	windstilte (de)	['wind·stiltə]
quiet, calm (adj)	kalm	[kalm]

pole	pool (de)	[pōl]
polar (adj)	polair	[pɔ'lɛr]

latitude	breedtegraad (de)	['brētə·xrāt]
longitude	lengtegraad (de)	['lɛŋtə·xrāt]
parallel	parallel (de)	[para'lɛl]
equator	evenaar (de)	['ɛvənār]

sky	hemel (de)	['heməl]
horizon	horizon (de)	['hɔrizɔn]
air	lucht (de)	[lʉxt]

lighthouse	vuurtoren (de)	['vūr·tɔrən]
to dive (vi)	duiken	['dœʏkən]
to sink (ab. boat)	zinken	['zinkən]
treasures	schatten	['sxatən]

199. Seas' and Oceans' names

Atlantic Ocean	Atlantische Oceaan (de)	[at'lantisə ɔse'ān]
Indian Ocean	Indische Oceaan (de)	['indisə ɔse'ān]

Pacific Ocean	**Stille Oceaan (de)**	['stilə ɔse'ān]
Arctic Ocean	**Noordelijke IJszee (de)**	['nōrdələkə 'ɛjs·zē]
Black Sea	**Zwarte Zee (de)**	['zwartə zē]
Red Sea	**Rode Zee (de)**	['rɔdə zē]
Yellow Sea	**Gele Zee (de)**	['xelə zē]
White Sea	**Witte Zee (de)**	['witə zē]
Caspian Sea	**Kaspische Zee (de)**	['kaspisə zē]
Dead Sea	**Dode Zee (de)**	['dɔdə zē]
Mediterranean Sea	**Middellandse Zee (de)**	['midəlandsə zē]
Aegean Sea	**Egeïsche Zee (de)**	[ɛ'xejsə zē]
Adriatic Sea	**Adriatische Zee (de)**	[adri'atisə zē]
Arabian Sea	**Arabische Zee (de)**	[a'rabisə zē]
Sea of Japan	**Japanse Zee (de)**	[ja'pansə zē]
Bering Sea	**Beringzee (de)**	['beriŋ·zē]
South China Sea	**Zuid-Chinese Zee (de)**	['zœyd-ʃi'nesə zē]
Coral Sea	**Koraalzee (de)**	[kɔ'rāl·zē]
Tasman Sea	**Tasmanzee (de)**	['tasman·zē]
Caribbean Sea	**Caribische Zee (de)**	[ka'ribisə zē]
Barents Sea	**Barentszzee (de)**	['barənts·zē]
Kara Sea	**Karische Zee (de)**	['karisə zē]
North Sea	**Noordzee (de)**	['nōrd·zē]
Baltic Sea	**Baltische Zee (de)**	['baltisə zē]
Norwegian Sea	**Noorse Zee (de)**	['nōrsə zē]

200. Mountains

mountain	**berg (de)**	[bɛrx]
mountain range	**bergketen (de)**	['bɛrx·'ketən]
mountain ridge	**gebergte (het)**	[xə'bɛrxtə]
summit, top	**bergtop (de)**	['bɛrx·tɔp]
peak	**bergpiek (de)**	['bɛrx·pik]
foot (~ of the mountain)	**voet (de)**	[vut]
slope (mountainside)	**helling (de)**	['heliŋ]
volcano	**vulkaan (de)**	[vʉl'kān]
active volcano	**actieve vulkaan (de)**	[ak'tivə vʉl'kān]
dormant volcano	**uitgedoofde vulkaan (de)**	['œytxədōfdə vyl'kān]
eruption	**uitbarsting (de)**	['œytbarstiŋ]
crater	**krater (de)**	['kratər]
magma	**magma (het)**	['maxma]
lava	**lava (de)**	['lava]

molten (~ lava)	gloeiend	['xlʉjənt]
canyon	kloof (de)	[klōf]
gorge	bergkloof (de)	['bɛrx·klōf]
crevice	spleet (de)	[splet]
abyss (chasm)	afgrond (de)	['afxrɔnt]
pass, col	bergpas (de)	['bɛrx·pas]
plateau	plateau (het)	[pla'tɔ]
cliff	klip (de)	[klip]
hill	heuvel (de)	['høvəl]
glacier	gletsjer (de)	['xletʃər]
waterfall	waterval (de)	['watər·val]
geyser	geiser (de)	['xɛjzər]
lake	meer (het)	[mẽr]
plain	vlakte (de)	['vlaktə]
landscape	landschap (het)	['landsxap]
echo	echo (de)	['ɛxɔ]
alpinist	alpinist (de)	[alpi'nist]
rock climber	bergbeklimmer (de)	['bɛrx·bə'klimər]
to conquer (in climbing)	trotseren	[trɔ'tserən]
climb (an easy ~)	beklimming (de)	[bə'klimiŋ]

201. Mountains names

The Alps	Alpen (de)	['alpən]
Mont Blanc	Mont Blanc (de)	[mɔn blan]
The Pyrenees	Pyreneeën (de)	[pirə'nẽən]
The Carpathians	Karpaten (de)	[kar'patən]
The Ural Mountains	Oeralgebergte (het)	[ural·xə'bɛrxtə]
The Caucasus Mountains	Kaukasus (de)	[kau'kazʉs]
Mount Elbrus	Elbroes (de)	[ɛlb'rus]
The Altai Mountains	Altaj (de)	[al'taj]
The Tian Shan	Tiensjan (de)	[ti'ençan]
The Pamir Mountains	Pamir (de)	[pa'mir]
The Himalayas	Himalaya (de)	[hima'laja]
Mount Everest	Everest (de)	['ɛverɛst]
The Andes	Andes (de)	['andɛs]
Mount Kilimanjaro	Kilimanjaro (de)	[kiliman'dʒarɔ]

202. Rivers

| river | rivier (de) | [ri'vir] |
| spring (natural source) | bron (de) | [brɔn] |

riverbed (river channel)	**rivierbedding (de)**	[ri'vir·'bɛdiŋ]
basin (river valley)	**rivierbekken (het)**	[ri'vir·'bɛkən]
to flow into ...	**uitmonden in ...**	['œʏtmɔndən in]
tributary	**zijrivier (de)**	[zɛj·ri'vir]
bank (of river)	**oever (de)**	['uvər]
current (stream)	**stroming (de)**	['strɔmiŋ]
downstream (adv)	**stroomafwaarts**	[strõm·'afwãrts]
upstream (adv)	**stroomopwaarts**	[strõm·'ɔpwãrts]
inundation	**overstroming (de)**	[ɔvər'strɔmiŋ]
flooding	**overstroming (de)**	[ɔvər'strɔmiŋ]
to overflow (vi)	**buiten zijn**	['bœʏtən zɛjn
	oevers treden	'uvərs 'trɛdən]
to flood (vt)	**overstromen**	[ɔvər'strɔmən]
shallow (shoal)	**zandbank (de)**	['zant·bank]
rapids	**stroomversnelling (de)**	[strõm·vər'sneliŋ]
dam	**dam (de)**	[dam]
canal	**kanaal (het)**	[ka'nãl]
reservoir (artificial lake)	**spaarbekken (het)**	['spãr·bɛkən]
sluice, lock	**sluis (de)**	['slœʏs]
water body (pond, etc.)	**waterlichaam (het)**	['watər·'lixãm]
swamp (marshland)	**moeras (het)**	[mu'ras]
bog, marsh	**broek (het)**	[bruk]
whirlpool	**draaikolk (de)**	['drãj·kɔlk]
stream (brook)	**stroom (de)**	[strõm]
drinking (ab. water)	**drink-**	[drink]
fresh (~ water)	**zoet**	[zut]
ice	**ijs (het)**	[ɛjs]
to freeze over	**bevriezen**	[bə'vrizən]
(ab. river, etc.)		

203. Rivers' names

Seine	**Seine (de)**	['sɛjnə]
Loire	**Loire (de)**	[lu'arə]
Thames	**Theems (de)**	['tɛjms]
Rhine	**Rijn (de)**	['rɛjn]
Danube	**Donau (de)**	['dɔnau]
Volga	**Wolga (de)**	['wɔlxa]
Don	**Don (de)**	[dɔn]
Lena	**Lena (de)**	['lena]

Yellow River	Gele Rivier (de)	['xelə ri'vir]
Yangtze	Blauwe Rivier (de)	['blauə ri'vir]
Mekong	Mekong (de)	[me'kɔŋ]
Ganges	Ganges (de)	['xaŋəs]

Nile River	Nijl (de)	['nɛjl]
Congo River	Kongo (de)	['kɔnxɔ]
Okavango River	Okavango (de)	[ɔka'vanxɔ]
Zambezi River	Zambezi (de)	[zam'bezi]
Limpopo River	Limpopo (de)	[lim'pɔpɔ]
Mississippi River	Mississippi (de)	[misi'sipi]

204. Forest

| forest, wood | bos (het) | [bɔs] |
| forest (as adj) | bos- | [bɔs] |

thick forest	oerwoud (het)	['urwaut]
grove	bosje (het)	['bɔɕə]
forest clearing	open plek (de)	['ɔpən plek]

| thicket | struikgewas (het) | ['strœʏk·xə'was] |
| scrubland | struiken | ['strœʏkən] |

| footpath (troddenpath) | paadje (het) | ['pādjə] |
| gully | ravijn (het) | [ra'vɛjn] |

tree	boom (de)	[bōm]
leaf	blad (het)	[blat]
leaves (foliage)	gebladerte (het)	[xə'bladərtə]

fall of leaves	vallende bladeren	['valəndə 'bladerən]
to fall (ab. leaves)	vallen	['valən]
top (of the tree)	boomtop (de)	['bōm·tɔp]

branch	tak (de)	[tak]
bough	ent (de)	[ɛnt]
bud (on shrub, tree)	knop (de)	[knɔp]
needle (of pine tree)	naald (de)	[nālt]
pine cone	dennenappel (de)	['dɛnən·'apəl]

hollow (in a tree)	boom holte (de)	[bōm 'hɔltə]
nest	nest (het)	[nɛst]
burrow (animal hole)	hol (het)	[hɔl]
trunk	stam (de)	[stam]
root	wortel (de)	['wortəl]
bark	schors (de)	[sxɔrs]
moss	mos (het)	[mɔs]
to uproot (remove trees or tree stumps)	ontwortelen	[ɔnt'wortələn]

to chop down	kappen	['kapən]
to deforest (vt)	ontbossen	[ɔn'bɔsən]
tree stump	stronk (de)	[strɔnk]

campfire	kampvuur (het)	['kampvūr]
forest fire	bosbrand (de)	['bɔs·brant]
to extinguish (vt)	blussen	['blʉsən]

forest ranger	boswachter (de)	[bɔs·'waxtər]
protection	bescherming (de)	[bə'sxɛrmiŋ]
to protect (~ nature)	beschermen	[bə'sxɛrmən]
poacher	stroper (de)	['strɔpər]
steel trap	val (de)	[val]

| to gather, to pick (vt) | plukken | ['plʉkən] |
| to lose one's way | verdwalen (de weg kwijt zijn) | [vərd'walən] |

205. Natural resources

natural resources	natuurlijke rijkdommen	[na'tūrləkə 'rɛjkdɔmən]
minerals	delfstoffen	['dɛlfstɔfən]
deposits	lagen	['laxən]
field (e.g., oilfield)	veld (het)	[vɛlt]

to mine (extract)	winnen	['winən]
mining (extraction)	winning (de)	['winiŋ]
ore	erts (het)	[ɛrts]
mine (e.g., for coal)	mijn (de)	[mɛjn]
shaft (mine ~)	mijnschacht (de)	['mɛjn·sxaxt]
miner	mijnwerker (de)	['mɛjn·wɛrkər]

| gas (natural ~) | gas (het) | [xas] |
| gas pipeline | gasleiding (de) | [xas·'lɛjdiŋ] |

oil (petroleum)	olie (de)	['ɔli]
oil pipeline	olieleiding (de)	['ɔli·'lɛjdiŋ]
oil well	oliebron (de)	['ɔli·brɔn]
derrick (tower)	boortoren (de)	[bōr·'tɔrən]
tanker	tanker (de)	['tankər]

sand	zand (het)	[zant]
limestone	kalksteen (de)	['kalkstēn]
gravel	grind (het)	[xrint]
peat	veen (het)	[vēn]
clay	klei (de)	[klɛj]
coal	steenkool (de)	['stēn·kōl]

| iron (ore) | ijzer (het) | ['ɛjzər] |
| gold | goud (het) | ['xaut] |

silver	zilver (het)	['zilvər]
nickel	nikkel (het)	['nikəl]
copper	koper (het)	['kɔpər]
zinc	zink (het)	[zink]
manganese	mangaan (het)	[man'xān]
mercury	kwik (het)	['kwik]
lead	lood (het)	[lōt]
mineral	mineraal (het)	[minə'rāl]
crystal	kristal (het)	[kris'tal]
marble	marmer (het)	['marmər]
uranium	uraan (het)	[ju'rān]

The Earth. Part 2

206. Weather

weather	**weer (het)**	[wĕr]
weather forecast	**weersvoorspelling (de)**	['wĕrs·vōr'spɛliŋ]
temperature	**temperatuur (de)**	[tɛmpəra'tūr]
thermometer	**thermometer (de)**	['tɛrmɔmetər]
barometer	**barometer (de)**	['barɔ'metər]
humid (adj)	**vochtig**	['vɔhtəx]
humidity	**vochtigheid (de)**	['vɔhtixhɛjt]
heat (extreme ~)	**hitte (de)**	['hitə]
hot (torrid)	**heet**	[hĕt]
it's hot	**het is heet**	[ət is hĕt]
it's warm	**het is warm**	[ət is warm]
warm (moderately hot)	**warm**	[warm]
it's cold	**het is koud**	[ət is 'kaut]
cold (adj)	**koud**	['kaut]
sun	**zon (de)**	[zɔn]
to shine (vi)	**schijnen**	['sxɛjnən]
sunny (day)	**zonnig**	['zɔnɛx]
to come up (vi)	**opgaan**	['ɔpxān]
to set (vi)	**ondergaan**	['ɔndərxān]
cloud	**wolk (de)**	[wɔlk]
cloudy (adj)	**bewolkt**	[bə'wɔlkt]
rain cloud	**regenwolk (de)**	['rexən·wɔlk]
somber (gloomy)	**somber**	['sɔmbər]
rain	**regen (de)**	['rexən]
it's raining	**het regent**	[ət 'rexənt]
rainy (~ day, weather)	**regenachtig**	['rexənaxtəx]
to drizzle (vi)	**motregenen**	['mɔtrexənən]
pouring rain	**plensbui (de)**	['plɛnsbœy]
downpour	**stortbui (de)**	['stɔrt·bœy]
heavy (e.g., ~ rain)	**hard**	[hart]
puddle	**plas (de)**	[plas]
to get wet (in rain)	**nat worden**	[nat 'wɔrdən]
fog (mist)	**mist (de)**	[mist]
foggy	**mistig**	['mistəx]

snow   sneeuw (de)   [snēw]
it's snowing   het sneeuwt   [ət 'snēwt]

207. Severe weather. Natural disasters

thunderstorm   noodweer (het)   ['nɔtwer]
lightning (~ strike)   bliksem (de)   ['bliksəm]
to flash (vi)   flitsen   ['flitsən]

thunder   donder (de)   ['dɔndər]
to thunder (vi)   donderen   ['dɔndərən]
it's thundering   het dondert   [ət 'dɔndərt]

hail   hagel (de)   ['haxəl]
it's hailing   het hagelt   [ət 'haxəlt]

to flood (vt)   overstromen   [ɔvər'strɔmən]
flood, inundation   overstroming (de)   [ɔvər'strɔmiŋ]

earthquake   aardbeving (de)   ['ārd·beviŋ]
tremor, quake   aardschok (de)   ['ārd·sxɔk]
epicenter   epicentrum (het)   [ɛpi'sɛntrʉm]
eruption   uitbarsting (de)   ['œytbarstiŋ]
lava   lava (de)   ['lava]

twister   wervelwind (de)   ['wɛrvəl·vint]
tornado   windhoos (de)   ['windhōs]
typhoon   tyfoon (de)   [taj'fōn]

hurricane   orkaan (de)   [ɔr'kān]
storm   storm (de)   [stɔrm]
tsunami   tsunami (de)   [tsʉ'nami]

cyclone   cycloon (de)   [si'klōn]
bad weather   onweer (het)   ['ɔnwēr]
fire (accident)   brand (de)   [brant]
disaster   ramp (de)   [ramp]
meteorite   meteoriet (de)   [meteɔ'rit]

avalanche   lawine (de)   [la'winə]
snowslide   sneeuwverschuiving (de) ['snēw·'fɛrsxœyviŋ]
blizzard   sneeuwjacht (de)   ['snēw·jaxt]
snowstorm   sneeuwstorm (de)   ['snēw·stɔrm]

208. Noises. Sounds

silence (quiet)   stilte (de)   ['stiltə]
sound   geluid (het)   [xə'lœyt]

noise	lawaai (het)	[la'wai]
to make noise	lawaai maken	[la'wai 'makən]
noisy (adj)	lawaaierig	[la'wājərəx]
loudly (to speak, etc.)	luid	['lœʏt]
loud (voice, etc.)	luid	['lœʏt]
constant (e.g., ~ noise)	aanhoudend	['ānhaudənt]
cry, shout (n)	schreeuw (de)	[sxrēw]
to cry, to shout (vi)	schreeuwen	['sxrēwən]
whisper	gefluister (het)	[xə'flœʏstər]
to whisper (vi, vt)	fluisteren	['flœʏstərən]
barking (dog's ~)	geblaf (het)	[xə'blaf]
to bark (vi)	blaffen	['blafən]
groan (of pain, etc.)	gekreun (het)	[xə'krøn]
to groan (vi)	kreunen	['krønən]
cough	hoest (de)	[hust]
to cough (vi)	hoesten	['hustən]
whistle	gefluit (het)	[xə'flœʏt]
to whistle (vi)	fluiten	['flœʏtən]
knock (at the door)	geklop (het)	[xə'klɔp]
to knock (at the door)	kloppen	['klɔpən]
to crack (vi)	kraken	['krakən]
crack (cracking sound)	gekraak (het)	[xə'krāk]
siren	sirene (de)	[si'renə]
whistle (factory ~, etc.)	fluit (de)	['flœʏt]
to whistle (ab. train)	fluiten	['flœʏtən]
honk (car horn sound)	toeter (de)	['tutər]
to honk (vi)	toeteren	['tutərən]

209. Winter

winter (n)	winter (de)	['wintər]
winter (as adj)	winter-	['wintər]
in winter	in de winter	[in də 'wintər]
snow	sneeuw (de)	[snēw]
it's snowing	het sneeuwt	[ət 'snēwt]
snowfall	sneeuwval (de)	['snēw·fal]
snowdrift	sneeuwhoop (de)	['snēw·hōp]
snowflake	sneeuwvlok (de)	['snēw·flɔk]
snowball	sneeuwbal (de)	['snēw·bal]
snowman	sneeuwman (de)	['snēw·man]
icicle	ijspegel (de)	['ɛjspexəl]

December	**december (de)**	[de'sɛmbər]
January	**januari (de)**	[janʉ'ari]
February	**februari (de)**	[febrʉ'ari]
frost (severe ~, freezing cold)	**vorst (de)**	[vɔrst]
frosty (weather, air)	**vries-**	[vris]
below zero (adv)	**onder nul**	['ɔndər nʉl]
first frost	**eerste vorst (de)**	['ērstə vɔrst]
hoarfrost	**rijp (de)**	[rɛjp]
cold (cold weather)	**koude (de)**	['kaudə]
it's cold	**het is koud**	[ət is 'kaut]
fur coat	**bontjas (de)**	[bɔnt jas]
mittens	**wanten**	['wantən]
to get sick	**ziek worden**	[zik 'wɔrdən]
cold (illness)	**verkoudheid (de)**	[vər'kauthɛjt]
to catch a cold	**verkouden raken**	[vər'kaudən 'rakən]
ice	**ijs (het)**	[ɛjs]
black ice	**ijzel (de)**	['ɛjzəl]
to freeze over (ab. river, etc.)	**bevriezen**	[bə'vrizən]
ice floe	**ijsschol (de)**	['ɛjs·sxɔl]
skis	**ski's**	[skis]
skier	**skiër (de)**	['skiər]
to ski (vi)	**skiën**	['skiən]
to skate (vi)	**schaatsen**	['sxātsən]

Fauna

210. Mammals. Predators

predator	roofdier (het)	['rōf·dīr]
tiger	tijger (de)	['tɛjxər]
lion	leeuw (de)	[lēw]
wolf	wolf (de)	[wɔlf]
fox	vos (de)	[vɔs]
jaguar	jaguar (de)	['jaguar]
leopard	luipaard (de)	['lœʏpārt]
cheetah	jachtluipaard (de)	['jaxt·lœʏpārt]
black panther	panter (de)	['pantər]
puma	poema (de)	['puma]
snow leopard	sneeuwluipaard (de)	['snēw·lœʏpārt]
lynx	lynx (de)	[links]
coyote	coyote (de)	[kɔ'jot]
jackal	jakhals (de)	['jakhals]
hyena	hyena (de)	[hi'ena]

211. Wild animals

animal	dier (het)	[dīr]
beast (animal)	beest (het)	[bēst]
squirrel	eekhoorn (de)	['ēkhōrn]
hedgehog	egel (de)	['exəl]
hare	haas (de)	[hās]
rabbit	konijn (het)	[kɔ'nɛjn]
badger	das (de)	[das]
raccoon	wasbeer (de)	['wasbēr]
hamster	hamster (de)	['hamstər]
marmot	marmot (de)	[mar'mɔt]
mole	mol (de)	[mɔl]
mouse	muis (de)	[mœʏs]
rat	rat (de)	[rat]
bat	vleermuis (de)	['vlēr·mœʏs]
ermine	hermelijn (de)	[hɛrmə'lɛjn]
sable	sabeldier (het)	['sabəl·dīr]

marten	marter (de)	['martər]
weasel	wezel (de)	['wezəl]
mink	nerts (de)	[nɛrts]

| beaver | bever (de) | ['bɛvər] |
| otter | otter (de) | ['ɔtər] |

horse	paard (het)	[pārt]
moose	eland (de)	['ɛlant]
deer	hert (het)	[hɛrt]
camel	kameel (de)	[ka'mēl]

bison	bizon (de)	[bi'zɔn]
aurochs	oeros (de)	['urɔs]
buffalo	buffel (de)	['bʉfəl]

zebra	zebra (de)	['zɛbra]
antelope	antilope (de)	[anti'lɔpə]
roe deer	ree (de)	[rē]
fallow deer	damhert (het)	['damhɛrt]
chamois	gems (de)	[xɛms]
wild boar	everzwijn (het)	['ɛvər·zwɛjn]

whale	walvis (de)	['walvis]
seal	rob (de)	[rɔb]
walrus	walrus (de)	['walrʉs]
fur seal	zeehond (de)	['zē·hɔnt]
dolphin	dolfijn (de)	[dɔl'fɛjn]

bear	beer (de)	[bēr]
polar bear	ijsbeer (de)	['ɛjs·bēr]
panda	panda (de)	['panda]

monkey	aap (de)	[āp]
chimpanzee	chimpansee (de)	[ʃimpan'sē]
orangutan	orang-oetan (de)	[ɔ'raŋ-utaŋ]
gorilla	gorilla (de)	[xɔ'rila]
macaque	makaak (de)	[ma'kāk]
gibbon	gibbon (de)	['xibɔn]

elephant	olifant (de)	['ɔlifant]
rhinoceros	neushoorn (de)	['nøshōrn]
giraffe	giraffe (de)	[xi'rafə]
hippopotamus	nijlpaard (het)	['nɛjl·pārt]

| kangaroo | kangoeroe (de) | ['kanxəru] |
| koala (bear) | koala (de) | [kɔ'ala] |

mongoose	mangoest (de)	[man'xust]
chinchilla	chinchilla (de)	[ʃin'ʃila]
skunk	stinkdier (het)	['stink·dīr]
porcupine	stekelvarken (het)	['stekəl·'varkən]

212. Domestic animals

cat	poes (de)	[pus]
tomcat	kater (de)	['katər]
horse	paard (het)	[pãrt]
stallion (male horse)	hengst (de)	[hɛŋst]
mare	merrie (de)	['mɛri]
cow	koe (de)	[ku]
bull	stier (de)	[stir]
ox	os (de)	[ɔs]
sheep (ewe)	schaap (het)	[sxãp]
ram	ram (de)	[ram]
goat	geit (de)	[xɛjt]
billy goat, he-goat	bok (de)	[bɔk]
donkey	ezel (de)	['ezəl]
mule	muilezel (de)	[mœɣlezəl]
pig, hog	varken (het)	['varkən]
piglet	biggetje (het)	['bixətʃə]
rabbit	konijn (het)	[kɔ'nɛjn]
hen (chicken)	kip (de)	[kip]
rooster	haan (de)	[hãn]
duck	eend (de)	[ēnt]
drake	woerd (de)	[wurt]
goose	gans (de)	[xans]
tom turkey, gobbler	kalkoen haan (de)	[kal'kun hãn]
turkey (hen)	kalkoen (de)	[kal'kun]
domestic animals	huisdieren	['hœɣs·'dĩrən]
tame (e.g., ~ hamster)	tam	[tam]
to tame (vt)	temmen, tam maken	['tɛmən], [tam 'makən]
to breed (vt)	fokken	['fɔkən]
farm	boerderij (de)	[burdə'rɛj]
poultry	gevogelte (het)	[xə'vɔxəltə]
cattle	rundvee (het)	['rʉntvē]
herd (cattle)	kudde (de)	['kʉdə]
stable	paardenstal (de)	['pãrdən·stal]
pigpen	zwijnenstal (de)	['zwɛjnən·stal]
cowshed	koeienstal (de)	['kujen·stal]
rabbit hutch	konijnenhok (het)	[kɔ'nɛjnən·hɔk]
hen house	kippenhok (het)	['kipən·hɔk]

213. Dogs. Dog breeds

dog	hond (de)	[hɔnt]
sheepdog	herdershond (de)	['hɛrdərs·hɔnt]
German shepherd	Duitse herdershond (de)	['dœʏtsə 'herdərs·hɔnt]
poodle	poedel (de)	['pudəl]
dachshund	teckel (de)	['tekəl]
bulldog	buldog (de)	['bʉldɔx]
boxer	boxer (de)	['bɔksər]
mastiff	mastiff (de)	[mas'tif]
Rottweiler	rottweiler (de)	[rɔt'wɛjlər]
Doberman	doberman (de)	['dɔberman]
basset	basset (de)	['basɛt]
bobtail	bobtail (de)	['bɔbtəjl]
Dalmatian	dalmatiër (de)	[dal'matʃər]
cocker spaniel	cockerspaniël (de)	['kɔkər·spani'el]
Newfoundland	newfoundlander (de)	[nʉ'faundləndər]
Saint Bernard	sint-bernard (de)	[sint-'bɛrnart]
husky	poolhond (de)	['pōlhɔnt]
Chow Chow	chowchow (de)	['tʃau·tʃau]
spitz	spits (de)	[spits]
pug	mopshond (de)	['mɔps·hɔnt]

214. Sounds made by animals

barking (n)	geblaf (het)	[xə'blaf]
to bark (vi)	blaffen	['blafən]
to meow (vi)	miauwen	[mi'auən]
to purr (vi)	spinnen	['spinən]
to moo (vi)	loeien	['lʉjən]
to bellow (bull)	brullen	['brʉlən]
to growl (vi)	grommen	['xrɔmən]
howl (n)	gehuil (het)	[xe'hœʏl]
to howl (vi)	huilen	['hœʏlən]
to whine (vi)	janken	['jankən]
to bleat (sheep)	mekkeren	['mekərən]
to oink, to grunt (pig)	knorren	['knɔrən]
to squeal (vi)	gillen	['xilən]
to croak (vi)	kwaken	['kwakən]
to buzz (insect)	zoemen	['zumən]
to chirp (crickets, grasshopper)	tjirpen	['tʃirpən]

215. Young animals

cub	jong (het)	[joŋ]
kitten	poesje (het)	['puɕə]
baby mouse	muisje (het)	[mœʏɕə]
puppy	puppy (de)	['pʉpi]
leveret	jonge haas (de)	[joŋə hās]
baby rabbit	konijntje (het)	[kɔ'nɛjntʃə]
wolf cub	wolfje (het)	['wolfjə]
fox cub	vosje (het)	['vɔɕə]
bear cub	beertje (het)	['bērtʃə]
lion cub	leeuwenjong (het)	['lēwən joŋ]
tiger cub	tijgertje (het)	['tɛjxərtʃə]
elephant calf	olifantenjong (het)	['ɔlifantən·joŋ]
piglet	biggetje (het)	['bixətʃə]
calf (young cow, bull)	kalf (het)	[kalf]
kid (young goat)	geitje (het)	['xɛjtʃə]
lamb	lam (het)	[lam]
fawn (young deer)	reekalf (het)	['rēkalf]
young camel	jonge kameel (de)	['joŋə ka'mēl]
snakelet (baby snake)	slangenjong (het)	['slaŋən·joŋ]
froglet (baby frog)	kikkertje (het)	['kikərtʃə]
baby bird	vogeltje (het)	['vɔxəltʃə]
chick (of chicken)	kuiken (het)	['kœʏkən]
duckling	eendje (het)	['ēndjə]

216. Birds

bird	vogel (de)	['vɔxəl]
pigeon	duif (de)	['dœʏf]
sparrow	mus (de)	[mʉs]
tit (great tit)	koolmees (de)	['kōlmēs]
magpie	ekster (de)	['ɛkstər]
raven	raaf (de)	[rāf]
crow	kraai (de)	[krāj]
jackdaw	kauw (de)	['kau]
rook	roek (de)	[ruk]
duck	eend (de)	[ēnt]
goose	gans (de)	[xans]
pheasant	fazant (de)	[fa'zant]
eagle	arend (de)	['arənt]
hawk	havik (de)	['havik]

falcon	valk (de)	[valk]
vulture	gier (de)	[xir]
condor (Andean ~)	condor (de)	['kɔndɔr]

swan	zwaan (de)	[zwãn]
crane	kraanvogel (de)	['krãn·vɔxəl]
stork	ooievaar (de)	['õjevãr]

parrot	papegaai (de)	[papə'xãj]
hummingbird	kolibrie (de)	[kɔ'libri]
peacock	pauw (de)	['pau]

ostrich	struisvogel (de)	['strœys·vɔxəl]
heron	reiger (de)	['rɛjxər]
flamingo	flamingo (de)	[fla'mingɔ]
pelican	pelikaan (de)	[peli'kãn]

| nightingale | nachtegaal (de) | ['nahtəxãl] |
| swallow | zwaluw (de) | ['zwaluv] |

thrush	lijster (de)	['lɛjstər]
song thrush	zanglijster (de)	[zaŋ·'lɛjstər]
blackbird	merel (de)	['merəl]

swift	gierzwaluw (de)	[xirz'waluv]
lark	leeuwerik (de)	['lẽwərik]
quail	kwartel (de)	['kwartəl]

woodpecker	specht (de)	[spɛxt]
cuckoo	koekoek (de)	['kukuk]
owl	uil (de)	['œyl]
eagle owl	oehoe (de)	['uhu]
wood grouse	auerhoen (het)	['auər·hun]
black grouse	korhoen (het)	['kɔrhun]
partridge	patrijs (de)	[pa'trɛjs]

starling	spreeuw (de)	[sprẽw]
canary	kanarie (de)	[ka'nari]
hazel grouse	hazelhoen (het)	['hazəlhun]
chaffinch	vink (de)	[vink]
bullfinch	goudvink (de)	['xaudvink]

seagull	meeuw (de)	[mẽw]
albatross	albatros (de)	[albatrɔs]
penguin	pinguïn (de)	['piŋgwin]

217. Birds. Singing and sounds

| to sing (vi) | fluiten, zingen | ['flœytən], ['ziŋən] |
| to call (animal, bird) | schreeuwen | ['sxrẽwən] |

to crow (rooster)	**kraaien**	['krãjən]
cock-a-doodle-doo	**kukeleku**	[kʉkelə'kʉ]
to cluck (hen)	**klokken**	['klɔkən]
to caw (vi)	**krassen**	['krasən]
to quack (duck)	**kwaken**	['kwakən]
to cheep (vi)	**piepen**	['pipən]
to chirp, to twitter	**tjilpen**	['tʃilpən]

218. Fish. Marine animals

bream	**brasem (de)**	['brasəm]
carp	**karper (de)**	['karpər]
perch	**baars (de)**	[bãrs]
catfish	**meerval (de)**	['mērval]
pike	**snoek (de)**	[snuk]
salmon	**zalm (de)**	[zalm]
sturgeon	**steur (de)**	['stør]
herring	**haring (de)**	['hariŋ]
Atlantic salmon	**atlantische zalm (de)**	[at'lantisə zalm]
mackerel	**makreel (de)**	[ma'krēl]
flatfish	**platvis (de)**	['platvis]
zander, pike perch	**snoekbaars (de)**	['snukbãrs]
cod	**kabeljauw (de)**	[kabə'ljau]
tuna	**tonijn (de)**	[tɔ'nɛjn]
trout	**forel (de)**	[fɔ'rɛl]
eel	**paling (de)**	[pa'liŋ]
electric ray	**sidderrog (de)**	['sidər·rɔx]
moray eel	**murene (de)**	[mʉ'rɛnə]
piranha	**piranha (de)**	[pi'ranja]
shark	**haai (de)**	[hãj]
dolphin	**dolfijn (de)**	[dɔl'fɛjn]
whale	**walvis (de)**	['walvis]
crab	**krab (de)**	[krab]
jellyfish	**kwal (de)**	['kwal]
octopus	**octopus (de)**	['ɔktɔpʉs]
starfish	**zeester (de)**	['zē·stər]
sea urchin	**zee-egel (de)**	[zē-'exəl]
seahorse	**zeepaardje (het)**	['zē·pãrtjə]
oyster	**oester (de)**	['ustər]
shrimp	**garnaal (de)**	[xar'nãl]
lobster	**kreeft (de)**	[krēft]
spiny lobster	**langoest (de)**	[lan'xust]

219. Amphibians. Reptiles

snake	**slang (de)**	[slaŋ]
venomous (snake)	**giftig**	['xiftəx]
viper	**adder (de)**	['adər]
cobra	**cobra (de)**	['kɔbra]
python	**python (de)**	['pitɔn]
boa	**boa (de)**	['bɔa]
grass snake	**ringslang (de)**	['riŋ·slaŋ]
rattle snake	**ratelslang (de)**	['ratəl·slaŋ]
anaconda	**anaconda (de)**	[ana'kɔnda]
lizard	**hagedis (de)**	['haxədis]
iguana	**leguaan (de)**	[lexʉ'ān]
monitor lizard	**varaan (de)**	[va'rān]
salamander	**salamander (de)**	[sala'mandər]
chameleon	**kameleon (de)**	[kamele'ɔn]
scorpion	**schorpioen (de)**	[sxɔrpi'un]
turtle	**schildpad (de)**	['sxildpat]
frog	**kikker (de)**	['kikər]
toad	**pad (de)**	[pat]
crocodile	**krokodil (de)**	[krɔkɔ'dil]

220. Insects

insect, bug	**insect (het)**	[in'sɛkt]
butterfly	**vlinder (de)**	['vlindər]
ant	**mier (de)**	[mir]
fly	**vlieg (de)**	[vlix]
mosquito	**mug (de)**	[mʉx]
beetle	**kever (de)**	['kevər]
wasp	**wesp (de)**	[wɛsp]
bee	**bij (de)**	[bɛj]
bumblebee	**hommel (de)**	['hɔməl]
gadfly (botfly)	**horzel (de)**	['hɔrsəl]
spider	**spin (de)**	[spin]
spiderweb	**spinnenweb (het)**	['spinən·wɛb]
dragonfly	**libel (de)**	[li'bɛl]
grasshopper	**sprinkhaan (de)**	['sprinkhān]
moth (night butterfly)	**nachtvlinder (de)**	['naxt·'vlindər]
cockroach	**kakkerlak (de)**	['kakərlak]
tick	**teek (de)**	[tẽk]

flea	vlo (de)	[vlɔ]
midge	kriebelmug (de)	['kribəl·mʉx]
locust	treksprinkhaan (de)	['trɛk·sprink'hān]
snail	slak (de)	[slak]
cricket	krekel (de)	['krekəl]
lightning bug	glimworm (de)	['xlim·wɔrm]
ladybug	lieveheersbeestje (het)	[livə'hērs·'bestʃə]
cockchafer	meikever (de)	['mɛjkəvər]
leech	bloedzuiger (de)	['blud·zœʏxər]
caterpillar	rups (de)	[rʉps]
earthworm	aardworm (de)	['ārd·wɔrm]
larva	larve (de)	['larvə]

221. Animals. Body parts

beak	snavel (de)	['snavəl]
wings	vleugels	['vløxəls]
foot (of bird)	poot (de)	[pōt]
feathers (plumage)	verenkleed (het)	[vərən·'klēt]
feather	veer (de)	[vēr]
crest	kuifje (het)	['kœʏfjə]
gills	kieuwen	['kiuən]
spawn	kuit, dril (de)	['kœʏt], [dril]
larva	larve (de)	['larvə]
fin	vin (de)	[vin]
scales (of fish, reptile)	schubben	['sxʉbən]
fang (canine)	slagtand (de)	['slax·tant]
paw (e.g., cat's ~)	poot (de)	[pōt]
muzzle (snout)	muil (de)	[mœʏl]
mouth (of cat, dog)	bek (de)	[bɛk]
tail	staart (de)	[stārt]
whiskers	snorharen	['snɔrharən]
hoof	hoef (de)	[huf]
horn	hoorn (de)	[hōrn]
carapace	schild (het)	[sxilt]
shell (of mollusk)	schelp (de)	[sxɛlp]
eggshell	eierschaal (de)	['ɛjer·sxāl]
animal's hair (pelage)	vacht (de)	[vaxt]
pelt (hide)	huid (de)	['hœʏt]

222. Actions of animals

to fly (vi)	vliegen	['vlixən]
to fly in circles	cirkelen	['sirkələn]
to fly away	wegvliegen	['wɛxvlixən]
to flap (~ the wings)	klapwieken	['klapwikən]
to peck (vi)	pikken	['pikən]
to sit on eggs	broeden	['brudən]
to hatch out (vi)	uitbroeden	['œytbrudən]
to build a nest	een nest bouwen	[en nɛst 'bauwən]
to slither, to crawl	kruipen	['krœypən]
to sting, to bite (insect)	steken	['stekən]
to bite (ab. animal)	bijten	['bɛjtən]
to sniff (vt)	snuffelen	['snʉfelən]
to bark (vi)	blaffen	['blafən]
to hiss (snake)	sissen	['sisən]
to scare (vt)	doen schrikken	[dun 'sxrikən]
to attack (vt)	aanvallen	['ānvalən]
to gnaw (bone, etc.)	knagen	['knaxən]
to scratch (with claws)	schrammen	['sxramən]
to hide (vi)	zich verbergen	[zih vər'bɛrxən]
to play (kittens, etc.)	spelen	['spelən]
to hunt (vi, vt)	jagen	['jaxən]
to hibernate (vi)	winterslapen	['wintər·'slapən]
to go extinct	uitsterven	['œytstɛrvən]

223. Animals. Habitats

habitat	leefgebied (het)	['lẽfxəbit]
migration	migratie (de)	[mi'xratsi]
mountain	berg (de)	[bɛrx]
reef	rif (het)	[rif]
cliff	klip (de)	[klip]
forest	bos (het)	[bɔs]
jungle	jungle (de)	[dʒəngl]
savanna	savanne (de)	[sa'vanə]
tundra	toendra (de)	['tundra]
steppe	steppe (de)	['stɛpə]
desert	woestijn (de)	[wus'tɛjn]
oasis	oase (de)	[ɔ'azə]
sea	zee (de)	[zẽ]

lake	meer (het)	[mēr]
ocean	oceaan (de)	[ɔse'ān]
swamp (marshland)	moeras (het)	[mu'ras]
freshwater (adj)	zoetwater-	[zut·'watər]
pond	vijver (de)	['vɛjvər]
river	rivier (de)	[ri'vir]
den (bear's ~)	berenhol (het)	['berənhɔl]
nest	nest (het)	[nɛst]
hollow (in a tree)	boom holte (de)	[bōm 'hɔltə]
burrow (animal hole)	hol (het)	[hɔl]
anthill	mierenhoop (de)	['mirən·hōp]

224. Animal care

zoo	dierentuin (de)	['dīrən·tœyn]
nature preserve	natuurreservaat (het)	[na'tūr·rezɛr'vāt]
breeder (cattery, kennel, etc.)	fokkerij (de)	[fɔkə'rɛj]
open-air cage	openluchtkooi (de)	['ɔpənlʉxt·'kōj]
cage	kooi (de)	[kōj]
doghouse (kennel)	hondenhok (het)	['hɔndən·hɔk]
dovecot	duiventil (de)	['dœyvən·'til]
aquarium (fish tank)	aquarium (het)	[ak'warijum]
dolphinarium	dolfinarium (het)	[dɔlfi'narijum]
to breed (animals)	fokken	['fɔkən]
brood, litter	nakomelingen	['nakɔməliŋən]
to tame (vt)	temmen, tam maken	['tɛmən], [tam 'makən]
to train (animals)	dresseren	[drɛ'serən]
feed (fodder, etc.)	voeding (de)	['vudiŋ]
to feed (vt)	voederen	['vudərən]
pet store	dierenwinkel (de)	['dīrən·'winkəl]
muzzle (for dog)	muilkorf (de)	[mœyl·kɔrf]
collar (e.g., dog ~)	halsband (de)	['hals·bant]
name (of animal)	naam (de)	[nām]
pedigree (of dog)	stamboom (de)	['stam·bōm]

225. Animals. Miscellaneous

pack (wolves)	meute (de)	['møtə]
flock (birds)	zwerm (de)	[zwɛrm]
shoal, school (fish)	school (de)	[sxōl]
herd (horses)	kudde (de)	['kʉdə]

male (n)	mannetje (het)	['manɛtʃə]
female (n)	vrouwtje (het)	['vrautʃə]
hungry (adj)	hongerig	['hɔŋərəh]
wild (adj)	wild	[wilt]
dangerous (adj)	gevaarlijk	[xe'vārlək]

226. Horses

horse	paard (het)	[pārt]
breed (race)	ras (het)	[ras]
foal	veulen (het)	['vølən]
mare	merrie (de)	['mɛri]
mustang	mustang (de)	[mʉstaŋ]
pony	pony (de)	['pɔni]
draft horse	koudbloed (de)	['kaut·blut]
mane	manen	['manən]
tail	staart (de)	[stārt]
hoof	hoef (de)	[huf]
horseshoe	hoefijzer (het)	[huf·'ɛjzər]
to shoe (vt)	beslaan	[bə'slān]
blacksmith	paardensmid (de)	[pārdən·'smit]
saddle	zadel (het)	['zadəl]
stirrup	stijgbeugel (de)	['stɛjx'bøxəl]
bridle	breidel (de)	['brɛjdəl]
reins	leidsels	['lɛjdsəls]
whip (for riding)	zweep (de)	[zwẽp]
rider	ruiter (de)	['rœʏtər]
to saddle up (vt)	zadelen	['zadələn]
to mount a horse	een paard bestijgen	[ən pārt bə'stɛjxə]
gallop	galop (de)	[xa'lɔp]
to gallop (vi)	galopperen	[xalɔ'perən]
trot (n)	draf (de)	[draf]
at a trot (adv)	in draf	[in draf]
to go at a trot	draven	['dravən]
racehorse	renpaard (het)	[ren'pārt]
horse racing	paardenrace (de)	['pārdən·rɛjs]
stable	paardenstal (de)	['pārdən·stal]
to feed (vt)	voederen	['vudərən]
hay	hooi (het)	[hõj]
to water (animals)	water geven	['watər 'xevən]

to wash (horse)	**wassen**	['wasən]
horse-drawn cart	**paardenkar (de)**	['pārdən·kar]
to graze (vi)	**grazen**	['xrazən]
to neigh (vi)	**hinniken**	['hinikən]
to kick (about horse)	**een trap geven**	[en trap 'xevən]

Flora

227. Trees

tree	**boom (de)**	[bõm]
deciduous (adj)	**loof-**	[lõf]
coniferous (adj)	**dennen-**	['dɛnən]
evergreen (adj)	**groenblijvend**	[xrun 'blɛjvənt]
apple tree	**appelboom (de)**	['apəl·bõm]
pear tree	**perenboom (de)**	['perən·bõm]
sweet cherry tree	**zoete kers (de)**	['zutə kɛrs]
sour cherry tree	**zure kers (de)**	['zʉrə kɛrs]
plum tree	**pruimelaar (de)**	[prœyməˑlãr]
birch	**berk (de)**	[bɛrk]
oak	**eik (de)**	[ɛjk]
linden tree	**linde (de)**	['lində]
aspen	**esp (de)**	[ɛsp]
maple	**esdoorn (de)**	['ɛsdõrn]
spruce	**spar (de)**	[spar]
pine	**den (de)**	[dɛn]
larch	**lariks (de)**	['lariks]
fir tree	**zilverspar (de)**	['zilvər·spar]
cedar	**ceder (de)**	['sedər]
poplar	**populier (de)**	[pɔpʉ'lir]
rowan	**lijsterbes (de)**	['lɛjstərbɛs]
willow	**wilg (de)**	[wilx]
alder	**els (de)**	[ɛls]
beech	**beuk (de)**	['bøk]
elm	**iep (de)**	[jep]
ash (tree)	**es (de)**	[ɛs]
chestnut	**kastanje (de)**	[kas'tanjə]
magnolia	**magnolia (de)**	[mah'nɔlija]
palm tree	**palm (de)**	[palm]
cypress	**cipres (de)**	[sip'rɛs]
mangrove	**mangrove (de)**	[man'xrɔvə]
baobab	**baobab (de)**	['baɔbap]
eucalyptus	**eucalyptus (de)**	[øka'liptʉs]
sequoia	**mammoetboom (de)**	[ma'mut·bõm]

228. Shrubs

bush	struik (de)	['strœyk]
shrub	heester (de)	['hēstər]
grapevine	wijnstok (de)	['wɛjn·stɔk]
vineyard	wijngaard (de)	['wɛjnxārt]
raspberry bush	frambozenstruik (de)	[fram'bɔsən·'strœyk]
blackcurrant bush	zwarte bes (de)	['zwartə bɛs]
redcurrant bush	rode bessenstruik (de)	['rɔdə 'bɛsən·strœyk]
gooseberry bush	kruisbessenstruik (de)	['krœys·'bɛsənstrœyk]
acacia	acacia (de)	[a'kaɕia]
barberry	zuurbes (de)	['zūr·bɛs]
jasmine	jasmijn (de)	[jas'mɛjn]
juniper	jeneverbes (de)	[je'nɛvərbɛs]
rosebush	rozenstruik (de)	['rɔzən·strœyk]
dog rose	hondsroos (de)	['hund·rōs]

229. Mushrooms

mushroom	paddenstoel (de)	['padənstul]
edible mushroom	eetbare paddenstoel (de)	['ētbarə 'padənstul]
poisonous mushroom	giftige paddenstoel (de)	['xiftixə 'padənstul]
cap (of mushroom)	hoed (de)	[hut]
stipe (of mushroom)	steel (de)	[stēl]
cep (Boletus edulis)	gewoon eekhoorntjesbrood (het)	[xə'wōn ē'hɔntʃes·brōt]
orange-cap boletus	rosse populierenboleet (de)	['rɔsə popʉ'lirən·bɔlēt]
birch bolete	berkenboleet (de)	['bɛrkən·bɔlēt]
chanterelle	cantharel (de)	[kanta'rɛl]
russula	russula (de)	[rʉ'sʉla]
morel	morielje (de)	[mɔ'rilje]
fly agaric	vliegenzwam (de)	['vlixən·zwam]
death cap	groene knolamaniet (de)	['xrunə 'knɔl·ama'nit]

230. Fruits. Berries

fruit	vrucht (de)	[vrʉxt]
fruits	vruchten	['vrʉxtən]
apple	appel (de)	['apəl]
pear	peer (de)	[pēr]

plum	pruim (de)	['prœʏm]
strawberry (garden ~)	aardbei (de)	['ārd·bɛj]
sour cherry	zure kers (de)	['zʉrə kɛrs]
sweet cherry	zoete kers (de)	['zutə kɛrs]
grape	druif (de)	[drœʏf]

raspberry	framboos (de)	[fram'bōs]
blackcurrant	zwarte bes (de)	['zwartə bɛs]
redcurrant	rode bes (de)	['rodə bɛs]
gooseberry	kruisbes (de)	['krœʏsbɛs]
cranberry	veenbes (de)	['vēnbɛs]

orange	sinaasappel (de)	['sināsapəl]
mandarin	mandarijn (de)	[manda'rɛjn]
pineapple	ananas (de)	['ananas]
banana	banaan (de)	[ba'nān]
date	dadel (de)	['dadəl]

lemon	citroen (de)	[si'trun]
apricot	abrikoos (de)	[abri'kōs]
peach	perzik (de)	['pɛrzik]
kiwi	kiwi (de)	['kiwi]
grapefruit	grapefruit (de)	['grepfrut]

berry	bes (de)	[bɛs]
berries	bessen	['bɛsən]
cowberry	vossenbes (de)	['vɔsənbɛs]
wild strawberry	bosaardbei (de)	[bɔs·ārdbɛj]
bilberry	bosbes (de)	['bɔsbɛs]

231. Flowers. Plants

| flower | bloem (de) | [blum] |
| bouquet (of flowers) | boeket (het) | [bu'kɛt] |

rose (flower)	roos (de)	[rōs]
tulip	tulp (de)	[tʉlp]
carnation	anjer (de)	['anjer]
gladiolus	gladiool (de)	[xladi'ōl]

cornflower	korenbloem (de)	['kɔrənblum]
harebell	klokje (het)	['klɔkjə]
dandelion	paardenbloem (de)	['pārdən·blum]
camomile	kamille (de)	[ka'milə]

aloe	aloë (de)	[a'lɔe]
cactus	cactus (de)	['kaktʉs]
rubber plant, ficus	ficus (de)	['fikʉs]
lily	lelie (de)	['leli]
geranium	geranium (de)	[xə'ranijum]

hyacinth	hyacint (de)	[hia'sint]
mimosa	mimosa (de)	[mi'mɔza]
narcissus	narcis (de)	[nar'sis]
nasturtium	Oostindische kers (de)	[ōst 'indisə kɛrs]

orchid	orchidee (de)	[ɔrxi'dē]
peony	pioenroos (de)	[pi'un·rōs]
violet	viooltje (het)	[vi'jōltʃə]
pansy	driekleurig viooltje (het)	[dri'klørəx vi'ōltʃə]
forget-me-not	vergeet-mij-nietje (het)	[vər'xēt-mɛj-'nitʃə]
daisy	madeliefje (het)	[madɛ'lifⁱə]

poppy	papaver (de)	[pa'pavər]
hemp	hennep (de)	['hɛnəp]
mint	munt (de)	[mʉnt]

| lily of the valley | lelietje-van-dalen (het) | ['leljetʃe-van-'dalən] |
| snowdrop | sneeuwklokje (het) | ['snēw·'klɔkjə] |

nettle	brandnetel (de)	['brant·netəl]
sorrel	veldzuring (de)	[vɛlt·'tsʉriŋ]
water lily	waterlelie (de)	['watər·leli]
fern	varen (de)	['varən]
lichen	korstmos (het)	['kɔrstmɔs]
greenhouse (tropical ~)	oranjerie (de)	[ɔranʒɛ'ri]
lawn	gazon (het)	[xa'zɔn]
flowerbed	bloemperk (het)	['blum·pɛrk]

plant	plant (de)	[plant]
grass	gras (het)	[xras]
blade of grass	grasspriet (de)	['xras·sprit]

leaf	blad (het)	[blat]
petal	bloemblad (het)	['blum·blat]
stem	stengel (de)	['stɛŋəl]
tuber	knol (de)	[knɔl]

| young plant (shoot) | scheut (de) | [sxøt] |
| thorn | doorn (de) | [dōrn] |

to blossom (vi)	bloeien	['blujən]
to fade, to wither	verwelken	[vər'wɛlkən]
smell (odor)	geur (de)	[xør]
to cut (flowers)	snijden	['snɛjdən]
to pick (a flower)	plukken	['plʉkən]

232. Cereals, grains

| grain | graan (het) | [xrān] |
| cereal crops | graangewassen | ['xrān·xɛ'wasən] |

ear (of barley, etc.)	**aar (de)**	[ār]
wheat	**tarwe (de)**	['tarwə]
rye	**rogge (de)**	['rɔxə]
oats	**haver (de)**	['havər]
millet	**gierst (de)**	[xirst]
barley	**gerst (de)**	[xɛrst]
corn	**maïs (de)**	[majs]
rice	**rijst (de)**	[rɛjst]
buckwheat	**boekweit (de)**	['bukwɛjt]
pea plant	**erwt (de)**	[ɛrt]
kidney bean	**boon (de)**	[bõn]
soy	**soja (de)**	['sɔja]
lentil	**linze (de)**	['linzə]
beans (pulse crops)	**bonen**	['bɔnən]

233. Vegetables. Greens

vegetables	**groenten**	['xruntən]
greens	**verse kruiden**	['vɛrsə 'krœydən]
tomato	**tomaat (de)**	[tɔ'māt]
cucumber	**augurk (de)**	[au'xʉrk]
carrot	**wortel (de)**	['wɔrtəl]
potato	**aardappel (de)**	['ārd·apəl]
onion	**ui (de)**	['œy]
garlic	**knoflook (de)**	['knõflɔk]
cabbage	**kool (de)**	[kõl]
cauliflower	**bloemkool (de)**	['blum·kõl]
Brussels sprouts	**spruitkool (de)**	['sprœyt·kõl]
broccoli	**broccoli (de)**	['brɔkɔli]
beetroot	**rode biet (de)**	['rɔdə bit]
eggplant	**aubergine (de)**	[ɔbɛr'ʒinə]
zucchini	**courgette (de)**	[kur'ʒɛt]
pumpkin	**pompoen (de)**	[pɔm'pun]
turnip	**knolraap (de)**	['knɔlrāp]
parsley	**peterselie (de)**	[petər'sɛli]
dill	**dille (de)**	['dilə]
lettuce	**sla (de)**	[sla]
celery	**selderij (de)**	['sɛldɛrɛj]
asparagus	**asperge (de)**	[as'pɛrʒə]
spinach	**spinazie (de)**	[spi'nazi]
pea	**erwt (de)**	[ɛrt]
beans	**bonen**	['bɔnən]
corn (maize)	**maïs (de)**	[majs]

kidney bean	**boon (de)**	[bōn]
pepper	**peper (de)**	['pepər]
radish	**radijs (de)**	[ra'dɛjs]
artichoke	**artisjok (de)**	[arti'çɔk]

REGIONAL GEOGRAPHY

Countries. Nationalities

234. Western Europe

Europe	**Europa (het)**	[ø'rɔpa]
European Union	**Europese Unie (de)**	[ørɔ'pezə 'juni]
European (n)	**Europeaan (de)**	[ørɔpe'ān]
European (adj)	**Europees**	[ørɔ'pēs]
Austria	**Oostenrijk (het)**	['ōstənrɛjk]
Austrian (masc.)	**Oostenrijker (de)**	['ōstənrɛjkər]
Austrian (fem.)	**Oostenrijkse (de)**	['ōstənrɛjksə]
Austrian (adj)	**Oostenrijks**	['ōstənrɛjks]
Great Britain	**Groot-Brittannië (het)**	[xrōt-bri'taniə]
England	**Engeland (het)**	['ɛŋɛlant]
British (masc.)	**Engelsman (de)**	['ɛŋɛlsman]
British (fem.)	**Engelse (de)**	['ɛŋɛlsə]
English, British (adj)	**Engels**	['ɛŋɛls]
Belgium	**België (het)**	['bɛlxiə]
Belgian (masc.)	**Belg (de)**	[bɛlx]
Belgian (fem.)	**Belgische (de)**	['bɛlxisə]
Belgian (adj)	**Belgisch**	['bɛlxis]
Germany	**Duitsland (het)**	['dœɤtslant]
German (masc.)	**Duitser (de)**	['dœɤtsər]
German (fem.)	**Duitse (de)**	['dœɤtsə]
German (adj)	**Duits**	['dœɤts]
Netherlands	**Nederland (het)**	['nedərlant]
Holland	**Holland (het)**	['hɔlant]
Dutch (masc.)	**Nederlander (de)**	['nedərlandər]
Dutch (fem.)	**Nederlandse (de)**	['nedərlandsə]
Dutch (adj)	**Nederlands**	['nedərlands]
Greece	**Griekenland (het)**	['xrikənlant]
Greek (masc.)	**Griek (de)**	[xrik]
Greek (fem.)	**Griekse (de)**	['xriksə]
Greek (adj)	**Grieks**	[xriks]
Denmark	**Denemarken (het)**	['denəmarkən]
Dane (masc.)	**Deen (de)**	[dēn]

Dane (fem.)	**Deense (de)**	['dēnsə]
Danish (adj)	**Deens**	[dēns]
Ireland	**Ierland (het)**	[ˈīrlant]
Irish (masc.)	**Ier (de)**	[īr]
Irish (fem.)	**Ierse (de)**	[ˈīrsə]
Irish (adj)	**Iers**	[īrs]
Iceland	**IJsland (het)**	[ˈɛjslant]
Icelander (masc.)	**IJslander (de)**	[ˈɛjslandər]
Icelander (fem.)	**IJslandse (de)**	[ˈɛjslandsə]
Icelandic (adj)	**IJslands**	[ˈɛjslandsə]
Spain	**Spanje (het)**	[ˈspanjə]
Spaniard (masc.)	**Spanjaard (de)**	[ˈspanjārt]
Spaniard (fem.)	**Spaanse (de)**	[ˈspānsə]
Spanish (adj)	**Spaans**	[spāns]
Italy	**Italië (het)**	[iˈtaliə]
Italian (masc.)	**Italiaan (de)**	[italiˈān]
Italian (fem.)	**Italiaanse (de)**	[italiˈānsə]
Italian (adj)	**Italiaans**	[italiˈāns]
Cyprus	**Cyprus (het)**	[ˈsiprʉs]
Cypriot (masc.)	**Cyprioot (de)**	[sipriˈōt]
Cypriot (fem.)	**Cypriotische (de)**	[sipriˈɔtisə]
Cypriot (adj)	**Cypriotisch**	[sipriˈɔtis]
Malta	**Malta (het)**	[ˈmalta]
Maltese (masc.)	**Maltees (de)**	[malˈtēs]
Maltese (fem.)	**Maltese (de)**	[malˈtezə]
Maltese (adj)	**Maltees**	[malˈtēs]
Norway	**Noorwegen (het)**	[ˈnōrwexən]
Norwegian (masc.)	**Noor (de)**	[nōr]
Norwegian (fem.)	**Noorse (de)**	[ˈnōrsə]
Norwegian (adj)	**Noors**	[nōrs]
Portugal	**Portugal (het)**	[portʉxal]
Portuguese (masc.)	**Portugees (de)**	[portʉˈxēs]
Portuguese (fem.)	**Portugese (de)**	[portʉˈxesə]
Portuguese (adj)	**Portugees**	[portʉˈxēs]
Finland	**Finland (het)**	[ˈfinlant]
Finn (masc.)	**Fin (de)**	[fin]
Finn (fem.)	**Finse (de)**	[ˈfinsə]
Finnish (adj)	**Fins**	[fins]
France	**Frankrijk (het)**	[ˈfrankrɛjk]
French (masc.)	**Fransman (de)**	[ˈfransman]
French (fem.)	**Française (de)**	[franˈsɛzə]
French (adj)	**Frans**	[frans]

Sweden	Zweden (het)	['zwedən]
Swede (masc.)	Zweed (de)	[zwẽt]
Swede (fem.)	Zweedse (de)	['zwẽtsə]
Swedish (adj)	Zweeds	[zwẽts]

Switzerland	Zwitserland (het)	['zwitsərlant]
Swiss (masc.)	Zwitser (de)	['zwitsər]
Swiss (fem.)	Zwitserse (de)	['zwitsərsə]
Swiss (adj)	Zwitsers	['zwitsərs]

Scotland	Schotland (het)	['sxɔtlant]
Scottish (masc.)	Schot (de)	[sxɔt]
Scottish (fem.)	Schotse (de)	['sxɔtsə]
Scottish (adj)	Schots	[sxɔts]

Vatican	Vaticaanstad (de)	[vati'kān·stat]
Liechtenstein	Liechtenstein (het)	['lixtɛnstɛjn]
Luxembourg	Luxemburg (het)	['lʉksɛmbʉrx]
Monaco	Monaco (het)	[mɔ'nakɔ]

235. Central and Eastern Europe

Albania	Albanië (het)	[al'baniə]
Albanian (masc.)	Albanees (de)	[alba'nẽs]
Albanian (fem.)	Albanese (de)	[alba'nesə]
Albanian (adj)	Albanees	[alba'nẽs]

Bulgaria	Bulgarije (het)	[bʉlxa'rɛjə]
Bulgarian (masc.)	Bulgaar (de)	[bʉl'xār]
Bulgarian (fem.)	Bulgaarse (de)	[bʉl'xārsə]
Bulgarian (adj)	Bulgaars	[bʉl'xārs]

Hungary	Hongarije (het)	[hɔnxa'rɛjə]
Hungarian (masc.)	Hongaar (de)	[hɔn'xār]
Hungarian (fem.)	Hongaarse (de)	[hɔn'xārsə]
Hungarian (adj)	Hongaars	[hɔn'xārs]

Latvia	Letland (het)	['lɛtlant]
Latvian (masc.)	Let (de)	[lɛt]
Latvian (fem.)	Letse (de)	['lɛtsə]
Latvian (adj)	Lets	[lɛts]

Lithuania	Litouwen (het)	[li'tauən]
Lithuanian (masc.)	Litouwer (de)	[li'tauər]
Lithuanian (fem.)	Litouwse (de)	[li'tausə]
Lithuanian (adj)	Litouws	[li'taus]

Poland	Polen (het)	['pɔlən]
Pole (masc.)	Pool (de)	[pōl]
Pole (fem.)	Poolse (de)	['pōlsə]

Polish (adj)	**Pools**	[pōls]
Romania	**Roemenië (het)**	[ru'meniə]
Romanian (masc.)	**Roemeen (de)**	[ru'mēn]
Romanian (fem.)	**Roemeense (de)**	[ru'mēnsə]
Romanian (adj)	**Roemeens**	[ru'mēns]

Serbia	**Servië (het)**	['sɛrviə]
Serbian (masc.)	**Serviër (de)**	['sɛrviər]
Serbian (fem.)	**Servische (de)**	['sɛrvisə]
Serbian (adj)	**Servisch**	['sɛrvis]

Slovakia	**Slowakije (het)**	[slɔwa'kɛjə]
Slovak (masc.)	**Slowaak (de)**	[slɔ'wāk]
Slovak (fem.)	**Slowaakse (de)**	[slɔ'wāksə]
Slovak (adj)	**Slowaakse**	[slɔ'wāksə]

Croatia	**Kroatië (het)**	[krɔ'asiə]
Croatian (masc.)	**Kroaat (de)**	[krɔ'āt]
Croatian (fem.)	**Kroatische (de)**	[krɔ'atisə]
Croatian (adj)	**Kroatisch**	[krɔ'atis]

Czech Republic	**Tsjechië (het)**	['tʃɛxiə]
Czech (masc.)	**Tsjech (de)**	[tʃɛx]
Czech (fem.)	**Tsjechische (de)**	['tʃɛxisə]
Czech (adj)	**Tsjechisch**	['tʃɛxis]

Estonia	**Estland (het)**	['ɛstlant]
Estonian (masc.)	**Est (de)**	[ɛst]
Estonian (fem.)	**Estse (de)**	['ɛstsə]
Estonian (adj)	**Ests**	['ɛsts]

Bosnia and Herzegovina	**Bosnië en Herzegovina (het)**	['bɔsniə ən hɛrzə'xɔvina]
Macedonia (Republic of ~)	**Macedonië (het)**	[make'dɔniə]
Slovenia	**Slovenië (het)**	[slɔ'vɛniə]
Montenegro	**Montenegro (het)**	[mɔntə'nɛxrɔ]

236. Former USSR countries

Azerbaijan	**Azerbeidzjan (het)**	[azərbej'dʒan]
Azerbaijani (masc.)	**Azerbeidzjaan (de)**	[azərbej'dʒān]
Azerbaijani (fem.)	**Azerbeidjaanse (de)**	[azərbej'dʒānsə]
Azerbaijani, Azeri (adj)	**Azerbeidjaans**	[azərbej'dʒāns]

Armenia	**Armenië (het)**	[ar'meniə]
Armenian (masc.)	**Armeen (de)**	[ar'mēn]
Armenian (fem.)	**Armeense (de)**	[ar'mēnsə]
Armenian (adj)	**Armeens**	[ar'mēns]
Belarus	**Wit-Rusland (het)**	[wit-'ruslant]
Belarusian (masc.)	**Wit-Rus (de)**	[wit-'rus]

Belarusian (fem.)	Wit-Russische (de)	[wit-'rʉsisə]
Belarusian (adj)	Wit-Russisch	[wit-'rʉsis]
Georgia	Georgië (het)	[xe'orxiə]
Georgian (masc.)	Georgiër (de)	[xe'orxiər]
Georgian (fem.)	Georgische (de)	[xe'orxisə]
Georgian (adj)	Georgisch	[xe'orxis]
Kazakhstan	Kazakstan (het)	[kazak'stan]
Kazakh (masc.)	Kazak (de)	[ka'zak]
Kazakh (fem.)	Kazakse (de)	[ka'zaksə]
Kazakh (adj)	Kazakse	[ka'zaksə]
Kirghizia	Kirgizië (het)	[kir'xiziə]
Kirghiz (masc.)	Kirgiziër (de)	[kir'xiziər]
Kirghiz (fem.)	Kirgizische (de)	[kir'xizisə]
Kirghiz (adj)	Kirgizische	[kir'xizisə]
Moldova, Moldavia	Moldavië (het)	[mɔl'daviə]
Moldavian (masc.)	Moldaviër (de)	[mɔl'daviər]
Moldavian (fem.)	Moldavische (de)	[mɔl'davisə]
Moldavian (adj)	Moldavisch	[mɔl'davis]
Russia	Rusland (het)	['rʉslant]
Russian (masc.)	Rus (de)	[rʉs]
Russian (fem.)	Russin (de)	[rʉ'sin]
Russian (adj)	Russisch	['rʉsis]
Tajikistan	Tadzjikistan (het)	[ta'dʒikistan]
Tajik (masc.)	Tadzjiek (de)	[ta'dʒik]
Tajik (fem.)	Tadzjiekse (de)	[ta'dʒiksə]
Tajik (adj)	Tadzjieks	[ta'dʒiks]
Turkmenistan	Turkmenistan (het)	[tʉrk'menistan]
Turkmen (masc.)	Turkmeen (de)	[tʉrk'mēn]
Turkmen (fem.)	Turkmeense (de)	[tʉrk'mēnsə]
Turkmenian (adj)	Turkmeens	[tʉrk'mēns]
Uzbekistan	Oezbekistan (het)	[uz'bekistan]
Uzbek (masc.)	Oezbeek (de)	[uz'bēk]
Uzbek (fem.)	Oezbeekse (de)	[uz'bēksə]
Uzbek (adj)	Oezbeeks	[uz'bēks]
Ukraine	Oekraïne (het)	[ukra'inə]
Ukrainian (masc.)	Oekraïner (de)	[ukra'inər]
Ukrainian (fem.)	Oekraïense (de)	[ukra'insə]
Ukrainian (adj)	Oekraïens	[ukra'ins]

237. Asia

Asia	Azië (het)	['āzijə]
Asian (adj)	Aziatisch	[azi'atis]

Vietnam	**Vietnam (het)**	[vjet'nam]
Vietnamese (masc.)	**Vietnamees (de)**	[vjetna'mēs]
Vietnamese (fem.)	**Vietnamese (de)**	[vjetna'mesə]
Vietnamese (adj)	**Vietnamees**	[vjetna'mēs]
India	**India (het)**	['india]
Indian (masc.)	**Indiër (de)**	['indier]
Indian (fem.)	**Indische (de)**	['indisə]
Indian (adj)	**Indisch**	['indis]
Israel	**Israël (het)**	['israɛl]
Israeli (masc.)	**Israëliër (de)**	[isra'ɛlier]
Israeli (fem.)	**Israëlische (de)**	[isra'ɛlisə]
Israeli (adj)	**Israëlisch**	[isra'ɛlis]
Jew (n)	**Jood (de)**	[jōt]
Jewess (n)	**Jodin (de)**	[jo'din]
Jewish (adj)	**Joods**	[jōds]
China	**China (het)**	['ʃina]
Chinese (masc.)	**Chinees (de)**	[ʃi'nēs]
Chinese (fem.)	**Chinese (de)**	[ʃi'nesə]
Chinese (adj)	**Chinees**	[ʃi'nēs]
Korean (masc.)	**Koreaan (de)**	[kɔre'ān]
Korean (fem.)	**Koreaanse (de)**	[kɔre'ānsə]
Korean (adj)	**Koreaans**	[kɔre'āns]
Lebanon	**Libanon (het)**	['libanɔn]
Lebanese (masc.)	**Libanees (de)**	[liba'nēs]
Lebanese (fem.)	**Libanese (de)**	[liba'nesə]
Lebanese (adj)	**Libanees**	[liba'nēs]
Mongolia	**Mongolië (het)**	[mɔn'xɔliə]
Mongolian (masc.)	**Mongool (de)**	[mɔn'xōl]
Mongolian (fem.)	**Mongoolse (de)**	[mɔn'xōlsə]
Mongolian (adj)	**Mongools**	[mɔn'xōls]
Malaysia	**Maleisië (het)**	[ma'lɛjziə]
Malaysian (masc.)	**Maleisiër (de)**	[ma'lɛjzier]
Malaysian (fem.)	**Maleisische (de)**	[ma'lɛjzisə]
Malaysian (adj)	**Maleisisch**	[ma'lɛjzis]
Pakistan	**Pakistan (het)**	['pakistan]
Pakistani (masc.)	**Pakistaan (de)**	[paki'stan]
Pakistani (fem.)	**Pakistaanse (de)**	[paki'stānsə]
Pakistani (adj)	**Pakistaans**	[paki'stāns]
Saudi Arabia	**Saoedi-Arabië (het)**	[sa'udi-a'rabiə]
Arab (masc.)	**Arabier (de)**	[ara'bir]
Arab (fem.)	**Arabische (de)**	[a'rabisə]
Arab, Arabic (adj)	**Arabisch**	[a'rabis]

Thailand	**Thailand (het)**	['tailant]
Thai (masc.)	**Thai (de)**	['tai]
Thai (fem.)	**Thaise (de)**	['taisə]
Thai (adj)	**Thai**	['tai]
Taiwan	**Taiwan (het)**	[taj'wan]
Taiwanese (masc.)	**Taiwanees (de)**	[tajwa'nēs]
Taiwanese (fem.)	**Taiwanese (de)**	[tajwa'nesə]
Taiwanese (adj)	**Taiwanees**	[tajwa'nēs]
Turkey	**Turkije (het)**	[tʉr'kɛjə]
Turk (masc.)	**Turk (de)**	[tʉrk]
Turk (fem.)	**Turkse (de)**	['tʉrksə]
Turkish (adj)	**Turks**	[tʉrks]
Japan	**Japan (het)**	[ja'pan]
Japanese (masc.)	**Japanner (de)**	[ja'panər]
Japanese (fem.)	**Japanse (de)**	[ja'pansə]
Japanese (adj)	**Japans**	[ja'pans]
Afghanistan	**Afghanistan (het)**	[afˈxanistan]
Bangladesh	**Bangladesh (het)**	[banhla'dɛʃ]
Indonesia	**Indonesië (het)**	[indɔ'nɛsiə]
Jordan	**Jordanië (het)**	[jor'daniə]
Iraq	**Irak (het)**	[i'rak]
Iran	**Iran (het)**	[i'ran]
Cambodia	**Cambodja (het)**	[kam'bɔdja]
Kuwait	**Koeweit (het)**	[ku'wɛjt]
Laos	**Laos (het)**	['laɔs]
Myanmar	**Myanmar (het)**	['mjanmar]
Nepal	**Nepal (het)**	[ne'pal]
United Arab Emirates	**Verenigde Arabische Emiraten**	[və'rɛnixdə a'rabisə ɛmi'ratən]
Syria	**Syrië (het)**	['siriə]
Palestine	**Palestijnse autonomie (de)**	[pale'stɛjnsə autɔnɔ'mi]
South Korea	**Zuid-Korea (het)**	['zœyd-kɔ'rea]
North Korea	**Noord-Korea (het)**	[nōrd-kɔ'rea]

238. North America

United States of America	**Verenigde Staten van Amerika**	[və'rɛnixdə 'statən van a'merika]
American (masc.)	**Amerikaan (de)**	[ameri'kān]
American (fem.)	**Amerikaanse (de)**	[ameri'kānsə]
American (adj)	**Amerikaans**	[ameri'kāns]
Canada	**Canada (het)**	['kanada]

Canadian (masc.)	Canadees (de)	[kana'dēs]
Canadian (fem.)	Canadese (de)	[kana'desə]
Canadian (adj)	Canadees	[kana'dēs]

Mexico	Mexico (het)	['meksikɔ]
Mexican (masc.)	Mexicaan (de)	[meksi'kān]
Mexican (fem.)	Mexicaanse (de)	[meksi'kānsə]
Mexican (adj)	Mexicaans	[meksi'kāns]

239. Central and South America

Argentina	Argentinië (het)	[arxɛn'tiniə]
Argentinian (masc.)	Argentijn (de)	[arxɛn'tɛjn]
Argentinian (fem.)	Argentijnse (de)	[arxɛn'tɛjnsə]
Argentinian (adj)	Argentijns	[arxɛn'tɛjns]

Brazil	Brazilië (het)	[bra'ziliə]
Brazilian (masc.)	Braziliaan (de)	[brazili'ān]
Brazilian (fem.)	Braziliaanse (de)	[brazili'ānsə]
Brazilian (adj)	Braziliaans	[brazili'āns]

Colombia	Colombia (het)	[kɔ'lɔmbia]
Colombian (masc.)	Colombiaan (de)	[kɔlɔmbi'ān]
Colombian (fem.)	Colombiaanse (de)	[kɔlɔmbi'ānsə]
Colombian (adj)	Colombiaans	[kɔlɔmbi'ānsə]

Cuba	Cuba (het)	['kʉba]
Cuban (masc.)	Cubaan (de)	[kʉ'bān]
Cuban (fem.)	Cubaanse (de)	[kʉ'bānsə]
Cuban (adj)	Cubaans	[kʉ'bāns]

Chile	Chili (het)	['ʃili]
Chilean (masc.)	Chileen (de)	[ʃi'lēn]
Chilean (fem.)	Chileense (de)	[ʃi'lēnsə]
Chilean (adj)	Chileens	[ʃi'lēns]

Bolivia	Bolivia (het)	[bɔ'livia]
Venezuela	Venezuela (het)	[venəzʉ'ɛla]
Paraguay	Paraguay (het)	['paragvaj]
Peru	Peru (het)	[pe'ru]
Suriname	Suriname (het)	[sʉri'namə]
Uruguay	Uruguay (het)	['urugvaj]
Ecuador	Ecuador (het)	[ɛkwa'dɔr]

The Bahamas	Bahama's	[ba'hamas]
Haiti	Haïti (het)	[ha'iti]
Dominican Republic	Dominicaanse Republiek (de)	[dɔmini'kānsə repʉ'blik]
Panama	Panama (het)	['panama]
Jamaica	Jamaica (het)	[ja'majka]

243

240. Africa

Egypt	Egypte (het)	[ɛ'xiptə]
Egyptian (masc.)	Egyptenaar (de)	[ɛ'xiptənār]
Egyptian (fem.)	Egyptische (de)	[ɛ'xiptisə]
Egyptian (adj)	Egyptisch	[ɛ'xiptis]
Morocco	Marokko (het)	[ma'rɔkɔ]
Moroccan (masc.)	Marokkaan (de)	[marɔ'kān]
Moroccan (fem.)	Marokkaanse (de)	[marɔ'kānsə]
Moroccan (adj)	Marokkaans	[marɔ'kāns]
Tunisia	Tunesië (het)	[tʉ'nɛziə]
Tunisian (masc.)	Tunesiër (de)	[tʉ'nɛziər]
Tunisian (fem.)	Tunesische (de)	[tʉ'nezisə]
Tunisian (adj)	Tunesisch	[tʉ'nezis]
Ghana	Ghana (het)	['xana]
Zanzibar	Zanzibar (het)	['zanzibar]
Kenya	Kenia (het)	['kenia]
Libya	Libië (het)	['libiə]
Madagascar	Madagaskar (het)	[mada'xaskar]
Namibia	Namibië (het)	[na'mibiə]
Senegal	Senegal (het)	[senexal]
Tanzania	Tanzania (het)	[tan'zania]
South Africa	Zuid-Afrika (het)	['zœʏd-'afrika]
African (masc.)	Afrikaan (de)	[afri'kān]
African (fem.)	Afrikaanse (de)	[afri'kānsə]
African (adj)	Afrikaans	[afri'kāns]

241. Australia. Oceania

Australia	Australië (het)	[ɔu'straliə]
Australian (masc.)	Australiër (de)	[ɔu'straliər]
Australian (fem.)	Australische (de)	[au'stralisə]
Australian (adj)	Australisch	[au'stralis]
New Zealand	Nieuw-Zeeland (het)	[niu-'zēlant]
New Zealander (masc.)	Nieuw-Zeelander (de)	[niu-'zēlandər]
New Zealander (fem.)	Nieuw-Zeelandse (de)	[niu-'zēlantsə]
New Zealand (as adj)	Nieuw-Zeelands	[niu-'zēlants]
Tasmania	Tasmanië (het)	[taz'maniə]
French Polynesia	Frans-Polynesië	[frans-pɔli'nɛziə]

242. Cities

Amsterdam	**Amsterdam**	[amstɛr'dam]
Ankara	**Ankara**	[ankara]
Athens	**Athene**	[a'tenə]
Baghdad	**Bagdad**	[bax'dat]
Bangkok	**Bangkok**	['baŋkɔk]
Barcelona	**Barcelona**	[barse'lɔna]
Beijing	**Peking**	['pekiŋ]
Beirut	**Beiroet**	['bɛjrut]
Berlin	**Berlijn**	[bɛr'lɛjn]
Mumbai (Bombay)	**Bombay, Mumbai**	[bɔm'bɛj], [mumbaj]
Bonn	**Bonn**	[bɔn]
Bordeaux	**Bordeaux**	[bɔr'dɔ]
Bratislava	**Bratislava**	[brati'slava]
Brussels	**Brussel**	['brʉsɛl]
Bucharest	**Boekarest**	[buka'rɛst]
Budapest	**Boedapest**	[buda'pɛst]
Cairo	**Caïro**	[ka'irɔ]
Kolkata (Calcutta)	**Calcutta**	[kal'kʉta]
Chicago	**Chicago**	[ɕi'kagɔ]
Copenhagen	**Kopenhagen**	[kɔpən'haxən]
Dar-es-Salaam	**Dar Es Salaam**	[dar ɛs sa'lãm]
Delhi	**Delhi**	['dɛlhi]
Dubai	**Dubai**	[dʉ'bai]
Dublin	**Dublin**	['dʉblin]
Düsseldorf	**Düsseldorf**	[dʉsəl'dɔrf]
Florence	**Florence**	[flɔ'rans]
Frankfurt	**Frankfort**	['frankfʉrt]
Geneva	**Genève**	[ʒe'nɛvə]
The Hague	**Den Haag**	[dɛn hãx]
Hamburg	**Hamburg**	['hambʉrx]
Hanoi	**Hanoi**	[ha'nɔj]
Havana	**Havana**	[ha'vana]
Helsinki	**Helsinki**	['hɛlsinki]
Hiroshima	**Hiroshima**	[hirɔ'ʃima]
Hong Kong	**Hongkong**	[hɔŋ'kɔŋ]
Istanbul	**Istanbul**	[istan'bul]
Jerusalem	**Jeruzalem**	[jeruza'lɛm]
Kyiv	**Kiev**	['kiev]
Kuala Lumpur	**Kuala Lumpur**	[kʉ'ala 'lʉmpʉr]
Lisbon	**Lissabon**	['lisabɔn]
London	**Londen**	['lɔndən]
Los Angeles	**Los Angeles**	[lɔs 'andʒələs]

Lyons	**Lyon**	[li'ɔn]
Madrid	**Madrid**	[mad'rit]
Marseille	**Marseille**	[mar'sɛjə]
Mexico City	**Mexico-Stad**	['meksikɔ-stat]
Miami	**Miami**	[ma'jami]
Montreal	**Montreal**	[mɔntrɛ'al]
Moscow	**Moskou**	['mɔskau]
Munich	**München**	['mʉnxən]
Nairobi	**Nairobi**	[naj'rɔbi]
Naples	**Napels**	['napɛls]
New York	**New York**	[nʉ jork]
Nice	**Nice**	[nis]
Oslo	**Oslo**	['ɔslɔ]
Ottawa	**Ottawa**	['ɔtawa]
Paris	**Parijs**	[pa'rɛjs]
Prague	**Praag**	[prãx]
Rio de Janeiro	**Rio de Janeiro**	[riɔ də ʒa'nɛjrɔ]
Rome	**Rome**	['rɔmə]
Saint Petersburg	**Sint-Petersburg**	[sint-'petərsbʉrx]
Seoul	**Seoel**	[sɛ'ul]
Shanghai	**Sjanghai**	[ɕan'xaj]
Singapore	**Singapore**	[sinxa'pɔrə]
Stockholm	**Stockholm**	[stɔk'hɔlm]
Sydney	**Sydney**	['sidnɛj]
Taipei	**Taipei**	[taj'pɛj]
Tokyo	**Tokio**	['tɔkiɔ]
Toronto	**Toronto**	[tɔ'rɔntɔ]
Venice	**Venetië**	[ve'nɛtsiə]
Vienna	**Wenen**	['wenən]
Warsaw	**Warschau**	['warʃʌu]
Washington	**Washington**	['waʃingtɔn]

243. Politics. Government. Part 1

politics	**politiek (de)**	[poli'tik]
political (adj)	**politiek**	[poli'tik]
politician	**politicus (de)**	[pɔ'litikʉs]
state (country)	**staat (de)**	[stãt]
citizen	**burger (de)**	['bʉrxər]
citizenship	**staatsburgerschap (het)**	['bʉrxərsxap]
national emblem	**nationaal wapen (het)**	[natsjɔ'nãl 'wapən]
national anthem	**volkslied (het)**	['vɔlkslit]
government	**regering (de)**	[re'xɛrin]

head of state	staatshoofd (het)	['stāts·hōft]
parliament	parlement (het)	[parle'mɛnt]
party	partij (de)	[par'tɛj]

| capitalism | kapitalisme (het) | [kapita'lismə] |
| capitalist (adj) | kapitalistisch | [kapita'listis] |

| socialism | socialisme (het) | [sɔʃia'lismə] |
| socialist (adj) | socialistisch | [sɔʃia'listis] |

communism	communisme (het)	[kɔmʉ'nismə]
communist (adj)	communistisch	[kɔmʉ'nistis]
communist (n)	communist (de)	[kɔmʉ'nist]

democracy	democratie (de)	[demɔkra'tsi]
democrat	democraat (de)	[demɔ'krāt]
democratic (adj)	democratisch	[demɔ'kratis]
Democratic party	democratische partij (de)	[demɔ'kratisə par'tɛj]

| liberal (n) | liberaal (de) | [libe'rāl] |
| liberal (adj) | liberaal | [libe'rāl] |

| conservative (n) | conservator (de) | [kɔnsər'vatɔr] |
| conservative (adj) | conservatief | [kɔnsərva'tif] |

republic (n)	republiek (de)	[repʉ'blik]
republican (n)	republikein (de)	[repʉbli'kɛjn]
Republican party	Republikeinse Partij (de)	[repʉbli'kɛjnsə par'tɛj]

elections	verkiezing (de)	[vər'kiziŋ]
to elect (vt)	kiezen	['kizən]
elector, voter	kiezer (de)	['kizər]
election campaign	verkiezings- campagne (de)	[vər'kiziŋs kam'panjə]

voting (n)	stemming (de)	['stɛmiŋ]
to vote (vi)	stemmen	['stɛmən]
suffrage, right to vote	stemrecht (het)	['stɛm·rɛxt]

candidate	kandidaat (de)	[kandi'dāt]
to be a candidate	zich kandideren	[zix kandi'derən]
campaign	campagne (de)	[kam'panjə]

| opposition (as adj) | oppositie- | [ɔpɔ'zitsi] |
| opposition (n) | oppositie (de) | [ɔpɔ'zitsi] |

visit	bezoek (het)	[bə'zuk]
official visit	officieel bezoek (het)	[ɔfi'ʃēl bə'zuk]
international (adj)	internationaal	[intərnatsjo'nāl]

| negotiations | onderhandelingen | ['ɔndər'handeliŋən] |
| to negotiate (vi) | onderhandelen | ['ɔndər'handelən] |

244. Politics. Government. Part 2

society	maatschappij (de)	[mãtsxa'pɛj]
constitution	grondwet (de)	['xrɔnt·wɛt]
power (political control)	macht (de)	[maxt]
corruption	corruptie (de)	[kɔ'rʉpsi]
law (justice)	wet (de)	[wɛt]
legal (legitimate)	wettelijk	['wɛtələk]
justice (fairness)	rechtvaardigheid (de)	[rɛxt'vãrdəxhɛjt]
just (fair)	rechtvaardig	[rɛxt'vãrdəx]
committee	comité (het)	[kɔmi'tɛ]
bill (draft law)	wetsvoorstel (het)	['wɛtsvõrstɛl]
budget	begroting (de)	[bə'xrɔtiŋ]
policy	beleid (het)	[bə'lɛjt]
reform	hervorming (de)	[hɛr'vɔrmiŋ]
radical (adj)	radicaal	[radi'kãl]
power (strength, force)	macht (de)	[maxt]
powerful (adj)	machtig	['mahtəx]
supporter	aanhanger (de)	['ãnhaŋər]
influence	invloed (de)	['invlut]
regime (e.g., military ~)	regime (het)	[re'ʒim]
conflict	conflict (het)	[kɔn'flikt]
conspiracy (plot)	samenzwering (de)	['samənzweriŋ]
provocation	provocatie (de)	[prɔvɔ'katsi]
to overthrow (regime, etc.)	omverwerpen	['ɔmvər'wɛrpən]
overthrow (of government)	omverwerping (de)	['ɔmvər'wɛrpiŋ]
revolution	revolutie (de)	[revɔ'lʉtsi]
coup d'état	staatsgreep (de)	['stãts·xrɛp]
military coup	militaire coup (de)	['militɛrə kup]
crisis	crisis (de)	['krisis]
economic recession	economische recessie (de)	[ɛkɔ'nɔmisə rɛ'sɛsi]
demonstrator (protester)	betoger (de)	[bə'tɔxər]
demonstration	betoging (de)	[bə'toxiŋ]
martial law	krijgswet (de)	['krɛjxs·wɛt]
military base	militaire basis (de)	['militɛrə 'bazis]
stability	stabiliteit (de)	[stabili'tɛjt]
stable (adj)	stabiel	[sta'bil]
exploitation	uitbuiting (de)	['œytbɛjtiŋ]
to exploit (workers)	uitbuiten	['œytbɛjtən]
racism	racisme (het)	[ra'sismə]

racist	racist (de)	[ra'sist]
fascism	fascisme (het)	[fa'ʃismə]
fascist	fascist (de)	[fa'ʃist]

245. Countries. Miscellaneous

foreigner	vreemdeling (de)	['vrēmdəliŋ]
foreign (adj)	buitenlands	['bœʏtənlants]
abroad	in het buitenland	[in ət 'bœʏtənlant]
(in a foreign country)		

emigrant	emigrant (de)	[ɛmi'xrant]
emigration	emigratie (de)	[ɛmi'xratsi]
to emigrate (vi)	emigreren	[ɛmi'xrerən]

the West	Westen (het)	['wɛstən]
the East	Oosten (het)	['ōstən]
the Far East	Verre Oosten (het)	['vɛrə 'ōstən]

civilization	beschaving (de)	[bə'sxaviŋ]
humanity (mankind)	mensheid (de)	['mɛnshɛjt]
the world (earth)	wereld (de)	['werəlt]
peace	vrede (de)	['vredə]
worldwide (adj)	wereld-	['werəlt]

homeland	vaderland (het)	['vadər·lant]
people (population)	volk (het)	[vɔlk]
population	bevolking (de)	[bə'vɔlkiŋ]
people (a lot of ~)	mensen	['mɛnsən]
nation (people)	natie (de)	['natsi]
generation	generatie (de)	[xenə'ratsi]

territory (area)	gebied (het)	[xə'bit]
region	regio, streek (de)	['rexiɔ], [strēk]
state (part of a country)	deelstaat (de)	['dēlstāt]

tradition	traditie (de)	[tra'ditsi]
custom (tradition)	gewoonte (de)	[xə'wōntə]
ecology	ecologie (de)	[ɛkɔlɔ'xi]

Indian (Native American)	Indiaan (de)	[indi'ān]
Gypsy (masc.)	zigeuner (de)	[zixønər]
Gypsy (fem.)	zigeunerin (de)	[zixøne'rin]
Gypsy (adj)	zigeuner-	[zixønər]

empire	rijk (het)	[rɛjk]
colony	kolonie (de)	[kɔ'lɔni]
slavery	slavernij (de)	[slavər'nɛj]
invasion	invasie (de)	[in'vazi]
famine	hongersnood (de)	['hɔŋərsnōt]

246. Major religious groups. Confessions

religion	**religie (de)**	[re'lixi]
religious (adj)	**religieus**	[relixiøs]
faith, belief	**geloof (het)**	[xə'lõf]
to believe (in God)	**geloven**	[xə'lɔvən]
believer	**gelovige (de)**	[xə'lɔvixə]
atheism	**atheïsme (het)**	[ate'izmə]
atheist	**atheïst (de)**	[ate'ist]
Christianity	**christendom (het)**	['kristəndɔm]
Christian (n)	**christen (de)**	['kristən]
Christian (adj)	**christelijk**	['kristələk]
Catholicism	**katholicisme (het)**	[katɔli'sismə]
Catholic (n)	**katholiek (de)**	[katɔ'lik]
Catholic (adj)	**katholiek**	[katɔ'lik]
Protestantism	**protestantisme (het)**	[prɔtɛstan'tismə]
Protestant Church	**Protestante Kerk (de)**	[prɔtɛ'stantə kɛrk]
Protestant (n)	**protestant (de)**	[prɔtɛ'stant]
Orthodoxy	**orthodoxie (de)**	[ɔrtɔdɔk'si]
Orthodox Church	**Orthodoxe Kerk (de)**	[ɔrtɔ'dɔksə kɛrk]
Orthodox (n)	**orthodox**	[ɔrtɔ'dɔks]
Presbyterianism	**presbyterianisme (het)**	[prɛsbitəria'nismə]
Presbyterian Church	**Presbyteriaanse Kerk (de)**	[prɛsbitəri'ānsə kɛrk]
Presbyterian (n)	**presbyteriaan (de)**	[prɛsbitəri'ān]
Lutheranism	**lutheranisme (het)**	[lʉtɛra'nismə]
Lutheran (n)	**lutheraan (de)**	[lʉtɛ'rān]
Baptist Church	**baptisme (het)**	[bap'tismə]
Baptist (n)	**baptist (de)**	[bap'tist]
Anglican Church	**Anglicaanse kerk (de)**	[anhli'kānsə kɛrk]
Anglican (n)	**anglicaan (de)**	[anhli'kān]
Mormonism	**mormonisme (het)**	[mɔrmɔ'nismə]
Mormon (n)	**mormoon (de)**	[mɔr'mõn]
Judaism	**Jodendom (het)**	['jodəndɔm]
Jew (n)	**jood (de)**	[jõt]
Buddhism	**boeddhisme (het)**	[bu'dismə]
Buddhist (n)	**boeddhist (de)**	[bu'dist]
Hinduism	**hindoeïsme (het)**	[hindu'ismə]

Hindu (n)	hindoe (de)	['hindu]
Islam	islam (de)	[is'lam]
Muslim (n)	islamiet (de)	[isla'mit]
Muslim (adj)	islamitisch	[isla'mitis]

| Shiah Islam | sjiisme (het) | [ɕi'ismə] |
| Shiite (n) | sjiiet (de) | [ɕi'it] |

| Sunni Islam | soennisme (het) | [su'nismə] |
| Sunnite (n) | soenniet (de) | [su'nit] |

247. Religions. Priests

| priest | priester (de) | ['pristər] |
| the Pope | paus (de) | ['paus] |

monk, friar	monnik (de)	['mɔnək]
nun	non (de)	[nɔn]
pastor	pastoor (de)	['pastõr]

abbot	abt (de)	[apt]
vicar (parish priest)	vicaris (de)	[vi'karis]
bishop	bisschop (de)	['bisxɔp]
cardinal	kardinaal (de)	[kardi'nãl]

preacher	predikant (de)	[prədi'kant]
preaching	preek (de)	[prẽk]
parishioners	kerkgangers	[kɛrk·'xaŋərs]

| believer | gelovige (de) | [xə'lovixə] |
| atheist | atheïst (de) | [ate'ist] |

248. Faith. Christianity. Islam

| Adam | Adam | ['adam] |
| Eve | Eva | ['ɛva] |

God	God (de)	[xɔt]
the Lord	Heer (de)	[hẽr]
the Almighty	Almachtige (de)	[al'mahtixə]

sin	zonde (de)	['zɔndə]
to sin (vi)	zondigen	['zɔndixən]
sinner (masc.)	zondaar (de)	['zɔndãr]
sinner (fem.)	zondares (de)	[zɔnda'rɛs]

| hell | hel (de) | [hɛl] |
| paradise | paradijs (het) | [para'dajs] |

Jesus	**Jezus**	['jezʉs]
Jesus Christ	**Jezus Christus**	['jezʉs 'kristʉs]
the Holy Spirit	**Heilige Geest (de)**	['hɛjlixə xēst]
the Savior	**Verlosser (de)**	[vər'lɔsə]
the Virgin Mary	**Maagd Maria (de)**	[māxt ma'ria]
the Devil	**duivel (de)**	['dœyvəl]
devil's (adj)	**duivels**	['dœyvəls]
Satan	**Satan**	['satan]
satanic (adj)	**satanisch**	[sa'tanis]
angel	**engel (de)**	['ɛŋəl]
guardian angel	**beschermengel (de)**	[bə'sxɛrm·'ɛŋəl]
angelic (adj)	**engelachtig**	['ɛŋəlaxtəx]
apostle	**apostel (de)**	[a'pɔstəl]
archangel	**aartsengel (de)**	[ārts'ɛŋəl]
the Antichrist	**antichrist (de)**	[anti'krist]
Church	**Kerk (de)**	[kɛrk]
Bible	**bijbel (de)**	['bɛjbəl]
biblical (adj)	**bijbels**	['bɛjbəls]
Old Testament	**Oude Testament (het)**	['audə tɛsta'mɛnt]
New Testament	**Nieuwe Testament (het)**	['niuə tɛsta'mɛnt]
Gospel	**evangelie (het)**	[ɛvaŋ'heli]
Holy Scripture	**Heilige Schrift (de)**	['hɛjlixə sxrift]
Heaven	**Hemel, Hemelrijk (de)**	['heməl], ['heməlrɛjk]
Commandment	**gebod (het)**	[hə'bɔt]
prophet	**profeet (de)**	[prɔ'fēt]
prophecy	**profetie (de)**	[prɔ'fetsi]
Allah	**Allah**	['ala]
Mohammed	**Mohammed**	[mɔ'hamət]
the Koran	**Koran (de)**	[kɔ'ran]
mosque	**moskee (de)**	[mɔs'kē]
mullah	**moellah (de)**	[mula]
prayer	**gebed (het)**	[xə'bɛt]
to pray (vi, vt)	**bidden**	['bidən]
pilgrimage	**pelgrimstocht (de)**	['pɛlxrims·tɔxt]
pilgrim	**pelgrim (de)**	['pɛlxrim]
Mecca	**Mekka**	['mɛka]
church	**kerk (de)**	[kɛrk]
temple	**tempel (de)**	['tɛmpəl]
cathedral	**kathedraal (de)**	[kate'drāl]
Gothic (adj)	**gotisch**	['xɔtis]
synagogue	**synagoge (de)**	[sina'xɔxə]

mosque	moskee (de)	[mɔs'keē]
chapel	kapel (de)	[ka'pɛl]
abbey	abdij (de)	[ab'dɛj]
convent	nonnenklooster (het)	['nɔnən·'klōstər]
monastery	mannenklooster (het)	['manən·'klōstər]
monastery	klooster (het)	['klōstər]

bell (church ~s)	klok (de)	[klɔk]
bell tower	klokkentoren (de)	['klɔkən·'tɔrən]
to ring (ab. bells)	luiden	['lœʏdən]

cross	kruis (het)	['krœʏs]
cupola (roof)	koepel (de)	['kupəl]
icon	icoon (de)	[i'kōn]

soul	ziel (de)	[zil]
fate (destiny)	lot, noodlot (het)	[lɔt], ['nōtlɔt]
evil (n)	kwaad (het)	['kwāt]
good (n)	goed (het)	[xut]

vampire	vampier (de)	[vam'pir]
witch (evil ~)	heks (de)	[hɛks]
demon	demoon (de)	[de'mōn]
spirit	geest (de)	[xēst]

| redemption (giving us ~) | verzoeningsleer (de) | [vər'zunəŋslēr] |
| to redeem (vt) | vrijkopen | [vrɛj'kɔpən] |

church service, mass	mis (de)	[mis]
to say mass	de mis opdragen	[də mis 'ɔpdraxən]
confession	biecht (de)	[bixt]
to confess (vi)	biechten	['bixtən]

saint (n)	heilige (de)	['hɛjlihə]
sacred (holy)	heilig	['hɛjləx]
holy water	wijwater (het)	['wɛj·watər]

ritual (n)	ritueel (het)	[ritʉ'ēl]
ritual (adj)	ritueel	[ritʉ'ēl]
sacrifice	offerande (de)	[ɔfɛ'randə]

superstition	bijgeloof (het)	['bɛjxəlōf]
superstitious (adj)	bijgelovig	['bɛjxəlɔvəx]
afterlife	hiernamaals (het)	[hir'na·māls]
eternal life	eeuwige leven (het)	['ēwəxə 'levən]

MISCELLANEOUS

249. Various useful words

background (green ~)	achtergrond (de)	['ahtər·xrɔnt]
balance (of situation)	balans (de)	[ba'lans]
barrier (obstacle)	hindernis (de)	['hindərnis]
base (basis)	basis (de)	['bazis]
beginning	begin (het)	[bə'xin]
category	categorie (de)	[katexɔ'ri]
cause (reason)	reden (de)	['redən]
choice	keuze (de)	['køzə]
coincidence	samenvallen (het)	['samənvalən]
comfortable (~ chair)	comfortabel	[kɔmfɔr'tabəl]
comparison	vergelijking (de)	[vɛrxə'lɛjkiŋ]
compensation	compensatie (de)	[kɔmpən'satsi]
degree (extent, amount)	graad (de)	[xrãt]
development	ontwikkeling (de)	[ɔnt'wikəliŋ]
difference	onderscheid (het)	['ɔndərsxɛjt]
effect (e.g., of drugs)	effect (het)	[ɛ'fɛkt]
effort (exertion)	inspanning (de)	['inspaniŋ]
element	element (het)	[ɛle'mɛnt]
end (finish)	einde (het)	['ɛjndə]
example (illustration)	voorbeeld (het)	['vōrbēlt]
fact	feit (het)	[fɛjt]
frequent (adj)	veelvuldig	[vēl'vʉldəx]
growth (development)	groei (de)	[x'rui]
help	hulp (de)	[hʉlp]
ideal	ideaal (het)	[ide'ãl]
kind (sort, type)	soort (de/het)	[sõrt]
labyrinth	labyrint (het)	[labi'rint]
mistake, error	fout (de)	['faut]
moment	moment (het)	[mɔ'mɛnt]
object (thing)	voorwerp (het)	['vōrwərp]
obstacle	hinderpaal (de)	['hindərpãl]
original (original copy)	origineel (het)	[oriʒi'nēl]
part (~ of sth)	deel (het)	[dēl]
particle, small part	deeltje (het)	['dēltʃə]
pause (break)	pauze (de)	['pauzə]

position	**positie (de)**	[pɔ'zitsi]
principle	**principe (het)**	[prin'sipə]
problem	**probleem (het)**	[prɔ'blēm]

process	**proces (het)**	[prɔ'sɛs]
progress	**voortgang (de)**	['vōrtxaŋ]
property (quality)	**eigenschap (de)**	['ɛjxənsxap]
reaction	**reactie (de)**	[re'aksi]
risk	**risico (het)**	['riziko]

secret	**geheim (het)**	[xə'hɛjm]
series	**serie (de)**	['seri]
shape (outer form)	**vorm (de)**	[vɔrm]
situation	**situatie (de)**	[situ'atsi]
solution	**oplossing (de)**	['ɔplɔsiŋ]

standard (adj)	**standaard**	['standārt]
standard (level of quality)	**standaard (de)**	['standārt]
stop (pause)	**stop (de)**	[stɔp]
style	**stijl (de)**	[stɛjl]

system	**systeem (het)**	[si'stēm]
table (chart)	**tabel (de)**	[ta'bɛl]
tempo, rate	**tempo (het)**	['tɛmpo]
term (word, expression)	**term (de)**	[tɛrm]

thing (object, item)	**ding (het)**	[diŋ]
truth (e.g., moment of ~)	**waarheid (de)**	['wārhɛjt]
turn (please wait your ~)	**beurt (de)**	['børt]
type (sort, kind)	**type (het)**	['tipə]
urgent (adj)	**dringend**	['driŋənt]

urgently (adv)	**dringend**	['driŋənt]
utility (usefulness)	**nut (het)**	[nʉt]
variant (alternative)	**variant (de)**	[vari'ant]
way (means, method)	**manier (de)**	[ma'nir]
zone	**zone (de)**	['zɔnə]

250. Modifiers. Adjectives. Part 1

additional (adj)	**additioneel**	[aditsjɔ'nēl]
ancient (~ civilization)	**eeuwenoude**	[ēwə'naudə]
artificial (adj)	**kunstmatig**	[kʉnst'matəx]
back, rear (adj)	**achter-**	['axtər]
bad (adj)	**slecht**	[slɛxt]

beautiful (~ palace)	**prachtig**	['prahtəx]
beautiful (person)	**mooi**	[mōj]
big (in size)	**groot**	[xrōt]

bitter (taste)	**bitter**	['bitər]
blind (sightless)	**blind**	[blint]
calm, quiet (adj)	**kalm**	[kalm]
careless (negligent)	**nalatig**	[na'latəx]
caring (~ father)	**zorgzaam**	['zɔrxzām]
central (adj)	**centraal**	[sɛn'trāl]
cheap (low-priced)	**goedkoop**	[xut'kōp]
cheerful (adj)	**vrolijk**	['vrɔlək]
children's (adj)	**kinder-**	['kindər]
civil (~ law)	**burgerlijk**	['burxərlək]
clandestine (secret)	**ondergronds**	['ɔndər'xrɔnts]
clean (free from dirt)	**schoon**	[sxōn]
clear (explanation, etc.)	**begrijpelijk**	[bə'xrejpələk]
clever (smart)	**slim**	[slim]
close (near in space)	**dicht**	[dixt]
closed (adj)	**gesloten**	[xə'slotən]
cloudless (sky)	**onbewolkt**	[ɔmbə'wɔlkt]
cold (drink, weather)	**koud**	['kaut]
compatible (adj)	**verenigbaar**	[və'rɛnixbār]
contented (satisfied)	**tevreden**	[təv'redən]
continuous (uninterrupted)	**onophoudelijk**	[ɔnɔp'haudələk]
cool (weather)	**koel**	[kul]
dangerous (adj)	**gevaarlijk**	[xe'vārlək]
dark (room)	**donker**	['donkər]
dead (not alive)	**dood**	[dōt]
dense (fog, smoke)	**dicht**	[dixt]
destitute (extremely poor)	**straatarm**	['strātarm]
different (not the same)	**anders**	['andərs]
difficult (decision)	**moeilijk**	['mujlək]
difficult (problem, task)	**lastig**	['lastəx]
dim, faint (light)	**dof**	[dɔf]
dirty (not clean)	**vuil**	[vœyl]
distant (in space)	**ver**	[vɛr]
dry (clothes, etc.)	**droog**	[drōx]
easy (not difficult)	**eenvoudig**	[ēn'vaudəx]
empty (glass, room)	**leeg**	[lēx]
even (e.g., ~ surface)	**glad**	[xlat]
exact (amount)	**precies**	[prə'sis]
excellent (adj)	**uitstekend**	['œytstekənt]
excessive (adj)	**overdreven**	[ɔvər'drevən]
expensive (adj)	**duur**	[dūr]
exterior (adj)	**buiten-**	['bœytən]
far (the ~ East)	**verst**	[vɛrst]

fast (quick)	**snel**	[snɛl]
fatty (food)	**vettig**	['vetəx]
fertile (land, soil)	**vruchtbaar**	['vrʉxtbār]
flat (~ panel display)	**plat**	[plat]
foreign (adj)	**buitenlands**	['bœytənlants]
fragile (china, glass)	**breekbaar**	['brēkbār]
free (at no cost)	**gratis**	['xratis]
free (unrestricted)	**vrij**	[vrɛj]
fresh (~ water)	**zoet**	[zut]
fresh (e.g., ~ bread)	**vers**	[vɛrs]
frozen (food)	**diepvries**	['dip·vris]
full (completely filled)	**vol**	[vɔl]
gloomy (house, forecast)	**somber**	['sɔmbər]
good (book, etc.)	**goed**	[xut]
good, kind (kindhearted)	**vriendelijk**	['vrindələk]
grateful (adj)	**dankbaar**	['dankbār]
happy (adj)	**gelukkig**	[xə'lʉkəx]
hard (not soft)	**hard**	[hart]
heavy (in weight)	**zwaar**	[zwār]
hostile (adj)	**vijandig**	[vɛ'jandəx]
hot (adj)	**heet**	[hēt]
huge (adj)	**enorm**	[ɛ'nɔrm]
humid (adj)	**vochtig**	['vɔhtəx]
hungry (adj)	**hongerig**	['hoŋərəh]
ill (sick, unwell)	**ziek**	[zik]
immobile (adj)	**onbeweeglijk**	[ɔnbə'wēxlək]
important (adj)	**belangrijk**	[bə'lanxrɛjk]
impossible (adj)	**onmogelijk**	[ɔn'mɔxələk]
incomprehensible	**onbegrijpelijk**	[ɔnbə'xrejpələk]
indispensable (adj)	**onontbeerlijk**	[ɔnɔnt'bērlək]
inexperienced (adj)	**onervaren**	[ɔnər'varən]
insignificant (adj)	**onbelangrijk**	[ɔmbə'laŋrɛjk]
interior (adj)	**binnen-**	['binən]
joint (~ decision)	**gezamenlijk**	[xə'zamənlək]
last (e.g., ~ week)	**vorig**	['vɔrəx]
last (final)	**laatst**	[lātst]
left (e.g., ~ side)	**linker**	['linkər]
legal (legitimate)	**wettelijk**	['wɛtələk]
light (in weight)	**licht**	[lixt]
light (pale color)	**licht**	[lixt]
limited (adj)	**beperkt**	[bə'pɛrkt]
liquid (fluid)	**vloeibaar**	['vlujbār]
long (e.g., ~ hair)	**lang**	[laŋ]

| loud (voice, etc.) | **luid** | ['lœʏt] |
| low (voice) | **zacht** | [zaxt] |

251. Modifiers. Adjectives. Part 2

main (principal)	**hoofd-**	[hõft]
matt, matte	**mat**	[mat]
meticulous (job)	**accuraat**	[akʉ'rāt]
mysterious (adj)	**mysterieus**	[mistɛ'røs]
narrow (street, etc.)	**smal**	[smal]

native (~ country)	**geboorte-**	[xə'bõrtə]
nearby (adj)	**dicht**	[dixt]
nearsighted (adj)	**bijziend**	[bɛj'zint]
needed (necessary)	**nodig**	['nɔdəx]
negative (~ response)	**ontkennend**	[ɔnt'kɛnənt]

neighboring (adj)	**naburig**	[na'bʉrəx]
nervous (adj)	**nerveus**	[nɛr'vøs]
new (adj)	**nieuw**	[niu]
next (e.g., ~ week)	**volgend**	['vɔlxənt]

nice (kind)	**vriendelijk**	['vrindələk]
nice (voice)	**prettig**	['pretəx]
normal (adj)	**normaal**	[nɔr'māl]
not big (adj)	**niet groot**	[nit xrõt]
not difficult (adj)	**niet moeilijk**	[nit 'mujlək]

obligatory (adj)	**verplicht**	[vər'plixt]
old (house)	**oud**	['aut]
open (adj)	**open**	['ɔpən]
opposite (adj)	**tegenovergesteld**	['texən·'ɔvərxəstɛlt]

ordinary (usual)	**gewoon**	[xə'wõn]
original (unusual)	**origineel**	[ɔriʒi'nēl]
past (recent)	**vorig**	['vɔrəx]
permanent (adj)	**permanent**	[perma'nɛnt]
personal (adj)	**persoonlijk**	[pɛr'sõnlək]

polite (adj)	**beleefd**	[bə'lēft]
poor (not rich)	**arm**	[arm]
possible (adj)	**mogelijk**	['mɔxələk]
present (current)	**huidig**	['hœʏdəx]
previous (adj)	**vorig**	['vɔrəx]

principal (main)	**voornaamste**	[võr'nāmstə]
private (~ jet)	**privë**	[pri've]
probable (adj)	**waarschijnlijk**	[wār'sxɛjnlək]
prolonged (e.g., ~ applause)	**langdurig**	[laŋ'dʉrəx]

public (open to all)	**openbaar**	[ɔpən'bār]
punctual (person)	**punctueel**	[pʉnktʉ'ēl]
quiet (tranquil)	**rustig**	['rʉstəx]
rare (adj)	**zeldzaam**	['zɛldzām]
raw (uncooked)	**rauw**	['rau]
right (not left)	**rechter**	['rɛxtər]
right, correct (adj)	**juist, correct**	[jœyst], [kɔ'rɛkt]
ripe (fruit)	**rijp**	[rɛjp]
risky (adj)	**riskant**	[ris'kant]
sad (~ look)	**droevig**	['druvəx]
sad (depressing)	**treurig**	['trørəx]
safe (not dangerous)	**veilig**	['vɛjləx]
salty (food)	**zout**	['zaut]
satisfied (customer)	**tevreden**	[təv'redən]
second hand (adj)	**tweedehands**	[twēdə'hants]
shallow (water)	**ondiep**	[ɔn'dip]
sharp (blade, etc.)	**scherp**	[sxɛrp]
short (in length)	**kort**	[kɔrt]
short, short-lived (adj)	**kort**	[kɔrt]
significant (notable)	**betekenisvol**	[bə'tekənisvɔl]
similar (adj)	**gelijkend**	[xə'lɛjkənt]
simple (easy)	**eenvoudig**	[ēn'vaudəx]
skinny	**mager**	['maxər]
small (in size)	**klein**	[klɛjn]
smooth (surface)	**glad**	[xlat]
soft (~ toys)	**zacht**	[zaxt]
solid (~ wall)	**stevig**	['stevəx]
sour (flavor, taste)	**zuur**	[zūr]
spacious (house, etc.)	**ruim**	[rœʏm]
special (adj)	**speciaal**	[speʃi'āl]
straight (line, road)	**recht**	[rɛxt]
strong (person)	**sterk**	[stɛrk]
stupid (foolish)	**dom**	[dɔm]
suitable (e.g., ~ for drinking)	**passend**	['pasənt]
sunny (day)	**zonnig**	['zɔnɛx]
superb, perfect (adj)	**uitstekend**	['œʏtstekənt]
swarthy (adj)	**getaand**	[xə'tānt]
sweet (sugary)	**zoet**	[zut]
tan (adj)	**gebruind**	[xə'brœʏnt]
tasty (delicious)	**lekker**	['lɛkər]
tender (affectionate)	**teder**	['tedər]
the highest (adj)	**hoogste**	['hōxstə]
the most important	**belangrijkst**	[bə'lanxrɛjkst]

the nearest	**dichtstbijzijnd**	['dixtstbɛj'zɛjnt]
the same, equal (adj)	**eender**	['ēndər]
thick (e.g., ~ fog)	**dicht**	[dixt]
thick (wall, slice)	**dik**	[dik]

thin (person)	**dun**	[dʉn]
tight (~ shoes)	**strak**	[strak]
tired (exhausted)	**moe**	[mu]
tiring (adj)	**vermoeiend**	[vər'mujənt]

transparent (adj)	**doorzichtig**	[dōr'zihtəx]
unclear (adj)	**onduidelijk**	[ɔn'dœʏdələk]
unique (exceptional)	**uniek**	[ju'nik]
various (adj)	**verschillende**	[vər'sxiləndə]

warm (moderately hot)	**warm**	[warm]
wet (e.g., ~ clothes)	**nat**	[nat]
whole (entire, complete)	**heel**	[hēl]
wide (e.g., ~ road)	**breed**	[brēt]
young (adj)	**jong**	[joŋ]

MAIN 500 VERBS

252. Verbs A-C

to accompany (vt)	**begeleiden**	[bəxə'lɛjdən]
to accuse (vt)	**beschuldigen**	[bə'sxʉldəxən]
to acknowledge (admit)	**erkennen**	[ɛr'kɛnən]
to act (take action)	**optreden**	['ɔptredən]
to add (supplement)	**bijvoegen**	[bɛj'fuxən]
to address (speak to)	**toespreken**	['tusprekən]
to admire (vi)	**bewonderen**	[bə'wɔndərən]
to advertise (vt)	**adverteren**	[advɛr'tɛrən]
to advise (vt)	**adviseren**	[atvi'zirən]
to affirm (assert)	**verklaren**	[vər'klarən]
to agree (say yes)	**instemmen**	['instɛmən]
to aim (to point a weapon)	**mikken op**	['mikən ɔp]
to allow (sb to do sth)	**toestaan**	['tustān]
to amputate (vt)	**amputeren**	[ampʉ'terən]
to answer (vi, vt)	**antwoorden**	['antwōrdən]
to apologize (vi)	**zich verontschuldigen**	[zih vərɔnt'sxʉldəxən]
to appear (come into view)	**verschijnen**	[vər'sxɛjnən]
to applaud (vi, vt)	**applaudisseren**	[aplaudi'serən]
to appoint (assign)	**aanstellen**	['ānstɛlən]
to approach (come closer)	**naderen**	['nadərən]
to arrive (ab. train)	**aankomen**	['ānkɔmən]
to ask (~ sb to do sth)	**verzoeken**	[vər'zukən]
to aspire to …	**aspireren**	[aspi'rɛrən]
to assist (help)	**assisteren**	[asi'sterən]
to attack (mil.)	**aanvallen**	['ānvalən]
to attain (objectives)	**bereiken**	[bə'rɛjkən]
to avenge (get revenge)	**wreken**	['wrekən]
to avoid (danger, task)	**ontlopen**	[ɔnt'lɔpən]
to award (give medal to)	**onderscheiden**	['ɔndər'sxɛjdən]
to battle (vi)	**strijden**	['strɛjdən]
to be (vi)	**zijn**	[zɛjn]
to be a cause of …	**veroorzaken …**	[və'rōrzakən]
to be afraid	**bang zijn**	['baŋ zɛjn]
to be angry (with …)	**boos zijn**	[bōs zɛjn]

to be at war	oorlog voeren	['ōrlɔx 'vurən]
to be based (on …)	zich baseerd op	[zix ba'zērt ɔp]
to be bored	zich vervelen	[zix vər'velən]
to be convinced	overtuigd worden	[ɔvər'tœyxt 'wordən]
to be enough	genoeg zijn	[xə'nux zɛjn]
to be envious	afgunstig zijn	['afxʉnstəx zɛjn]
to be indignant	verontwaardigd zijn	[vərɔnt'wārdixt zɛjn]
to be interested in …	zich interesseren voor …	[zix interə'serən vōr]
to be lost in thought	peinzen	['pɛjnzən]
to be lying (~ on the table)	liggen	['lixən]
to be needed	nodig zijn	['nɔdəx zɛjn]
to be perplexed (puzzled)	verbouwereerd zijn	[vərbau'wɛrērt zɛjn]
to be preserved	geconserveerd zijn	[xəkɔnsər'vērt zɛjn]
to be required	onmisbaar zijn	[ɔn'misbār zɛjn]
to be surprised	verbaasd zijn	[vər'bāst zɛjn]
to be worried	bezorgd zijn	[bə'zɔrxt zɛjn]
to beat (to hit)	slaan	[slān]
to become (e.g., ~ old)	worden	['wordən]
to behave (vi)	zich gedragen	[zih xə'draxən]
to believe (think)	geloven	[xə'lovən]
to belong to …	toebehoren aan …	['tubəhorən ān]
to berth (moor)	aanleggen	['ānlexən]
to blind (other drivers)	verblinden	[vər'blindən]
to blow (wind)	blazen	['blazən]
to blush (vi)	blozen	['blozən]
to boast (vi)	opscheppen	['ɔpsxepən]
to borrow (money)	lenen	['lenən]
to break (branch, toy, etc.)	breken	['brekən]
to breathe (vi)	ademen	['adəmən]
to bring (sth)	brengen	['brɛŋən]
to burn (paper, logs)	verbranden	[vər'brandən]
to buy (purchase)	kopen	['kɔpən]
to call (~ for help)	roepen	['rupən]
to call (yell for sb)	roepen	['rupən]
to calm down (vt)	kalmeren	[kal'merən]
can (v aux)	kunnen	['kʉnən]
to cancel (call off)	afzeggen	['afzɛxən]
to cast off (of a boat or ship)	wegvaren	['wɛxvarən]
to catch (e.g., ~ a ball)	vangen	['vaŋən]
to change (~ one's opinion)	veranderen	[və'randərən]
to change (exchange)	verwisselen	[vər'wisələn]
to charm (vt)	charmeren	[ʃʌr'mɛrən]
to choose (select)	kiezen	['kizən]

to chop off (with an ax)	afhakken	['afhakən]
to clean (e.g., kettle from scale)	reinigen	['rɛjnixən]
to clean (shoes, etc.)	schoonmaken	['sxōn·makən]

to clean up (tidy)	schoonmaken	['sxōn·makən]
to close (vt)	sluiten	['slœytən]
to comb one's hair	het haar kammen	[ət hār 'kamən]
to come down (the stairs)	afdalen	['afdalən]

to come out (book)	verschijnen	[vər'sxɛjnən]
to compare (vt)	vergelijken	[vɛrxə'lɛjkən]
to compensate (vt)	compenseren	[kɔmpən'zerən]
to compete (vi)	concurreren	[kɔnkju'rerən]

to compile (~ a list)	samenstellen, maken	['samənstelən], ['makən]
to complain (vi, vt)	klagen	['klaxən]
to complicate (vt)	compliceren	[kɔmpli'serən]
to compose (music, etc.)	componeren	[kɔmpo'nerən]

to compromise (reputation)	compromitteren	[kɔmprɔmi'terən]
to concentrate (vi)	zich concentreren	[zix kɔnsən'trerən]
to confess (criminal)	bekennen	[bə'kenən]
to confuse (mix up)	verwarren	[vər'warən]

to congratulate (vt)	feliciteren	[felisi'terən]
to consult (doctor, expert)	raadplegen	['rātplexən]
to continue (~ to do sth)	vervolgen	[vər'vɔlxən]
to control (vt)	controleren	[kɔntro'lerən]

to convince (vt)	overtuigen	[ɔvər'tœyxən]
to cooperate (vi)	coöpereren	[koope'rerən]
to coordinate (vt)	coördineren	[koordi'nerən]
to correct (an error)	corrigeren	[kori'dʒɛrən]

to cost (vt)	kosten	['kɔstən]
to count (money, etc.)	tellen	['tɛlən]
to count on ...	rekenen op ...	['rekənən ɔp]
to crack (ceiling, wall)	barsten	['barstən]

to create (vt)	creëren	[kre'jerən]
to crush, to squash (~ a bug)	verpletteren	[vər'pletərən]
to cry (weep)	huilen	['hœylən]
to cut off (with a knife)	afsnijden	['afsnɛjdən]

253. Verbs D-G

| to dare (~ to do sth) | durven | ['dʉrvən] |
| to date from ... | gedateerd zijn | [xeda'tērt zɛjn] |

to deceive (vi, vt)	**bedriegen**	[bə'drixən]
to decide (~ to do sth)	**beslissen**	[bə'slisən]
to decorate (tree, street)	**versieren, decoreren**	[vər'sirən], [dekɔ'rɛrən]
to dedicate (book, etc.)	**toewijden**	['tuwɛjdən]
to defend (a country, etc.)	**verdedigen**	[vər'dedixən]
to defend oneself	**zich verdedigen**	[zih vər'dedixən]
to demand (request firmly)	**eisen**	['ɛjsən]
to denounce (vt)	**verklikken**	[vər'likən]
to deny (vt)	**ontkennen**	[ɔnt'kɛnən]
to depend on ...	**afhangen van ...**	['afhaŋən van]
to deprive (vt)	**ontnemen**	[ɔnt'nemən]
to deserve (vt)	**verdienen**	[vər'dinən]
to design (machine, etc.)	**ontwerpen**	[ɔnt'wɛrpən]
to desire (want, wish)	**wensen**	['wɛnsən]
to despise (vt)	**minachten**	['minaxtən]
to destroy (documents, etc.)	**vernietigen**	[vər'nitixən]
to differ (from sth)	**verschillen**	[vər'sxilən]
to dig (tunnel, etc.)	**graven**	['xravən]
to direct (point the way)	**de weg wijzen**	[də wɛx 'vɛjzən]
to disappear (vi)	**verdwijnen**	[vərd'wɛjnən]
to discover (new land, etc.)	**ontdekken**	[ɔn'dɛkən]
to discuss (vt)	**bespreken**	[bə'sprekən]
to distribute (leaflets, etc.)	**verspreiden**	[vər'sprɛjdən]
to disturb (vt)	**storen**	['stɔrən]
to dive (vi)	**duiken**	['dœʏkən]
to divide (math)	**delen**	['delən]
to do (vt)	**doen**	[dun]
to do the laundry	**de was doen**	[də was dun]
to double (increase)	**verdubbelen**	[vər'dʉbələn]
to doubt (have doubts)	**twijfelen**	['twɛjfelən]
to draw a conclusion	**een conclusie trekken**	[en kɔnk'lʉzi 'trɛkən]
to dream (daydream)	**dromen**	['drɔmən]
to dream (in sleep)	**dromen**	['drɔmən]
to drink (vi, vt)	**drinken**	['drinkən]
to drive a car	**een auto besturen**	[en 'autɔ bə'stʉrən]
to drive away (scare away)	**wegjagen**	['wɛx jaxən]
to drop (let fall)	**laten vallen**	['latən 'valən]
to drown (ab. person)	**verdrinken**	[vər'drinkən]
to dry (clothes, hair)	**drogen**	['drɔxən]
to eat (vi, vt)	**eten**	['etən]
to eavesdrop (vi)	**afluisteren**	['aflœʏstərən]

to emit (diffuse - odor, etc.)	**verspreiden**	[vər'sprɛjdən]
to enjoy oneself	**plezier hebben**	[plɛ'zir 'hɛbən]
to enter (on the list)	**opschrijven**	['ɔpsxrɛjvən]
to enter (room, house, etc.)	**binnengaan**	['binənxān]
to entertain (amuse)	**amuseren**	[amʉ'zerən]
to equip (fit out)	**uitrusten**	['œytrystən]
to examine (proposal)	**onderzoeken**	['ɔndər'zukən]
to exchange (sth)	**wisselen**	['wisələn]
to excuse (forgive)	**excuseren**	[ɛkskʉ'zerən]
to exist (vi)	**existeren**	[ɛksis'tɛrən]
to expect (anticipate)	**verwachten**	[vər'waxtən]
to expect (foresee)	**voorzien**	[võr'zin]
to expel (from school, etc.)	**uitsluiten**	['œytslœytən]
to explain (vt)	**verklaren**	[vər'klarən]
to express (vt)	**uitdrukken**	['œydrykən]
to extinguish (a fire)	**blussen**	['blʉsən]
to fall in love (with …)	**verliefd worden**	[vər'lift 'wordən]
to feed (provide food)	**voederen**	['vudərən]
to fight (against the enemy)	**strijden**	['strɛjdən]
to fight (vi)	**vechten**	['vɛxtən]
to fill (glass, bottle)	**vullen**	['vʉlən]
to find (~ lost items)	**vinden**	['vindən]
to finish (vt)	**beëindigen**	[be'ɛjndəxən]
to fish (angle)	**vissen**	['visən]
to fit (ab. dress, etc.)	**passen**	['pasən]
to flatter (vt)	**vleien**	['vlɛjən]
to fly (bird, plane)	**vliegen**	['vlixən]
to follow … (come after)	**volgen**	['vɔlxən]
to forbid (vt)	**verbieden**	[vər'bidən]
to force (compel)	**verplichten**	[vər'plixtən]
to forget (vi, vt)	**vergeten**	[vər'xetən]
to forgive (pardon)	**vergeven**	[vər'xevən]
to form (constitute)	**vormen**	['vɔrmən]
to get dirty (vi)	**vies worden**	[vis 'wordən]
to get infected (with …)	**besmet worden met …**	[bə'smɛt 'wordən mɛt]
to get irritated	**zich ergeren**	[zih 'ɛrxərən]
to get married	**trouwen**	['trauən]
to get rid of …	**zich bevrijden van …**	[zix bəv'rɛjdən van]
to get tired	**vermoeid raken**	[vər'mujt 'rakən]
to get up (arise from bed)	**opstaan**	['ɔpstān]

| to give (vt) | geven | ['xevən] |
| to give a bath (to bath) | een bad geven | [en bat 'xevən] |

to give a hug, to hug (vt)	omhelzen	[ɔm'hɛlzən]
to give in (yield to)	toegeven	['tuxevən]
to glimpse (vt)	opmerken	['ɔpmɛrkən]
to go (by car, etc.)	rijden	['rɛjdən]

to go (on foot)	gaan	[xān]
to go for a swim	gaan zwemmen	[xān 'zwɛmən]
to go out (for dinner, etc.)	uitgaan	['œʏtxān]
to go to bed (go to sleep)	gaan slapen	[xān 'slapən]

to greet (vt)	verwelkomen	[vər'wɛlkomən]
to grow (plants)	kweken	['kwekən]
to guarantee (vt)	garanderen	[xaran'derən]
to guess (the answer)	goed raden	[xut 'radən]

254. Verbs H-M

to hand out (distribute)	uitdelen	['œʏtdelən]
to hang (curtains, etc.)	ophangen	['ɔphaŋən]
to have (vt)	hebben	['hɛbən]
to have a try	proberen	[prɔ'berən]
to have breakfast	ontbijten	[ɔn'bɛjtən]

to have dinner	souperen	[su'perən]
to have lunch	lunchen	['lʉnʃən]
to head (group, etc.)	aanvoeren	['ānvurən]
to hear (vt)	horen	['hɔrən]
to heat (vt)	verwarmen	[vər'warmən]

to help (vt)	helpen	['hɛlpən]
to hide (vt)	verbergen	[vər'bɛrxən]
to hire (e.g., ~ a boat)	huren	['hʉrən]
to hire (staff)	huren	['hʉrən]
to hope (vi, vt)	hopen	['hɔpən]

to hunt (for food, sport)	jagen	['jaxən]
to hurry (vi)	zich haasten	[zix 'hāstən]
to imagine (to picture)	zich indenken	[zix 'indənkən]
to imitate (vt)	imiteren	[imi'terən]
to implore (vt)	smeken	['smekən]
to import (vt)	importeren	[impɔr'terən]
to increase (vi)	toenemen	['tunemən]
to increase (vt)	vergroten	[vər'xrɔtən]
to infect (vt)	besmetten	[bə'smetən]
to influence (vt)	beïnvloeden	[bə'invludən]
to inform (e.g., ~ the police about)	melden	['meldən]

to inform (vt)	informeren	[infɔr'merən]
to inherit (vt)	erven	['ɛrvən]
to inquire (about ...)	informeren naar ...	[infɔr'merən nãr]
to insert (put in)	inlassen	[in'lasən]
to insinuate (imply)	zinspelen	['zinspelən]
to insist (vi, vt)	aandringen	['ãndriŋən]
to inspire (vt)	inspireren	[inspi'rerən]
to instruct (teach)	onderwijzen	['ɔndər'vɛjzən]
to insult (offend)	beledigen	[bə'ledəxən]
to interest (vt)	interesseren	[intərə'serən]
to intervene (vi)	tussenbeide komen	[tʉsən'bɛjdə 'kɔmən]
to introduce (sb to sb)	voorstellen	['võrstɛlən]
to invent (machine, etc.)	uitvinden	['œytvindən]
to invite (vt)	uitnodigen	['œytnɔdixən]
to iron (clothes)	strijken	['strɛjkən]
to irritate (annoy)	irriteren	[iri'terən]
to isolate (vt)	isoleren	[izɔ'lerən]
to join (political party, etc.)	lid worden	[lid 'wɔrdən]
to joke (be kidding)	grappen maken	['xrapən 'makən]
to keep (old letters, etc.)	bewaren	[bə'warən]
to keep silent	zwijgen	['zwɛjxən]
to kill (vt)	doden	['dɔdən]
to knock (at the door)	kloppen	['klɔpən]
to know (sb)	kennen	['kɛnən]
to know (sth)	weten	['wetən]
to laugh (vi)	lachen	['laxən]
to launch (start up)	opstarten	['ɔpstartən]
to leave (~ for Mexico)	vertrekken	[vər'trɛkən]
to leave (forget sth)	vergeten	[vər'xetən]
to leave (spouse)	verlaten	[vər'latən]
to liberate (city, etc.)	bevrijden	[bə'vrɛjdən]
to lie (~ on the floor)	liggen	['lixən]
to lie (tell untruth)	liegen	['lixən]
to light (campfire, etc.)	aansteken	['ãnstekən]
to light up (illuminate)	verlichten	[vər'lixtən]
to like (I like ...)	bevallen	[bə'valən]
to limit (vt)	beperken	[bə'pɛrkən]
to listen (vi)	luisteren	['lœysterən]
to live (~ in France)	leven	['levən]
to live (exist)	bestaan	[bə'stãn]
to load (gun)	laden	['ladən]
to load (vehicle, etc.)	laden	['ladən]
to look (I'm just ~ing)	kijken	['kɛjkən]
to look for ... (search)	zoeken	['zukən]

to look like (resemble)	gelijken	[xə'lɛjkən]
to lose (umbrella, etc.)	verliezen	[vər'lizən]
to love (e.g., ~ dancing)	houden van	['haudən van]

to love (sb)	liefhebben	['lifhɛbən]
to lower (blind, head)	neerlaten	['nĕrlatən]
to make (~ dinner)	klaarmaken	['klār·makən]
to make a mistake	zich vergissen	[zih vər'xisən]
to make angry	boos maken	[bōs 'makən]

to make easier	verlichten	[vər'lixtən]
to make multiple copies	kopieën maken	[kɔ'pin makən]
to make the acquaintance	kennismaken	['kɛnis·makən]
to make use (of ...)	gebruiken	[xə'brœykən]
to manage, to run	beheren	[bə'herən]

to mark (make a mark)	markeren	[mar'kerən]
to mean (signify)	betekenen	[bə'tekənən]
to memorize (vt)	memoriseren	[memɔri'zɛrən]
to mention (talk about)	vermelden	[vər'mɛldən]
to miss (school, etc.)	verzuimen	[vər'zœymən]

to mix (combine, blend)	mengen	['mɛŋən]
to mock (make fun of)	uitlachen	['œytlaxən]
to move (to shift)	verplaatsen	[vər'plātsən]
to multiply (math)	vermenigvuldigen	[vər'menix·'vʉldixən]
must (v aux)	moeten	['mutən]

255. Verbs N-R

to name, to call (vt)	noemen	['numən]
to negotiate (vi)	onderhandelen	['ɔndər'handələn]
to note (write down)	noteren	[nɔ'tɛrən]
to notice (see)	opmerken	['ɔpmɛrkən]

to obey (vi, vt)	gehoorzamen	[xə'hōrzamən]
to object (vi, vt)	weerspreken	[wĕr'sprekən]
to observe (see)	waarnemen	['wārnemən]
to offend (vt)	beledigen	[bə'ledəxən]
to omit (word, phrase)	weglaten	['wɛxlatən]

to open (vt)	openen	['ɔpənən]
to order (in restaurant)	bestellen	[bə'stɛlən]
to order (mil.)	bevelen	[bə'velən]
to organize (concert, party)	organiseren	[ɔrxani'zerən]
to overestimate (vt)	overschatten	[ɔvər'sxatən]
to own (possess)	bezitten	[bə'zitən]
to participate (vi)	deelnemen	['dĕlnemən]
to pass through (by car, etc.)	passeren	[pa'serən]

to pay (vi, vt)	**betalen**	[bə'talən]
to peep, spy on	**gluren**	['xlʉrən]
to penetrate (vt)	**penetreren**	[pene'trɛrən]
to permit (vt)	**toestaan**	['tustān]
to pick (flowers)	**plukken**	['plʉkən]
to place (put, set)	**plaatsen**	['plātsən]
to plan (~ to do sth)	**plannen**	['planən]
to play (actor)	**spelen**	['spelən]
to play (children)	**spelen**	['spelən]
to point (~ the way)	**aanwijzen**	['ānwɛjzən]
to pour (liquid)	**gieten**	['xitən]
to pray (vi, vt)	**bidden**	['bidən]
to prefer (vt)	**prefereren**	[prəfe'rerən]
to prepare (~ a plan)	**klaarmaken**	['klār·makən]
to present (sb to sb)	**voorstellen**	['vōrstɛlən]
to preserve (peace, life)	**bewaren**	[bə'warən]
to prevail (vt)	**overheersen**	[ɔvər'hērsən]
to progress (move forward)	**vorderen**	['vɔrdərən]
to promise (vt)	**beloven**	[bə'lɔvən]
to pronounce (vt)	**uitspreken**	['œʏtsprekən]
to propose (vt)	**voorstellen**	['vōrstɛlən]
to protect (e.g., ~ nature)	**beschermen**	[bə'sxɛrmən]
to protest (vi)	**protesteren**	[prɔtɛ'sterən]
to prove (vt)	**bewijzen**	[bə'wɛjzən]
to provoke (vt)	**provoceren**	[prɔvɔ'ʃerən]
to pull (~ the rope)	**trekken**	['trɛkən]
to punish (vt)	**bestraffen**	[bə'strafən]
to push (~ the door)	**duwen**	['dʉwən]
to put away (vt)	**opbergen**	['ɔpbɛrxən]
to put in order	**op orde brengen**	[ɔp 'ɔrdə 'brɛŋən]
to put, to place	**plaatsen**	['plātsən]
to quote (cite)	**citeren**	[si'terən]
to reach (arrive at)	**bereiken**	[bə'rɛjkən]
to read (vi, vt)	**lezen**	['lezən]
to realize (a dream)	**verwezenlijken**	[vər'wezənləkən]
to recognize (identify sb)	**herkennen**	[hɛr'kɛnən]
to recommend (vt)	**aanbevelen**	['āmbəvelən]
to recover (~ from flu)	**zich herstellen**	[zix hɛr'ʃtɛlən]
to redo (do again)	**overdoen**	['ɔvərdun]
to reduce (speed, etc.)	**verminderen**	[vɛr'mindərən]
to refuse (~ sb)	**weigeren**	['wɛjxərən]
to regret (be sorry)	**betreuren**	[bə'trørən]

to reinforce (vt)	**versterken**	[vər'stɛrkən]
to remember (Do you ~ me?)	**herinneren**	[hɛ'rinərən]
to remember (I can't ~ her name)	**zich herinneren**	[zix hɛ'rinərən]
to remind of …	**herinneren aan …**	[hɛ'rinərən ãn]
to remove (~ a stain)	**verwijderen**	[vər'wɛjdərən]
to remove (~ an obstacle)	**verwijderen**	[vər'wɛjdərən]
to rent (sth from sb)	**huren**	['hʉrən]
to repair (mend)	**herstellen**	[hɛr'stɛlən]
to repeat (say again)	**herhalen**	[hɛr'halən]
to report (make a report)	**rapporteren**	[rapor'terən]
to reproach (vt)	**verwijten**	[vər'wɛjtən]
to reserve, to book	**reserveren**	[rezɛr'verən]
to restrain (hold back)	**bedwingen**	[bə'dwiŋən]
to return (come back)	**terugkeren**	[te'rʉx·kerən]
to risk, to take a risk	**riskeren**	[ris'kerən]
to rub out (erase)	**uitwissen**	['œʏtwisən]
to run (move fast)	**rennen**	['renən]
to rush (hurry sb)	**haasten**	['hãstən]

256. Verbs S-W

to satisfy (please)	**bevredigen**	[bə'vredixən]
to save (rescue)	**redden**	['rɛdən]
to say (~ thank you)	**zeggen**	['zexən]
to scold (vt)	**uitvaren tegen**	['œʏtvarən 'texən]
to scratch (with claws)	**schrammen**	['sxramən]
to select (to pick)	**selecteren**	[selɛk'terən]
to sell (goods)	**verkopen**	[vɛr'kopən]
to send (a letter)	**sturen**	['stʉrən]
to send back (vt)	**terugsturen**	[te'rʉx·stʉrən]
to sense (~ danger)	**aanvoelen**	['ãnvulən]
to sentence (vt)	**veroordelen**	[və'rõrdələn]
to serve (in restaurant)	**bedienen**	[bə'dinən]
to settle (a conflict)	**regelen**	['rexələn]
to shake (vt)	**schudden**	['sxʉdən]
to shave (vi)	**zich scheren**	[zix 'sxerən]
to shine (gleam)	**glimmen**	['xlimən]
to shiver (with cold)	**rillen**	['rilən]
to shoot (vi)	**schieten**	['sxitən]
to shout (vi)	**schreeuwen**	['sxrẽwən]

to show (to display)	tonen	['tonən]
to shudder (vi)	huiveren	['hœyvərən]
to sigh (vi)	zuchten	['zʉxtən]
to sign (document)	ondertekenen	['ɔndər'tekənən]
to signify (mean)	beduiden	[bə'dœydən]
to simplify (vt)	simplificeren	[simplifi'sɛrən]
to sin (vi)	zondigen	['zɔndixən]
to sit (be sitting)	zitten	['zitən]
to sit down (vi)	gaan zitten	[xãn 'zitən]
to smell (emit an odor)	ruiken	[rœykən]
to smell (inhale the odor)	ruiken	[rœykən]
to smile (vi)	glimlachen	['xlimlahən]
to snap (vi, ab. rope)	breken	['brekən]
to solve (problem)	oplossen	['ɔplɔsən]
to sow (seed, crop)	zaaien	['zãjən]
to spill (liquid)	morsen	['mɔrsən]
to spill out, scatter (flour, etc.)	zich verspreiden	[zix vər'ʃprɛjdən]
to spit (vi)	spuwen	['spʉwən]
to stand (toothache, cold)	verdragen	[vər'draxən]
to start (begin)	beginnen	[bə'xinən]
to steal (money, etc.)	stelen	['stelən]
to stop (for pause, etc.)	stoppen	['stɔpən]
to stop (please ~ calling me)	ophouden	['ɔphaudən]
to stop talking	verstommen	[vər'stɔmən]
to stroke (caress)	aaien	['ãjən]
to study (vt)	studeren	[stʉ'derən]
to suffer (feel pain)	lijden	['lɛjdən]
to support (cause, idea)	steunen	['stønən]
to suppose (assume)	veronderstellen	[vərɔndər'stɛlən]
to surface (ab. submarine)	opduiken	['ɔpdœykən]
to surprise (amaze)	verbazen	[vər'bazən]
to suspect (vt)	verdenken	[vər'dɛnkən]
to swim (vi)	zwemmen	['zwɛmən]
to take (get hold of)	nemen	['nemən]
to take a bath	een bad nemen	[en bat 'nemən]
to take a rest	rusten	['rʉstən]
to take away (e.g., about waiter)	wegdragen	['wɛxdraxən]
to take off (airplane)	opstijgen	['ɔpstɛjxən]
to take off (painting, curtains, etc.)	afnemen	['afnemən]

to take pictures	**foto's maken**	['fɔtos 'makən]
to talk to ...	**spreken met ...**	['sprekən mɛt]
to teach (give lessons)	**leren**	['lerən]
to tear off, to rip off (vt)	**afrukken**	['afrʉkən]
to tell (story, joke)	**vertellen**	[vər'tɛlən]
to thank (vt)	**danken**	['dankən]
to think (believe)	**vinden**	['vindən]
to think (vi, vt)	**denken**	['dɛnkən]
to threaten (vt)	**bedreigen**	[bə'drɛjxən]
to throw (stone, etc.)	**gooien**	['xõjən]
to tie to ...	**vastbinden aan ...**	['vastbindən ãn]
to tie up (prisoner)	**binden**	['bindən]
to tire (make tired)	**vermoeien**	[vər'mujən]
to touch (one's arm, etc.)	**aanraken**	['ãnrakən]
to tower (over ...)	**uittorenen**	['œʏttɔrənən]
to train (animals)	**dresseren**	[drɛ'serən]
to train (sb)	**trainen**	['trɛjnən]
to train (vi)	**zich trainen**	[zix 'trɛjnən]
to transform (vt)	**transformeren**	[transfɔr'merən]
to translate (vt)	**vertalen**	[vər'talən]
to treat (illness)	**behandelen**	[bə'handələn]
to trust (vt)	**vertrouwen**	[vər'trauwən]
to try (attempt)	**proberen**	[prɔ'berən]
to turn (e.g., ~ left)	**afslaan**	['afslãn]
to turn away (vi)	**wegdraaien**	['wɛxdrãjən]
to turn off (the light)	**uitdoen**	['œʏtdun]
to turn on (computer, etc.)	**aanzetten**	['ãnzɛtən]
to turn over (stone, etc.)	**omkeren**	['ɔmkerən]
to underestimate (vt)	**onderschatten**	['ɔndər'sxatən]
to underline (vt)	**onderstrepen**	['ɔndər'strepən]
to understand (vt)	**begrijpen**	[bə'xrɛjpən]
to undertake (vt)	**ondernemen**	['ɔndər'nemən]
to unite (vt)	**verenigen**	[və'rɛnixən]
to untie (vt)	**losbinden**	[lɔs'bindən]
to use (phrase, word)	**gebruiken**	[xə'brœʏkən]
to vaccinate (vt)	**inenten**	['inɛntən]
to vote (vi)	**stemmen**	['stɛmən]
to wait (vt)	**wachten**	['waxtən]
to wake (sb)	**wekken**	['wɛkən]
to want (wish, desire)	**willen**	['wilən]
to warn (of the danger)	**waarschuwen**	['wãrsxjuvən]
to wash (clean)	**wassen**	['wasən]

to water (plants)	**begieten**	[bə'xitən]
to wave (the hand)	**zwaaien**	['zwājən]
to weigh (have weight)	**wegen**	['wexən]
to work (vi)	**werken**	['wɛrkən]
to worry (make anxious)	**bezorgd maken**	[bə'zɔrxt 'makən]
to worry (vi)	**bezorgd zijn**	[bə'zɔrxt zɛjn]
to wrap (parcel, etc.)	**inpakken**	[in'pakən]
to wrestle (sport)	**worstelen**	['wɔrstələn]
to write (vt)	**schrijven**	['sxrɛjvən]
to write down	**opschrijven**	['ɔpsxrɛjvən]